SCIENCE in the World Around Us

Other Books by William C. Vergara

SCIENCE

William C. Vergara

in the World Around Us

1817

Harper & Row, Publishers

New York, Evanston, San Francisco, London

To Robert E. Vergara

500
V58s
84367
aug 1973

FIRST EDITION

STANDARD BOOK NUMBER: 06–014766–0

LIBRARY OF CONGRESS CATALOG CARD NUMBER: 72–79699

Preface

This is a book about science, its effect on our lives, and its relation to the world in which we live. I have tried to tell the general reader what scientists are up to, what they have discovered, and how scientific knowledge fits into our everyday frame of reference.

I have followed the question-and-answer format of my first three books—a technique that many readers seem to enjoy. So the book is really a continuation of that earlier series on science, mathematics, and electronics.

In the past, readers have written to suggest questions or topics for future use. I am indebted to all of these individuals, and am happy to include many of their questions in this book. The questions and answers are arranged randomly to add interest and to help the reader pick and choose. The index is the key to the book for those seeking specific reference material. I have tried to avoid duplication, so questions not covered here can often be found in one of my earlier books.

It's an unfortunate fact of our time that the general reader feels increasingly lost as the body of scientific knowledge grows daily larger and more complex. The knowledge that these scientific discoveries may profoundly affect his life—even the very existence of life as we know it—merely adds to his desire to be informed. There is a need, therefore, for books that communicate scientific principles and general ideas with clarity and simplicity. So, in this book, I have often avoided the absolute precision of scientific terminology in order to express scientific concepts in a way that is understandable to the general reader. I have made free use of illustrative examples and analogies, and have eliminated much pertinent, but intricate, detail. If the book should stimulate further reading in the fascinating field of science, it will have been worth the writing.

Finally, my purpose in writing this book has been to entertain as well as to instruct, so I have included many sidelights that I hope will seem interesting and relevant to the reader. And, where appropriate, I have not hesitated to editorialize on society's apparent misuse, or lack of use, of scientific knowledge. I have tried to be objective in such matters and hope the reader will forgive these intrusions in a book on science. While I cannot offer "equal time" for opposing points of view, I will welcome any comments that readers care to make.

WILLIAM C. VERGARA

Towson, Maryland

Editor's Note: All comments should be sent to William C. Vergara, c/o Harper & Row, Publishers, 10 East 53 Street, New York, N.Y. 10022.

Does dew fall in the desert?

Until recent times, dew was an unsuspected source of desert water. When scientists began measuring dew, they found that in many areas it can often equal as much as 10 inches of annual rainfall. Surprisingly enough, they also learned that—except in the driest deserts—there is as much dew in arid and semiarid lands as in humid coastal regions.

Dew is a result of the condensation of moisture from the air. As air cools, it is able to hold progressively smaller amounts of water vapor. Depending upon the relative humidity, a critically low temperature—the dew point—can be reached, at which the air is saturated with water vapor. At lower temperatures, the air deposits the excess water on surfaces, and in the early morning hours, when the temperature has fallen far below the previous day's high, dew can be deposited on the ground. In many humid places, the temperature rarely drops low enough at night to produce condensation. And when a city is covered with smog, it gets little dew because the particles in the air act like a heat blanket over the city.

Studies on dew have provided an answer for the puzzling observation that crops like tomatoes and watermelons do well in dry regions where there has been little rain. Similarly, research in Africa and Pakistan indicate that some crops prosper in arid lands with only a slight sprinkling of water to supplement dew. Quite possibly desert plants have always supplemented their meager water rations with dew. If so, perhaps dew research may lead to a new kind of irrigation involving the sprinkling of fine mist. This requires much less water than conventional irrigation, and could open up large arid regions for cultivation.

Why do things smell the way they do?

The world is full of smells, some pleasant, some horrible—but each is closely associated with the substance that produces it. One whiff tells us what is cooking on the stove, or which perfume came from which bottle. How can our sense of smell distinguish so clearly between so many different odors?

We can think of the sense of smell as an array of many doors, each with a different lock. When a certain door is opened, we smell onions. From another comes the odor of gasoline; from a third, dead fish. Each door lock requires a different key to open it. These "keys" are molecules, which evaporate from the substance and reach the nerve endings in the nose. And because these molecules differ from each other, they give rise to different sensations of smell.

Oddly enough, scientists believe that the odor of a substance depends on the positions of the atoms in the substance rather than upon the kinds of atoms of which it is composed. This is like saying that only the shape of the key determines which lock it will open— and not whether it is made of brass, iron, gold, or whatever.

2

To illustrate, let's consider the camphor molecule. Camphor has what to many people is a pleasant, fragrant odor. It is an organic compound consisting of ten carbon and seventeen hydrogen atoms. But these atoms are arranged in a very specific way in the molecule. If the shape theory is correct, camphor smells like camphor because of the way its shape or contour touches the smelling apparatus in the nose. Why not create a man-made "camphor," the atoms of which are different chemically, but which has the same shape as the true camphor molecule? Smelling such a compound should trick the nose into thinking it has smelled camphor.

Such an experiment has been performed by substituting chlorine atoms for some of the carbon and hydrogen atoms in camphor. Although the chemical properties of this new compound are entirely different from camphor, the two smell exactly the same!

Someday, when scientists learn more about the sense of smell, they will surely be able to produce new odors at will, or to reproduce expensive perfumes that now come from such rare sources as whales and musk deer. Before this can be done, however, science must learn a great deal more about which molecular shapes the nose seems to like best.

How do birds navigate over great distances?

One of the most remarkable accomplishments of many creatures is their uncanny ability to navigate with great accuracy over long distances. Some animals somehow know when a low sun means east and when it means west. Bees, for example, use solar navigation to find flowers more than a mile away from the hive. A forager bee searches the region until he finds the flowers. He then flies back to the hive and performs an elaborate dance, which communicates to the other bees the direction of the food source by giving its angle with respect to the sun. But although studies show that the sun does guide many species, that alone is not enough. The bees can find the blooming flowers even after the sun has moved across the sky. In some way, they compensate in their navigation for the continual movement of the sun.

3

Although bees are good navigators, some birds are truly amazing in finding their way over enormous distances. One bird—the migrating golden plover—is so accurate in its direction finding that it flies over more than 2,000 miles of open Pacific Ocean to land unerringly in Hawaii. Another bird, the wheatear, has just as impressive a record. A young bird of this species, hatched in summer in far northern Greenland, flies through many lonely nights to countries thousands of miles away in western Africa. Or consider the petrels that breed on Tristan da Cunha: in the fall they swarm all over the Atlantic region, yet find their way back to their tiny island in the spring.

Scientists are beginning to learn the methods these migrants use to perform such feats. In one experiment, the German zoologist Gustav Kramer built a special circular aviary for starlings. It was lighted by the sun, which reached the interior only through vertical slits in the walls. When the season for migration arrived, the birds did an amazing thing. Most of them perched facing along the compass course they would have followed had they been free. But as time passed, and as the sun moved across the sky, the birds made allowances for the change—as they would have to do in flight to maintain a straight course. Clearly some internal biological "clock" was helping them navigate. Just like a woodsman, they found their way by comparing the position of the sun with the time of day.

Kramer then carried the experiment a step further, in order to find out whether it was really the sun or some other unknown factor that guides the birds. He set up mirrors outside the aviary so that the apparent direction of the sun was suddenly changed by 90 degrees. He found that the perching birds "changed course" by exactly the same amount—clearly showing that they used the sun as their guide.

Perhaps even more remarkable was a similar series of experiments performed later by another German scientist, E. G. F. Sauer, who proved that some birds can navigate by the stars! He found that, on clear nights during the migration season, lesser whitethroat warblers in his aviary faced southeast, as they normally would to cross the Balkans and Mediterranean to Egypt. Furthermore, they maintained that direction hour after hour, as the stars rotated from east to west overhead. This could not be a learned trait, because Sauer obtained precisely the same results with a bird that had spent his entire life in a cage and had never flown in free flight under the stars. Like Kramer's starlings, Sauer's warblers used an internal biological clock to compensate for celestial motions. When the sky was overcast, however, with no stars shining overhead, the birds fluttered around in a random, disoriented manner.

Such experiments leave no doubt that birds, aided by an internal clock, use methods of celestial navigation to accomplish their brilliant feats of migration. They apparently have a remarkable hereditary mechanism that orients them by the heavenly bodies, coupled with a precise sense of time that relates the rotating heavens to the geography of the earth.

Before leaving the subject of migration, experiments have shown that, while some navigating ability is innate, other ability is learned. Each year, Baltic starlings fly in a southwesterly direction from the Baltic Sea toward England. One year, some of them were caught part way to England and transported to Geneva, Switzerland, far to the south of their normal course. When they were released, young birds continued on their southwesterly course, ending up in Spain. But older birds, who had made the trip before, realized they were off course and flew northwest toward England. Apparently, the young birds had not yet learned to make corrections for events that took them far off course.

The way in which the starling's chronometer and other animal clocks work is still obscure. In some way, with the help of the nervous system and certain hormone-secreting glands, the rising sun seems to reset these clocks. But, in any event, research is continuing in an attempt to discover more about migration, one of nature's best-kept secrets.

How does a seismograph work?

The seismograph was developed in 1855 to record the shock waves produced by earthquakes. As shown in the diagram, it consists of two metal frames firmly anchored in bedrock. A heavy

5

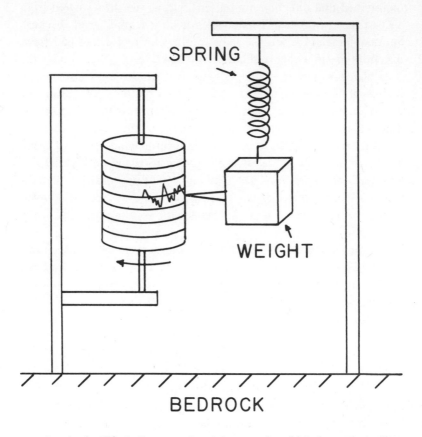

SPRING

WEIGHT

BEDROCK

FIG. 1. A simplified diagram of a seismograph, which is used to draw records of earthquake tremors. The rotating drum on the left moves up and down when the ground shakes, but the weight on the right is isolated from the earth tremors by its supporting spring. Attached to the stationary weight is a pen which traces out the motion of the drum.

weight is freely suspended from one of these frames by a spring. When an earth tremor shakes the support, the flexible spring keeps the bedrock motions from reaching the suspended weight. The weight, therefore, tends to hold its original position, despite the presence of earth tremors.

The other frame supports a rotating drum covered with graph

6

paper, as shown in the sketch. Because the drum is rigidly connected to the bedrock, it faithfully follows the movements caused by the earthquake. A pen mounted on the stationary weight then traces the movements of the drum on the unfurling graph paper—thus providing an accurate measure of the earthquake's force.

One of the first fruits of this new instrument was the observation that an earthquake's shock is transmitted around the world in several different forms. The slowest is called a *surface wave,* which moves like an ocean wave along the earth's thin, curved crust. Other waves, whose existence was unsuspected before seismographs revealed them, move straight into the earth at substantially higher speeds than the surface wave.

These speedy waves are of two kinds: *primary* or *P waves* and *secondary* or *S waves.* P waves are the faster and more penetrating of the two, moving easily through the earth's dense interior. The slower S waves have a transverse motion—like that of a plucked guitar string. S waves travel well enough through solids, but die out rapidly when they enter liquids or gases.

At a seismograph station, the first notice of a distant earthquake is given by the arrival of a train of P waves—the fastest ones. Later the S waves arrive. The interval between the two depends on the distance from the focus of the earthquake to the station. Still later the slowest waves, the surface waves, arrive, journeying along the thin, curved medium of the earth's crust.

Pinpointing an earthquake's place of origin, or *epicenter,* is done by three or more seismic stations in different cities. Each station determines the time interval between the arrival of the fast P waves and the slower S waves. From these data, estimates are made of the distances the waves traveled. Three circles are then drawn on a map, with the three distances as radii. At their intersection is the epicenter of the earthquake.

By analyzing data from seismographs, geophysicists are able to deduce a great deal of information about the earth. When a powerful earthquake occurs, a complete set of shock-wave travel times is obtained from the seismological observatories that dot the earth. From these it is possible to infer the speeds of P and S waves at various depths in the earth. We know, for example, that these speeds tend to increase gradually as the waves approach the center of the earth. Also, there are several depths at which sudden shifts in the speed of travel occur. Scientists know that such shifts must signify radical changes in the properties of the earth's matter at such levels. The boundaries that these levels mark between layers of different kinds of material are called *discontinuities.*

The topmost discontinuity is called the *Mohorovičić discontinuity,* after its discoverer. Above this discontinuity lies only the crust of the earth, a thin shell of rock about 3 miles thick under the ocean floors, but with an average thickness of about 20 miles under the continents.

Above the Mohorovičić discontinuity, the P and S waves travel at 4.3 and 2.4 miles per second, respectively. Below it they travel at 5.0 and 2.9 miles per second. Their speed then increases steadily for the next 1,800 miles downward, reaching 8.5 and 4.5 miles per second respectively. At the 1,800-mile depth, the speed of the P wave suddenly drops to 5 miles per second and its direction of travel changes abruptly, while the S waves disappear entirely. Evidently, there is a discontinuity at this 1,800-mile boundary between the earth's mantle of rock and its core.

Scientists believe that the region of the earth below 1,800 miles is made up of molten iron, perhaps mixed with some nickel and cobalt. First of all, the core must be very dense to account for the earth's great weight. And iron is the only heavy element that exists abundantly throughout the universe. Moreover, at the estimated pressures and temperatures of the core, iron would be a molten liquid. The earth's core must be liquid because the earthquake S waves cannot pass through it—their transverse vibrations can only pass through solids. Finally, the existence of the earth's magnetic field can most readily be understood in terms of an electric current generated in a mass of liquid metal.

Some geophysicists believe there is also an inner core some 800 miles from the center of the earth. This discontinuity might be a transition to a slightly different alloy of iron and nickel, or perhaps a change in state from liquid to solid.

Why do you sometimes feel a strange sensation when an elevator starts up?

The elevators in many tall buildings are designed to travel at high speed in order to get to the upper floors in a reasonable length of time. Oddly enough, it is not the high speed that causes the strange sensation in the pit of one's stomach; it is the rapid acceleration required to reach the high speed.

Velocity is a familiar concept in our everyday experience; acceleration is not. *Acceleration* is a measure of the rate at which an object's velocity is changing. To illustrate, imagine an automobile traveling along a straight road at 30 miles per hour. Its acceleration is zero, because its velocity is not changing. Now imagine that it speeds up uniformly so that its velocity increases by 10 miles per hour at the end of each second. After one second of acceleration its velocity is 40 mph; after two seconds it is 50 mph; after three seconds 60 mph, and so on. The acceleration is 10 miles per hour per second, because the car speeds up by 10 miles per hour in each second.

Much the same sort of thing happens in an elevator. Suppose an elevator starts up from the ground floor and accelerates at a rate of 3 feet per second per second. This means that its speed at the end of each succeeding second is 3, 6, 9, 12 feet per second and so forth. A person standing on a scale in the elevator would notice that his weight had increased by about 10 percent as a result of this acceleration. Furthermore, the muscles of his body would have to work somewhat harder to keep his frame erect and control the location of various internal organs. It is this sort of unaccustomed muscular activity that shows up as "that feeling in the pit of the stomach."

The same effect takes place, of course, when the elevator starts down. In that case, the scale shows the person's weight to be about 10 percent less than its stationary figure.

Acceleration can also be produced by the force of gravity. If we neglect air resistance, a falling object has an acceleration toward the center of the earth of about 32 feet per second per second. In other words, a falling object's speed increases steadily by 32 feet per second for each successive second until it reaches the ground.

This effect leads to a famous "thought experiment," which we can perform without leaving our comfortable easy chair. Imagine a man standing in an elevator atop the Empire State Building when the cable breaks and the elevator begins its uncontrolled descent toward ground level. (For the sake of our unfortunate passenger, let's assume that an automatic braking system will bring the elevator to a soft landing before it hits bottom!) We can see under these conditions that the apparent effect of gravity on the man is temporarily eliminated. From his point of view, and from the point of view of a scale he is standing on, he is quite weightless all the time that the elevator is falling. His feet are no longer planted firmly on the floor of the elevator by the force of gravity; instead, both he and the elevator are accelerating downward at the same rate. He finds himself floating freely this way and that in the air. The man's apparent "loss of gravity" is identical to the "weightlessness" experienced by astronauts in orbit around the earth. Both the man in the elevator and the astronaut in a space capsule are in a state of *free fall,* in which gravity seems to have been eliminated and objects have no weight.

Of course, we know that nothing has changed the gravitational field tugging at both the elevator and its passenger. Only the *effect* of gravity has disappeared, at least as far as the passenger is concerned. To an outside observer, there is no doubt that gravity is still doing its job; the man and elevator are both falling with steadily increasing velocity. Who, then, is right—the man in the elevator or the outside observer?

According to modern physical theory, both are right. This is the conclusion that Einstein's theory forces us to accept; no one can say with certainty which is right—it all depends upon the point of view.

Now let's carry this thought experiment a step further. Instead of falling, suppose the elevator with its passenger is located in empty space, far from any force of gravity. Suppose further that the elevator is attached by a cable to a sort of celestial skyhook that is accelerating it upward at a rate of 32 feet per second every second. (This is precisely the same as the acceleration of a falling object on earth.) With the elevator accelerating through space at this rate, what would the passenger observe?

Einstein concluded that the elevator might as well be standing motionless back on earth as far as the passenger is concerned. Instead of being weightless, the passenger's feet are planted firmly on the floor of the elevator. When he steps on the scale he finds his weight to be exactly right. His body presses down with exactly the same force that gravity would produce if he were on earth. If he drops a pencil, it falls to the floor just as on earth. If he slips and falls, he drops to the floor in a heap. In fact, if he didn't know better, he would think he is standing in a stalled elevator on earth. Yet an outside observer would notice that the elevator is accelerating steadily with respect to the earth.

So once again we may ask who is right—the distant observer or the passenger in the elevator? And once again the answer is that each is right according to his own point of view.

The "weight" of the passenger in the accelerating elevator is called an *inertial force;* it is produced by the acceleration acting with respect to the passenger's inertia. The weight of the man on earth is a gravitational force—a force of attraction between the man and the earth. Einstein concluded that both of these forces (or "weights," if you prefer) *describe precisely the self-same thing.* They are merely two different ways of expressing the same physical effect.

From a simple beginning we have come far afield; from a queasy stomach to the so-called principle of equivalence—the idea that gravitational forces and inertial forces are identical and equivalent in every way. The important implication of all of this is simply that *any kind of motion, whether constant or accelerated, is entirely relative;* and hence the notion of relativity theory. There is no such thing as "absolute motion" if by that term we mean motion of an object that is always observed to be the same by every possible observer.

Why is beach sand usually white?

Beach sand gets its color from quartz, of which it is largely composed. Quartz is a mineral made up of silicon (which is used to make transistors) and the oxygen we breathe. Its chemical formula is SiO_2.

Several factors combine to make quartz particles so plentiful on our beaches. First of all is the matter of abundance of quartz in nature. The following chart gives the average chemical composition of the surface of the earth.

ABUNDANCE OF THE ELEMENTS NEAR THE EARTH'S SURFACE

Element	Abundance by Weight (percentage)	Element	Abundance by Weight (percentage)
Oxygen	46.60	Fluorine	0.070
Silicon	27.70	Sulfur	0.052
Aluminum	8.13	Strontium	0.045
Iron	5.00	Barium	0.040
Calcium	3.63	Carbon	0.032
Sodium	2.83	Chlorine	0.020
Potassium	2.59	Chromium	0.020
Magnesium	2.09	Zirconium	0.016
Titanium	0.44	Rubidium	0.012
Hydrogen	0.14	Vanadium	0.011
Phosphorus	0.12	Others	0.312
Manganese	0.10		

The data show that oxygen and silicon are the two most abundant elements, consisting together almost three-fourths of the substance of the earth near the surface. Also, silicon and oxygen join together readily to produce quartz. So it's reasonable to expect to find a great deal of quartz on the earth.

Another important factor is the relative insolubility of quartz in water. Quartz is essentially insoluble under ordinary conditions. If it happens to be located in a rock, it is left as a residue of sandy soil after the more soluble minerals are carried away by the water.

Finally, of all ordinary rocks quartz is best able to resist the weathering effects of ocean waves. As other less durable rocks are pounded together, they quickly crumble into extremely fine particles that become suspended in the water and are carried off to be deposited as silt on the ocean bottom. This leaves a beach composed of small particles of quartz, with its familiar white color.

While we are on the subject, it is worth noting that 99 percent of the earth's crust is made up of only eight elements: oxygen, silicon, aluminum, iron, calcium, sodium, potassium, and magnesium. Some metals of great commercial value, on the other hand, are really quite rare. The following table lists the abundance of some commercially useful rare metals.

ABUNDANCE OF SOME RARE METALS NEAR THE EARTH'S SURFACE

Metal	Percent by Weight
Nickel, zinc, cobalt, lead, copper, thorium	0.001 to 0.01
Baron, beryllium, arsenic, tin, uranium, tungsten	0.0001 to 0.001
Mercury, silver, cadmium	0.00001 to 0.0001
Gold, platinum, rhodium, osmium, iridium	0.0000001 to 0.000001

It happens that the interior of the earth differs considerably from the crust, so the average chemical makeup of the whole earth must differ from the estimates given above. The following table is an estimate of the average composition of the whole earth.

ABUNDANCE OF THE ELEMENTS IN THE WHOLE EARTH

Element	Percent by Weight	Element	Percent by Weight
Iron	35.40	Cobalt	0.20
Oxygen	27.80	Sodium	0.14
Magnesium	17.00	Manganese	0.09
Silicon	12.60	Potassium	0.07
Sulfur	2.74	Titanium	0.04
Nickel	2.70	Phosphorus	0.03
Calcium	0.61	Chromium	0.01
Aluminum	0.44		

What makes it rain?

Scientists are still searching for a satisfactory explanation of rainfall. At the present time, meteorologists know there are at least two very different kinds of rainstorms and perhaps many more. And each of these may have a different explanation.

Much of our rain is nothing more than melted snowflakes. The basic process runs something like this: A cloud of water droplets rises through the atmosphere to a height at which the temperature is below freezing. Even so, tiny droplets often do not freeze until the temperature reaches ten or twenty degrees below freezing. (The cloud is said to be "supercooled" when liquid droplets exist at temperatures below freezing.) At some crucial temperature a few tiny ice crystals form among the super-cooled droplets of water. The stage is then set for an amazing performance—the droplets transfer their water through the air to the ice crystals.

How does this happen? Scientists know that water molecules escape much more easily from the surface of water droplets than from the surface of ice crystals. (In scientific terms, the *vapor pressure* of super-cooled water is said to be greater than that of ice at the same temperature.) So the water drops evaporate and the molecules of water condense on the ice. The ice crystals grow at the expense of the droplets.

Snowflakes form as the ice crystals fall and collide with others. The snowflakes then head for the ground and, upon reaching the lower, warmer region of the atmosphere, melt into raindrops.

But there's another kind of rain, called warm rain to distinguish it from the cold rain we discussed above. We know that rain can fall from clouds whose temperatures are warmer than freezing. There can be no ice crystals in such warm clouds. The problem, then, is to explain how the droplets get big and heavy enough to fall to earth. Tiny cloud droplets either evaporate before they fall very far or else are held aloft by gentle updrafts.

Meteorologists are beginning to get a good idea of just what goes on in certain clouds to produce so-called warm rain. It has to do with sea salt.

14

The churning oceans are like a giant salt shaker that continually fills the atmosphere with countless particles of sea salt—as many as 1 million per cubic yard of air over the sea! This is important, because sea salt absorbs a great amount of water vapor from the air. Substances that absorb water in this way are said to be *hygroscopic*.

As air currents carry these salt particles up into a cloud, they absorb water vapor from the humid air and become nuclei upon which raindrops can grow. When enough water has collected on a salt particle, it begins to fall through the cloud among the much more numerous, but smaller cloud droplets. In this way, it strikes and captures many small drops in its path, getting larger as it falls. It grows just as a snowball rolling downhill grows by gathering up some of the snow in its path. So each raindrop has its beginning as an extra large cloud drop that forms on a tiny bit of sea salt.

This explanation of warm rain is not yet fully proven, but it does seem to be the leading contender in explaining the existence of warm rain in maritime regions.

Do any animals hibernate in the summer?

Some animals escape life's difficult periods by sleeping through them. All birds and mammals are thought of as *homoiothermic,* or "warm-blooded." They have built-in biological thermostats that keep their body temperature at or near a normal level. In man, this temperature regulator is very precise—keeping the body temperature between 98°F. and 99°F. except for such abnormal conditions as illness or strenuous exercise. But in many wild animals there is a great deal more latitude, and the body temperatures of some drop far below normal into a state of dormancy.

There are important advantages for survival in dormancy. If food is in short supply, an animal can live much longer by lowering its body temperature. This conserves energy by lowering the rate at which the body uses up its stored food—because it takes fuel to keep the body processes going. This is especially true of small animals. They are quite easily heated or cooled by their environment, so they use up relatively more stored fuel to stabilize their body temperature and keep it functioning than do the larger animals. That is why most of the hibernators are small in size.

Scientists have learned a great deal about the pocket mouse, a tiny desert hibernator. It stores seeds in its burrow, and gets all its food and water from them. It never needs to supplement its diet with green vegetation. When the weather is extremely cold—or extremely hot and dry—the pocket mouse sees no particular advantage in using up its hard-earned seeds merely to stay awake. So it falls asleep, and its body temperature drops almost to the temperature of its burrow. In summer, the ground is somewhat warm, even in a burrow twelve inches below the surface, so the sleep is not so deep as in winter.

Summer hibernation of this kind is called *estivation*. The body temperature of a pocket mouse, when awake, varies between 91°F. and 102°F., depending upon his state of activity. During estivation it falls to the vicinity of 60°F. to 67°F. Scientists can induce this state experimentally, and maintain it for many days, by withholding food. If the temperature of the air falls to near freezing, the mouse falls into a state of deep hibernation, and its body temperature is maintained as low as 43°F. Breathing almost stops at this temperature, and the "burning" of body fuel is reduced to an extremely low rate. What little energy is needed is supplied by fat deposits in the body. The pocket mouse and other hibernators spend the cold winter months in this state. When warm weather arrives, they awake as good as new.

Some birds use this same method of energy conservation. Swifts, for example, frequently nest on desert cliffs and forage each day for flying insects, which are their only food. But sometimes the insects are grounded for several days or more by wind and rain. The birds and their young would probably starve during that period of food shortage if they maintained normal body temperature. Instead, the swifts and their young become dormant, apparently as a result of the lack of food. Then, when the insects take flight again, the birds revive spontaneously. Swifts can recover completely only if their body temperature falls no lower than 64° F., which seems to be the critical temperature.

16

Why do artificial fabrics dry so quickly?

Nylon is a *polymer,* or giant molecule, which has been formed by joining together many (*poly*) small parts (*mers*). The "small parts" capable of polymerization are called *monomers.* Some polymers, such as polyethane, are made of just one kind of monomer. Others may use a variety of monomers. Polymeric materials are found throughout the plant and animal kingdoms: the cellulose of tree trunks; the protein of animal tissue; and the cotton, wool, and rubber so common in the modern world.

Synthetic polymers have also become a part of our everyday lives. Their most useful feature, perhaps, is the ease with which they can be formed into almost any shape. For many plastics, the chemical reaction that joins the polymer together occurs as the article is being formed. Thus the object itself—such as nylon thread—may be one giant molecule. This characteristic leads both to the great strength of nylon, and to the ease with which it drys and even sheds water.

During formation of the nylon molecule, one long chain of attached monomers, called a *polymer chain,* is cross-linked to another chain much as the vertical parts of a ladder are attached by the rungs. This same manner of linking takes place with other chains until all are effectively linked together into one compact bundle. Because of this monomolecular feature of the nylon molecule, there are few places left in the molecule to which water molecules are attracted. Thus, water has little adhesion to nylon and tends to run off easily. The same characteristic—strong, water-shedding polymer chains—is shared by Orlon, Acrilan, and many other man-made fibers.

Cotton, which is also a polymer, does not share this feature. On the contrary, it has many places in its structure that are capable of attracting water molecules. Hence cotton garments dry less quickly than nylon ones.

Why does ice float?

Of all the compounds found in nature, water most often seems to follow a set of natural laws all its own. But it behaves most outlandishly when it freezes to form ice, for, unlike most compounds, water is lighter in its solid form than it is as a liquid. Consequently, it floats when it freezes.

Even as it cools toward the freezing temperature, water acts contrary to expectations. At first it behaves in the fashion of normal, well-behaved compounds: it contracts as it cools, growing heavier and more dense. Then, as 39°F. is reached, it suddenly begins to grow lighter and less dense, expanding in volume as the temperature drops further.

The reason for this unexpected behavior lies in the way water molecules attach themselves to each other. Each molecule of water has 2 hydrogen atoms and 1 oxygen atom, which join together to form an asymmetrical structure. The hydrogen atoms are located at one end and the oxygen atom at the other. Thus, the molecule is said to be polarized, with a distribution of positive charge on one end and negative charge on the other. Negative to positive, these polar molecules link together like so many tiny magnets. This electrical attraction is called a *hydrogen bond,* and in it the positively charged hydrogen end of one molecule hitches most readily to the negatively charged oxygen side of a neighbor.

Because water molecules have two positive "terminals" and only one negative "terminal," they join together to build specific patterns—such as the six-pointed structures in snowflakes. In general, an ice crystal is created whenever a water molecule bonds with four other water molecules, which in turn bond with still others. The pattern of molecules forms an elongated pyramid. The inside of the pyramid, however, contains empty space instead of water molecules. As a result, a given number of water molecules takes up more room after freezing than they did before. That is why ice, or solid water, is less dense than liquid water. In solidifying, the molecules shape themselves into a lightweight open structure that is held rigid by hydrogen bonds.

The hydrogen bond also accounts for the odd expansion of liquid water when its temperature changes from 32°F. to 39°F. To understand why, imagine that a piece of ice has melted and reached a temperature of, say, 33°F. Some—but not all—of the hydrogen bonds break apart and the well-ordered pattern begins to collapse. The molecules of water can then move more closely together, and the resulting liquid water is denser than the ice from which it formed. This increase in density, caused by the breakup of hydrogen bonds, continues from the melting point of ice, 32°F., to about 39°F. Within this narrow temperature range some of the molecules are still clumped together in their pyramidal patterns, while others —their bonds broken—are free to wander around with ever-increasing speed as the temperature is raised. At 39°F. enough molecules are moving at a great enough speed to cause water to expand, becoming less dense as the temperature increases further—just as other substances do.

Is there intelligent life on other planets?

Yes, there almost certainly is intelligent life on other planets, but this extraterrestrial life must be very, very far away indeed.

Scientists tell us that life is a chemical affair, the study of which has given birth to a new science—biochemistry. Life has to do with the activities of many kinds of large molecules, or macromolecules, which contain thousands of atoms. When these macromolecules divide in such a way that they duplicate themselves in structure as well as behavior, we have the thing called life.

The atoms that appear most often in living things are oxygen, carbon, and hydrogen. In the human body the atomic distribution is as follows: oxygen, 65 percent; carbon, 18 percent; hydrogen, 10 percent; nitrogen, 3 percent; calcium, 2 percent; phosphorus, 1 percent; all others, 1 percent. The percentages are much the same for animals.

Scientists point out that the high percentage of oxygen is significant. In the sun and stars, and in outer space, the quantity of oxygen is extremely small—much less than 1 percent. But oxygen is the most plentiful element in the crust of the earth—nearly 50 percent, with silicon just about half as plentiful. The ocean, believe it or not, is 89 percent oxygen, and most of the rest is hydrogen, with a trace of various salts thrown in for good measure. The air we breathe is over 20 percent oxygen.

So, although oxygen is rare in the universe at large, it is a dominating factor in water, rocks, air and the living things of this planet. We may wonder, of course, whether there may be kinds of life completely different from that which we know here on earth. Scientists have wondered, for example, whether silicon might be used in place of carbon in the living things of some far-off planet.

Anything is possible, of course, but the general opinion seems to be a qualified no—at least for the present. Although carbon and silicon have many things in common, biochemists tell us that life is not one of them. On earth, they see no evidence of silicon taking the place of carbon in the important business of life. By analysis of the light of stars, scientists have learned that there is a universal chemistry—the same elements everywhere in space. Most scientists now believe that there is also a universal biochemistry based on carbon.

With this background, we can ask ourselves whether life can exist on the other planets of our solar system. First of all, can there be life on the sun? Certainly not. The surface of the sun is much too hot—about 10,000°F. The "cooler" sunspots are at 6,000°F., and the inside of the sun runs up into the millions of degrees. At such temperatures living molecules would tear themselves apart, and even simple water—H_2O—could not exist. So the sun and all the stars are out as far as life is concerned.

Mercury, the nearest planet to the sun, is also a poor choice for life. It is believed to rotate so slowly on its axis that it is extremely hot on one side, perhaps 800°F., and very far below zero on the other side. So no liquid water can exist on the planet.

In the twilight region of Mercury—between the frigid wastes and the searing deserts—the temperature might be right for life, but other problems exist. Because of its small size, Mercury's gravitational pull is too weak to hold an atmosphere. Life, as we think of it, needs not only water, but air. So Mercury, therefore, must be a desolate, lifeless planet.

Venus, the second planet, also offers little hope of supporting life. Through the use of the radio telescope, many scientists have come to believe that Venus is very hot with temperatures up to 600°F. The radio telescope can "see" the surface of Venus because it can detect long radio waves coming from its surface. Visual light rays, on the other hand, are completely blocked by the heavy cloud layer in the atmosphere of Venus. Although the question is still far from settled, most scientists seem to agree that Venus is just too hot for life.

Mars, the planet just beyond the earth in the solar system, may well support a primitive sort of life. Telescopic observation shows clear seasonal changes on the Martian surface, and one interpretation of these changes tells us that they are biological.

The Martian air is thin, oxygen is scarce, the temperature is very cold (−40°F. on the average), and there is just enough water vapor to produce the thin polar ice caps we see. But in the summer season there may be enough liquid water to support simple forms of life.

The seasonal changes observed in Mars have been ascribed by some scientists to dust storms, lava flows, and other nonliving factors. Nevertheless, the answer to the question of life on Mars seems to be "possibly."

Jupiter was long thought to be too cold to support life. But because of the "greenhouse effect," some scientists now feel that Jupiter may have some sort of life on its surface. The moderate temperature of Jupiter is thought to be due to its thick atmosphere, which acts like the glass of a greenhouse, letting warm sunlight in but cutting down the radiation of heat upward from the surface.

The other planets of the sun—Saturn, Uranus, Neptune, and Pluto—are much too cold to support life.

Astronomers tell us that there are at least 40,000 nearby stars much like the sun in size, color, temperature, motion, and light intensity. And in our own Milky Way, there must be millions of duplicates of our own sun—and the same thing, of course, holds true for billions of other galaxies! A large fraction of these stars undoubtedly have planets. Certainly many millions must have planetary twins of our earth, similar to it in all respects. So there is little doubt that there must be intelligent life scattered all over outer space. At least, that's what many scientists think.

Why is carbon monoxide poisonous?

The animal and vegetable kingdoms depend heavily upon each other; the oxygen given off by plants is needed by animals, and the carbon dioxide given off by animals is used by plants in making food. Animals and men satisfy their energy needs—principally for body heat and movements—by the combustion of oxygen in their bodies. They obtain the necessary oxygen by breathing air into the lungs. From there, the oxygen is transported around the body by the bloodstream. The carrier that transports the oxygen in the blood is called *hemoglobin,* a giant protein molecule made up of carbon, hydrogen, iron, nitrogen, oxygen, and sulfur.

The hemoglobin molecule can readily attach itself to an oxygen molecule in the lung, and just as readily release it again in the body muscle. Here, the muscle tissue burns up its carbohydrates by combining them with oxygen. The by-product, carbon dioxide, is given to the hemoglobin, which carries it back to the lung to be breathed out into the atmosphere. Once released into the air, carbon dioxide is again available for use by plants.

Hemoglobin is of use in carrying carbon dioxide back to the lungs because it can also attach loosely to its molecule. Unfortunately, hemoglobin attaches much more firmly to carbon monoxide, a poisonous compound of carbon and oxygen. A person who breathes in enough carbon monoxide gas soon finds his hemoglobin saturated with tenacious carbon monoxide, and the hemoglobin can no longer carry oxygen. This causes suffocation, and that is how carbon monoxide poisons a person who breathes it.

Why do chrysanthemums wait until autumn to flower?

In the temperate and polar regions, there is a seasonal shift from the long, warm days of summer to the short, cold days of winter that poses a vital challenge to plants and animals. In order to survive, they must anticipate the shift. The Canadian snowshoe rabbit, for example, has to begin growing a white camouflage coat weeks before the first snowfall. Failure to do so would make him easy prey to owl or fox.

In order to meet these seasonal pressures, many plants and animals anticipate the seasons by keeping track of the relative amount of daylight and darkness—which, of course, is directly tied to the seasons. This response to different periods of daylight and darkness is called *photoperiodism,* and it has been found both in plants and animals. The snowshoe rabbit, for example, normally starts growing a white coat in August, as the period of daylight shortens. But if the animal is blindfolded for part of the day during the longer days of July, the shortened period of his day brings on the white fur several weeks earlier.

Flowering and fruiting in many plants is also controlled by photoperiodism, and experiments have shown that the length of nighttime is often just as important as the length of day. The chrysanthemum, for example, needs an uninterrupted period of about thirteen hours of darkness of an autumn night before it will flower. Commercial flower growers make use of this characteristic to delay the blossoming of chrysanthemums for a more profitable market. All they have to do is illuminate the plants briefly at night to break up the period of darkness.

The difference in the daylight-to-darkness ratio helps to explain why some plants cannot flourish in all latitudes. Take that scourge of hay fever sufferers, ragweed, for instance. Ragweed cannot begin to flower until summer nights have lengthened to about nine and a half hours. In the latitude of Baltimore, Maryland, this length of nighttime darkness occurs around July 1. Then, by the middle of August, the flowers have matured and scattered their pollen—to the intense discomfort of persons allergic to it. Happily, vacationers in northern Maine are free of this problem because ragweed has not been able to flourish in such northern latitudes. The reason is not that the climate is too cold in Maine; a transported ragweed plant does very well. But the days of midsummer are longer in Maine than in Maryland, so the critical nine-and-a-half-hour period of darkness does not occur until August 1, about a month later than in Baltimore. Fortunately for hay fever sufferers, this "tells" the plant to start its flowering process too late. Before the seeds have time to mature, they are killed by the first September frost. So if you want to have ragweed in Maine, you will have to plant seeds each year.

Can fish see out of water?

On a calm day, when the surface of the water is free of motion, a fish should have no trouble seeing objects in the air above. Never-

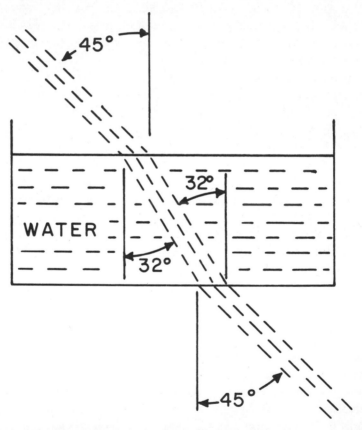

FIG. 2. A beam of light is bent into the water—or toward the perpendicular line—when it enters the tank, and in the opposite direction when it leaves the water.

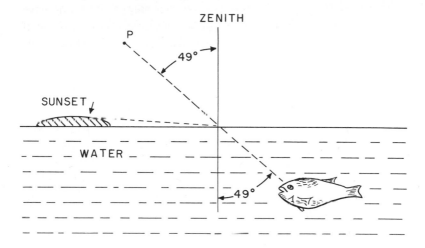

FIG. 3. A fish sees the setting sun at point *P,* only 49 degrees from the vertical direction. The entire atmospheric world of the fish, therefore, is compressed into a cone having an angle of 98 degrees.

theless, because of a scientific principle called the *law of refraction,* the fish's sky appears quite a bit different from our own.

Refraction is the bending of a beam of light when it passes from one transparent medium to another. If you have access to an aquarium tank with glass sides, you can demonstrate this bending as shown in figure 2. A beam of light is bent into the water when it enters the tank, and outwards when it passes into the air again. In general, a light beam is bent or *refracted* toward the perpendicular when it enters a denser medium, and away from the perpendicular when it enters a less dense medium.

Returning to the "heavens" as seen by the marine world, refraction compresses the fish's sky into a narrow cone, as shown in figure 3. As far as the fish are concerned, the sun seems to set at an angle of 49 degrees from the zenith instead of 90 degrees as is actually the case. When the sun is just about to dip beneath the horizon, its rays enter the water at nearly 90 degrees from the vertical. Upon entering the water they are bent to an angle of 49 degrees from the vertical. The result is that the rays reach the fish's eyes as though they originated in the direction of *P* in the diagram. So, from the fish's point of view, the entire terrestrial world is compressed into a cone having an angle of 2 × 49 degrees, or 98 degrees.

Why is DDT dangerous to animal life?

Certain organic pollutants, such as DDT, are extremely dangerous because of a process called *biological magnification*. Oysters, clams, and other shellfish tend to filter out and concentrate a wide variety of substances from their watery environment. This concentration is vital, of course, in obtaining needed food and nutrients from the dilute seawater. Unfortunately, the same biological ingenuity that sustains life can concentrate zinc, copper, and other trace mineral wastes into dangerous levels.

In a tragic incident in Japan, over a hundred villagers died after eating shellfish that had concentrated lethal amounts of a mercury compound that had been dumped into Minamata Bay by a nearby chemical plant. A lesson to be learned here is that the concentrated mercury was lethal, not to the shellfish, but rather to the unsuspecting people who ate the shellfish. The danger is greatest for predators at the top of the food chain, such as birds and human beings, where the biological concentration of toxic substances is greatest.

Scientists tell us that DDT is related to high infant mortality in a number of seabirds. It is believed that DDT residues upset enzyme processes and weaken eggshells. This effect threatens the very survival of such birds as the Bermuda petrel, the brown pelican, the osprey, and the peregrine falcon. These unfortunate creatures at the top of the food chain are fated to dine on shellfish that can store DDT at a level 70,000 times greater than that of the sea they live in.

DDT, the first man-made organic pesticide, was marketed in 1944. Today there are some 500 insecticides, pesticides, herbicides, and fungicides incorporated into the about 50,000 formulations that are registered for use in the United States. Unfortunately, it may take decades—as with DDT—to discover which of these are potential health hazards, either to animals or to man himself.

How much water is there?

Of all nine planets in the solar system, the earth is unique in having large quantities of water in the liquid state. The earth's supply—a staggering 326 million cubic miles of water—would, if poured on the United States, submerge the country to a depth of almost 100 miles. Also unique among the planets is the earth's ability to maintain vast amounts of water in all three of its fundamental states—as a vapor, liquid, and solid. Water, in fact, is the only common and abundant material that exists naturally in all three states on earth. This accident of nature has determined the course of life on our planet.

Almost all of the world's water is found in the oceans—some 97.2 percent, to be exact. The ice caps and glaciers account for another 2.15 percent, so that 99.35 percent of all the water is tied up either in the oceans or in the frozen parts of the earth. The remaining .65 percent is distributed among all the other manifestations of water. Included in that amount are the water of all the great lakes and rivers of the world; the inland seas; the brooks, streams, and swamps; the pools, puddles, bogs, sewers, and reservoirs, the snow and vapor in the atmosphere; the moisture in the land; and the groundwater that supplies our wells and helps feed our streams and rivers. Groundwater, in fact, accounts for the lion's share—97 percent—of that small, usable amount of water, the amount that is left when the oceans, ice caps, and glaciers are subtracted from the world total.

Scientists know that water follows a continuous cycle in which evaporation from the surface is followed by rainfall around the globe. The water going out from the surface of the earth must come back in equal amount—a perpetual hydrologic cycle with no beginning, middle, or end. In order to maintain this cycle there must be distributed, at any moment, an average of 3,100 cubic miles of water throughout the global atmosphere. This water, of course, is in the form of vapor or droplets. Although the amount seems substantial, it is only one-thousandth of one percent of the world supply, and is actually quite small compared with the size of the atmosphere. If all of the atmospheric water vapor and cloud droplets suddenly fell as rain, the 3,100 cubic miles of water would cover the earth with merely an inch of precipitation. Luckily, the turnover of atmospheric water is rapid. On the average, all of the water falls from the sky in twelve days and is continuously replaced by evaporation from the surface.

How do computers translate languages?

A number of experimental computers have been designed to translate from one language to another. The input of a typical computer is a keyboard whose keys bear the symbols of one language, say Russian, while the output is printed in another language, say English. The operator, who has no knowledge of Russian, merely types out the Russian character, key by key and word by word. Although the translation would win no literary prizes, such machines can usually produce a fairly intelligible translation.

Stored in the memory of the computer is an electronic dictionary of over 100,000 Russian phrases and words with their English equivalents. The computer searches its memory until it finds a match between a phrase or word that is to be translated and an entry in its electronic dictionary. When a match is found, it types out the English translation and goes on to the next phrase.

Translation machines face two major problems that must be solved. The first is the time required to scan its stored dictionary, even at the high speed of electronics. To reduce this time, the machine is taught to "skip pages"—just as we do—until it gets close to the desired phrase. Then it examines that page in detail—as we do—until it finds a match.

Another major stumbling block is the fact that many words in each language have a number of unrelated meanings. Take the word *line* for example. *Webster's Collegiate Dictionary* lists over sixty definitions for this one word! Obviously a machine cannot pick out the correct meaning if it works with only one word at a time. By and large, word-for-word translation is incomprehensible.

The computer solves this problem by working with groups of words, or phrases, just as human beings do. If it finds no match it drops off a word and tries again, going to shorter phrases, then words until a match is found. By this method it can deal with *all* words, common or unusual. The last resort, a letter-by-letter output, is not a translation, but rather a transliteration. Nevertheless, it is useful to the human reader in understanding the machine's output.

Why is glass transparent?

The explanation of why some substances are opaque and others transparent involves the interaction of materials with light. Scientists tell us that light is energy in the form of electromagnetic waves. Thus light and radio waves are the same kind of phenomenon, differing only in detail, not in principle.

In 1860 James Clerk Maxwell proposed the idea that such waves are moving electric and magnetic fields generated by the vibration of an electric charge. This causes an "energy message" to move out from the vibration in all directions. The wave, he pointed out, would oscillate at a rate equal to the rate of vibration of the electric charge. This, then, is the essential difference between light, radio waves, ultraviolet radiation, and infrared radiation: all have differing rates or frequencies of oscillation.

So all electromagnetic waves are oscillating electric and magnetic fields. What is of importance to transparency is the effect of matter on these fields. All matter is composed of electrically charged particles, so there is almost bound to be some interaction when the electromagnetic waves try to pass through a piece of matter, and in the usual case there is.

All of the particles in a solid body are held together in some way or other—molecules attracted to molecules, atoms to atoms, or electrons to nuclei of atoms. And all of these particles oscillate or vibrate back and forth in the solid structure. The stronger the linkage force between particles, the higher the natural frequency of vibration. Some molecules, for example, oscillate at a frequency of about 10^{13} (1 followed by 13 zeroes) oscillations per second. Electrons oscillate about 100 times faster, and nuclear particles oscillate about 100,000 times faster still.

If the frequency of the electromagnetic waves striking our piece of matter is the same as the natural frequencies of the body's linked particles, the latter will sway in tune with the waves, much as a piano hums back at you when you sing into the strings. The electrons begin to oscillate in time, absorbing a part of the light energy contained in the electromagnetic wave. When this happens in a material, the electromagnetic light waves cannot get through and the substance turns out to be opaque. But if the frequency of the light waves is appreciably different from the natural frequencies of the linked particles, there is little or no absorption. At most, the radiation is dispersed a little and penetrates right through the substance. Thus visible light goes through a transparent substance with little absorption because the substance has no constituents that can oscillate at the same frequency as the electromagnetic waves we call light.

Glass is not transparent for other frequencies—ultraviolet rays, for example. You cannot get a suntan behind a glass window because glass blocks out the invisible ultraviolet that gives you the tan.

Also related to transparency is the matter of color. Visible light is a mixture of electromagnetic waves of frequencies (or colors) from about 3.9 to 8.4×10^{14} oscillations per second. It appears white to the eye only if it contains all of these frequencies in more or less equal quantities. But many substances can selectively absorb light of certain specific frequencies. Thus, light of that color is removed from the spectrum and the mixture of the remaining colors no longer appears white. If yellow light is absorbed, for example, the remaining mixture looks violet to us. So we say the substance has a violet color.

What caused the Ice Age?

About a million years ago, the earth's average temperature fell about six degrees, or perhaps even less. But that small drop in temperature was enough to upset the delicate balance of water and ice in the world—a balance that had remained relatively stable for hundreds of millions of years. The reduced temperature was enough to produce a little more snow each year than the amount that melted. Thus, with the cycle out of kilter, the passage of time allowed the growing glaciers to spread great distances to the south, and the earth entered the Pleistocene era, or Ice Age.

The storage of so much additional water on the land caused the level of the oceans to lower by as much as 300 feet. As a result, about 2.5 million square miles of land were added to the East and Gulf coasts of North America. In addition, Alaska and Asia were connected by a land bridge, as were Europe and the British Isles.

The weight of the ice cap caused a secondary effect. Parts of the earth's crust under the ice caps sank considerably—as much as 3,000 feet in places. Then as the glaciers melted, and their ice ran back to the ocean as water, the depressed areas slowly rose again. Some localities have risen as much as 1,000 feet since the ice retreated, and the movement is continuing today at a measurable rate.

The last major expansion of glaciers began around 25,000 years ago, proceeding south at an average rate of 100 to 200 feet per year. The glaciers reached their furthest advance to the south about 17,000 years ago and then began to shrink. After various reexpansions toward the south, one of which blanketed much of the Great Lakes region 11,000 years ago, the shrinking ice had disappeared from most areas by 5,000 years ago. Other advances of the glaciers, both in Europe and America, took place around 40,000 and 60,000 years ago. Little is known about the timing of earlier periods of glaciation.

The climates that existed between the advances of the glaciers were cooler than the present climate. The last really nonglacial period of time, with climates comparable in warmth to today's, seems to have ended about 70,000 years ago. Much earlier, other glacial ages had occurred around 200 million and 600 million years ago—and there probably were others before that.

During the four major advances of the present Ice Age, the glaciers from the north wore down the Appalachian Mountains, gouged out basins of the Great Lakes—and thousands of others—and pushed up great heaps of earth and rock to form the New England hills. At their greatest extent, the ice sheets, often many thousands of feet thick, blanketed most of North America, down to the sites of New York City, Saint Louis, and Cleveland.

The glaciers began their last retreat only about 10,000 years ago, and are still receding. During the last 120 years there has been a general warming trend amounting to as much as 1.8°F.

The earth may finally have reestablished a normal balance between water and ice—but there is no way of knowing whether the Ice Age is over. The main causes of the climatic fluctuation responsible for the glacial ages are not known, but many scientists believe they lie outside the earth, perhaps in variations of solar energy output.

Can a person's aching joints predict weather changes?

Although aching joints probably cannot predict the weather, it does seem clear that some people can feel the weather changing. This weather sensitivity often stems from scar tissue.

In spite of modern surgical skill, scar tissue is merely nature's patch job, and is not in perfect harmony with the adjacent, older parts of the body. Consisting of regenerated skin and muscle tissue, scars often react differently to environmental changes than the older tissue. This sets up internal stresses, which can cause pain. People with a missing limb often complain that the missing part hurts. Although such pains are labeled "phantom pains," they are far from imaginary, as any sufferer will attest.

Records have been kept on a large group of persons suffering from this sort of pain. The data show that the pains have a seasonal trend. They are more common in months of wet, stormy weather than during dry, sunny times. On a day-to-day basis, poor weather and high humidity invariably accompany the weather miseries.

By far the largest group of weather sufferers is made up of people having rheumatism. Many rheumatics feel sharp pains when falling temperatures occur. They can often be helped by dry heat, and the treatment many times includes moving to a warm, dry climate.

Rheumatoid arthritis, with involvement in the joints, is also closely related to the weather. It is much more prevalent in cold, moist, stormy climates than in warm, dry, calm ones. People in poor housing are more susceptible than those in well-heated homes. The environment seems, in some mysterious way, to thicken fluids in joints and tendons, thereby providing more resistance to motion.

If all of this smacks of magic and witchcraft, consider the following experiments in which hospitalized arthritis patients were subjected to controlled atmospheric changes. They were placed in a room that was isolated from the outside weather. All elements of the atmospheric environment in this "climatron" could be separately controlled. The researchers recorded the subjective reactions of the patients and measured such factors as swelling of joints. The results proved that the existence of weather pains is supported by clinical evidence and is not a figment of the imagination. When the barometric pressure was reduced while relative humidity was raised, the typical arthritic complaints and symptoms were provoked. These, of course, are characteristic of the cold, wet weather mentioned earlier. Research continues in these fields, and may one day lead to a better understanding of weather-related diseases.

Can fish "speak" and hear?

Not only do fish make sounds in the water, but they have ears or hearing organs that pick up sound vibrations from the water. These ears are enclosed in auditory capsules on each side of the head, behind the eyes. Some persons with aquarium fish have trained their fish to come for food at feeding time. They tap the water before the food is placed in the aquarium, and the fish are attracted by the vibration.

The noises made by many fish can be heard clearly by the human ear. They cover a wide range of pitches and intensities. Among the noisier fish are the croakers, drums, grunts, tigerfish, catfish, and filefish. Drums and croakers make sounds similar to a drum roll. Grunts grunt! And the sound of the tigerfish is made by rotating fin spines.

Certain catfish use their air bladder to produce sound. Gas in the bladder is forced back and forth past taut membranes, causing them to vibrate. Fish with air bladders seem to be more sensitive to sound than those without air bladders. Some scientists suspect that sound may be amplified by the air bladder.

What is coke?

Coke is the residue—mostly carbon—that is left when coal gas is produced from coal. In the manufacture of coal gas, coal is heated to about 1800°F. in a large vessel or retort. At that high temperature a gas is produced that escapes from the red-hot coal. After several hours, all of the gas has been extracted from the coal, leaving a porous form of carbon called *coke*.

The coal gas leaving the retort contains many impurities, which must be removed before the gas can be piped into homes or factories. These include a considerable amount of tar and such materials as benzene, naphthalene, and ammonia. In a typical process, a ton of coal yields about 15,000 cubic feet of gas, 11 gallons of tar, and 1,500 pounds of coke.

In addition to its use as fuel, coke is also used to make an inflammable gas called *water gas*. Water in the form of steam is added to incandescent coke (carbon) and the chemical reaction between the two yields a mixture of hydrogen and carbon monoxide gas. Both of these gases burn in air, so water gas can be used as fuel.

Can an artificial satellite stay up forever?

Scientists speak of "permanent" and "temporary" satellite orbits. Both terms mean just what they say. A satellite in permanent orbit will remain in space indefinitely, while another, in temporary orbit, will remain in space only for a limited period of time.

The distinction between permanent and temporary depends only on one factor: the height of the nearest point, or *perigee,* from the ground. For perigees closer than about 250 miles the orbit is said to be temporary.

Our atmosphere is usually said to have a height of 100 miles, but it can obviously have no sharp upper boundary. Up to about 250 miles a satellite will still encounter some retardation from cosmic dust particles and small numbers of gas particles. At greater altitudes a satellite encounters practically no resistance in its orbit and stays there indefinitely.

So-called orbital decay of a satellite works something like this. After passing through the resisting atmosphere (at the perigee), the satellite continues along its orbit and reaches the highest point, or *apogee*. But because the satellite has previously lost some of its momentum by the action of air resistance, the apogee will not be quite as far up as it was on the previous orbit. Each time the satellite dips through the perigee it loses more momentum, and each succeeding apogee is closer to the earth. This causes the orbit to shrink until all of it is as low as the perigee was originally. The satellite then encounters resistance all the way around and sinks lower and lower in the atmosphere. When it reaches the denser layers it burns up.

Why can't we see the stars in the daytime?

In ancient times, man thought that the stars were lanterns lit by the gods to beautify the nighttime sky. When dawn approached the gods would pull the stars up through holes in the sky and extinguish them.

We now know, of course, that the stars and planets shine both in daytime and at night. In fact, if you know where to look, you can sometimes see Venus during the daytime. Venus is the brightest object in the sky, after the sun and moon.

We do not see the stars during the daytime because of the brightness of the sky. Stars are so clearly visible at night because we see them against a dark background. That is to say, there is a great difference in light intensity between a star and the region of the sky adjacent to it. The star is *many times* brighter than the darkened sky. During the daytime, however, this is not true. Particles of air, dust, and water vapor in the atmosphere scatter the sun's light, thereby giving the sky its brightness. Our eyes can detect no discernible difference in light intensity between the stars and the illuminated sky.

If we were to travel above the earth's atmosphere, we would see the stars against a dark background at all times. The sun and moon would look like bright disks against the blackness of outer space.

During a total eclipse of the sun, the brighter stars become visible as the atmosphere darkens. The same thing happens at dusk as the sun sets.

Why is the center of the earth hot?

Scientists are not in complete agreement on this question, mainly because they do not agree on how the earth was formed. The older theory tells us that the earth was originally a great ball of molten material ejected by the sun, or perhaps a molten fragment of some celestial explosion. This explanation accounts for the molten center of the earth, and for its uneven, rocky crust. In cooling, the earth would probably shrink and become wrinkled, thereby producing the mountains.

Another theory, accepted by most geophysicists, holds that the earth was cold at its formation, which slowly took place as gravity brought together vast clouds of interstellar dust. As the planet grew, its gravitational attraction would have become stronger and the process would have continued until all of the nearby matter had been attracted into one ball. Even today meteorites—mostly dust particles from outer space—continue to pelt the earth at a rate of 730,000 tons a year.

The dust-cloud theory leads scientists to believe that the earth may be heating up rather than cooling off, and it may even be expanding. The heat inside the earth is attributed to energy given off by radioactive materials in rocks. Radioactive elements such as uranium in the earth "decay," or decompose, discharging atomic particles and giving off heat energy. Calculations convince most scientists that, after the earth solidified, the decaying radioactive elements in its interior produced heat faster than it could escape through hundreds of miles of insulating rock to the earth's surface. If this is true, the earth would have begun to heat up.

Temperatures near the bottom of the mantle, about 1,800 miles down, are estimated to be in the range of 3,600°F. to 9,000°F.

The center of the earth is probably no more than 900°F. hotter than the lower mantle.

Does the moon cause tides in the land as well as the ocean?

With the advent of new kinds of instruments, scientists are learning more about earthquakes and other less dramatic examples of movement within the earth's crust. A strain meter, for example, deep in a mountain tunnel uses a seventy-five-foot-long quartz rod to measure crustal expansion and contraction. With such devices, scientists have made the amazing discovery that the moon creates tides on solid land just as it does in the oceans! There are two land tides per day; with each tide, a point on the earth may rise and fall several inches or more.

It has also been learned that for days after a severe earthquake the earth vibrates at certain frequencies like a struck gong. These frequencies, of course, are far too low to be heard—one of the "tones" is twenty octaves below middle C—but they are extremely powerful. It is possible that these vibrations even move the earth's inner core a fraction of an inch. Scientists are investigating still other earth movements along earthquake fault lines, in the hope that new discoveries may lead to accurate forecasting of when and where earthquakes will strike.

You may wonder how it is possible to measure the tidal rise and fall of the earth's rocky surface. The measurement was first made in a most clever way by the American physicist, Albert A. Michelson. He knew that the earth's deformation was certainly less than the ocean's, so the "tides in rocks" must be smaller than the tides in the oceans. Since both go up and down under the lunar influence, the tides we observe at the seashore must result from the difference between the heights of the two tides. We can easily measure this difference, but the independent measurement of the separate heights of the two tides is not a simple matter.

Michelson built a small version of the ocean, a carefully leveled iron pipe 500 feet long that was half filled with water. He found that there were small vertical displacements of the water level at each end of the pipe, just as in the oceans. They were so small, however—only twenty millionths of an inch at their maxima— that he could observe them only with the help of a sensitive optical device.

Comparing the observed height of these "microtides" with theoretical values—which he could easily calculate for his simple experiment, he found that they amounted to only 69 percent of the expected effect. The remaining 31 percent was evidently masked by tidal motion of the earth's surface under his pipe. So he concluded that the observed ocean tides must represent only 69 percent of the total rise of the water. And since the tides in open oceans amount to 2.5 feet, the total rise of water must be 3.6 feet. The difference, 1.1 feet, evidently corresponds to the up-and-down motion of the earth's crust. So, strange as it seems, the ground under our feet periodically rises and falls twice a day, with all of the cities, mountains, and valleys of the earth.

Why don't clouds fall to earth?

Except for fog, almost all clouds are formed as a result of rising air. When air ascends to higher altitudes, it becomes colder, which causes its relative humidity to increase. When the relative humidity becomes high enough, water molecules condense on solid particles in the air. The enormous number of tiny droplets produced in that way constitutes a cloud.

Most clouds don't fall to earth because rising air currents offset their tendency to fall. The following table lists the approximate falling speeds of water droplets of various sizes at sea level. (Smoke and dust particles are also included, for purposes of comparison.)

APPROXIMATE FALLING SPEED OF PARTICLES

Drop Diameter (in inches)	Description	Terminal Speed (feet per second)
0.00004	Smoke, dust	0.0001
0.0004	Cloud droplet	0.01
0.004	Drizzle	1.0
0.04	Rain	15.0

As you can see, cloud droplets fall only one-hundredth of a foot in a second. That amounts to falling only 36 feet in an hour. It doesn't take much vertical air motion to keep tiny cloud droplets from reaching the ground. (In the absence of updrafts, tiny cloud droplets usually evaporate before reaching the ground.)

Smoke particles fall at a speed that is about one one-hundredth as fast as cloud droplets. For all practical purposes, they can be thought of as not falling at all. Air currents carry them through all parts of the atmosphere until rain or snow sweeps them down to earth. Meteorologists often say that precipitation "scrubs" the atmosphere, or "washes it out."

The smallest raindrops, about one-hundredth of an inch in diameter, fall at a rate of about 3 feet per second. "Average" drops, perhaps one-tenth inch in diameter, fall about 20 feet per second. Large drops—a quarter-inch in diameter or larger—fall about 30 feet per second.

Raindrops fall at different speeds because of air resistance. When any object falls through the air, two forces act upon it: one is the force of gravity; the other is a frictional force called air resistance. While gravity pulls the object down, air resistance pushes up, and tends to slow it down.

To understand how this works, imagine a raindrop falling through the air. Our raindrop falls because of gravity and starts to speed up. As it does, the force of air resistance in the opposite direction becomes greater and greater. Finally, the two forces become equal and the drop's speed remains constant as it falls through the air. This speed is called its *terminal velocity*.

It turns out that large drops have greater terminal velocities than small drops. This is because, as the raindrop gets bigger, the pull of gravity on a drop goes up faster than the frictional force of air resistance.

Why does "bottom English" cause a cue ball to roll back after contact?

Hitting a cue ball below dead center imparts two distinct motions to it: the first is the normal forward motion tending to make it roll

BILLIARD BALL

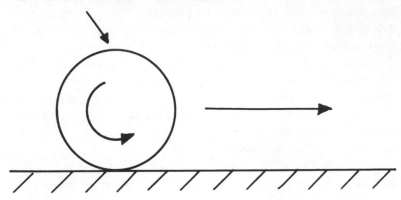

FIG. 4. Hitting a billiard ball with "bottom English" imparts two distinct motions to it: a forward translational movement, and a backward spin. After impact with another ball, the back spin causes the first ball to roll backwards.

or skid toward the object ball; the second is a spinning motion about a horizontal axis, which tends to impede its forward motion. To understand these motions, imagine an automobile sliding down a hill with its powered wheels spinning in reverse. The rear wheels have a forward motion (down the hill), and a reverse spin tending to stop the car. Bottom or reverse English gives much the same motion to a cue ball: although it moves forward, as illustrated in the diagram, it has a backward spin tending to slow it down.

When such a cue ball strikes the object ball head-on, or nearly so, its forward motion is transferred to the object ball. But the back-spin is not transferred and so causes the cue ball to roll backwards, away from the point of impact.

Much the same sort of thing happens with "side English." Here the cue ball is struck somewhat to the right or left of center as desired, to affect the angle taken by the ball after impact.

English is also used by bowlers to affect the direction taken by the bowling ball after it strikes the first pin. The English is imparted by a twisting motion of the hand as the bowling ball is released.

40

What is plankton?

The oceans and seas are teeming with tiny plants and animals called *plankton,* of which more than 15,000 kinds are known. The animal types are often larger than the plant plankton upon which they feed.

Plant plankton contain chlorophyll, and need sunlight to grow. For that reason they are found near the water's surface. They constitute the lowest link in the important food chain of the sea. Animal plankton eat plant plankton, and both are eaten by the smaller fish. Larger fish eat the smaller fish, and so on. Without plant plankton, the sea animals would soon run out of food, and perish.

Why does wood rot?

Damp wood is a natural breeding ground for bacteria and fungi, which break up the chemical substances of which wood is composed. Another type of decay, called *dry rot,* is also produced by several species of fungi.

The substance that wood-loving microbes seem to enjoy most is *cellulose,* the chief constituent of cell walls in plants and trees. Cellulose comprises one-third of all the vegetable matter in the entire world, which makes it the most abundant organic compound in the world. The chemical formula for cellulose is $C_6H_{10}O_6$. Dry wood contains up to 50 percent cellulose, while cotton is 90 percent cellulose. As mentioned above, a variety of bacteria, fungi, and protozoa are able to consume cellulose, giving off carbon dioxide and water in the process. Horses and ruminants are also able to digest cellulose—probably because their stomachs contain cellulose-decomposing bacteria and fungi. Human beings, however, cannot use cellulose as food.

In addition to microbes and horses, cellulose is also a favorite feature in the diet of many insects. Some of the more important are the deathwatch beetle, the powder-post beetle, and the common furniture beetle. In warm regions of the earth, termites are wood's greatest enemy. In the sea, certain crustaceans and marine molluscs such as the teredo destroy wood construction in seawater.

To combat its cellulose-craving enemies, wood is usually impregnated with antiseptic substances that protect it against microbes and insects. These fall into two groups: oils and salts. The most popular oil is creosote, a coal- and wood-tar product. The salt most often used is zinc chloride. They are applied in such a way that the wood absorbs as much of the material as possible in order to provide adequate and lasting protection.

How does a Xerox copier work?

The word *Xerox* stems from xerography, a word that means "dry writing." The Xerox machine produced a complete revolution in the office copying machine industry by providing a high-quality copy quickly, at low cost, and without the use of messy, smelly chemicals.

The Xerox machine uses an electric charge to help reproduce the image. A typed page, a page of a book, or any page to be copied is laid face down on the glass window of the machine. A button is pushed, and a copy comes out an instant later on any kind of paper you care to use.

The inventor, Chester Carlson, turned to electric charge and a *photoconductive* material to produce his new kind of copy. A photoconductive material will retain its electric charge in the dark, but will lose it whenever it is exposed to light. In the present machine, a selenium roll is given a uniform electric charge. A bright light then illuminates the original page, and a lens system projects its image on the selenium roll. Wherever the image is bright, the charge disappears; where the image is dark, the charge remains. In this way, the pattern of electric charge left on the roll corresponds point by point with the original page. A special dust is then applied to the roll and sticks to it only where there is an electric charge This image in dust is then transferred from roll to paper, and fused to the paper by a momentary application of heat. The result is a precise copy, identical to the original in all respects, and often of higher quality and easier to read.

Xerography is also used in high-speed printing machines that turn out thousands of copies per hour. And an analogous process is used to print mailing labels for a national magazine at a rate of 135,000 labels per hour.

Where did the moon come from?

Most of us have wondered at one time or another about the origin of the moon. Where did it come from? Has it changed much in the course of time? Is it changing or evolving even now?

Scientists have come up with many theories about the origin of the moon, but none of them are completely satisfactory. One suggests that the earth and moon were formed at the same time and from the same materials from which all of the planets were formed. This suggestion implies that the earth and moon were never a single planet but have always been a double planet, circling about each other as the pair circles the sun.

Some scientists also believe that the moon was born somewhere else and was "captured" by the earth's gravitational field—a pretty difficult feat to imagine.

Another well-known theory tells us that the moon came out of the Pacific Ocean in the early history of our planet, flung out by the earth's rapid rotation. There is some evidence for this theory. The rocks near the earth's surface are similar in density to the entire moon. The expulsion theory would also account well enough for the depth and size of the Pacific Ocean.

In his book, *Tides and Ages,* George Darwin—son of Charles Darwin, who gave us the Theory of Evolution—discusses the effects of the tides on the long-term motions of the earth and moon.

The tides exert a braking action on the earth, slowing it down ever so slightly over the years. To understand how this can happen, imagine that we are observing the earth from a point on the moon. We notice, first of all, that the earth spins on its axis once a day. We also observe two tidal bulges of water in the earth's oceans that point steadily toward and away from the moon as the earth spins under them. These tides transform some of the earth's rotational energy to heat by means of friction. A considerable amount of energy is used up by the internal friction of the water, by the friction of moving tidal flows against sea bottoms, and by the impact of the moving bulges of water against continents standing in their way. This dissipation of energy causes a slowing down of the earth's rotational motion.

The slowing down of the earth by the tides can amount to only 13 seconds per century, but this agrees well with astronomical observations. When astronomers measure the positions of the planets with respect to the stars, they find that they are ahead of time compared with the positions calculated a hundred years ago. These puzzling discrepancies can be explained by the slowing down of the earth's rotation.

Because the rotation of the earth is slowing down, the motion of the moon around the earth must be speeding up. This is a direct consequence of a fundamental law of science known as the *law of conservation of angular momentum*. And if the moon is speeding up, it must also be moving away from the earth. Scientists calculate that each new moon sees the moon 4 inches farther away. Here again, 4 inches is not very large compared with the earth-moon distance of 238,860 miles. But we are interested in the accumulated change in distance over billions of years. In that period of time the inches can add up to a considerable distance.

George Darwin reasoned that if the moon is moving away from the earth, it must once have been much closer. Carrying the moon's motion backward in time about 4.5 billion years, the moon must have been just about touching the earth's surface. In addition, both the length of the day and of the month would have been about five hours long. Thus, back in the early days of the solar system, we find the moon revolving around the earth at a low altitude, with a month equal in duration to a day. Why, then, not assume that they were once a single body that broke into two pieces? No one knows, of course, if that actually happened.

None of these hypotheses seems to account for the fact that the moon always turns the same face toward the earth. This peculiarity might just turn out to be an accident of nature, but it hardly seems likely. Perhaps further lunar exploration will yield additional clues to the moon's origin.

Can the growing of food be made more efficient?

With the population explosion and all of its implications, it is good to know that scientists are learning how to raise more food on less land than is possible with conventional farming methods. The key to food production, of course, is *photosynthesis*—the chemical reduction of carbon dioxide to form a sugar, and the splitting of water to produce oxygen. We can think of a kind of machine in the chlorophyll of green plants into which we dump water and carbon dioxide. The sun provides energy that runs the machine, and out come sugar (glucose) and oxygen. All of this is wonderful for mankind, of course, who eats the plant's food and breathes its oxygen.

But, unfortunately, the chlorophyll machine is like the goose that lays the golden eggs. Whenever scientists cut into it to see how it works, they destroy the machine and learn little for their pains.

Despite the fact that photosynthesis is largely a mystery to scientists, they have learned how to make it more efficient. To illustrate, we know that corn is about the most efficient plant user of sunshine, yet it has an efficiency of only 0.3 percent. This means that an acre of corn plants "wastes" about 99.7 percent of the sunlight that reaches it. Other plants are even less efficient by a factor of 2 or 3.

In spite of this low efficiency, normal crop production averages about 3 tons per acre per year. If plant efficiency could be raised to that of an electric motor, it would be possible theoretically to raise 3 tons of crops per acre in a single day or less! Incredible? Scientists have already begun to produce more food per acre by giving nature a helping hand. The plants used in this photochemical research are algaes such as *Chlorella pyrenoidosa*.

To most of us, algae are the green scum growing on ponds or the seaweed growing near the shore. At first glance they don't seem particularly appealing as food. But neither was the tomato, which was long thought to be poisonous before man accepted it as food.

Scientists have grown algae in plastic-covered tanks into which air containing 5 percent or more of carbon dioxide is fed. This is far above nature's provision of .03 percent carbon dioxide in the air. In addition, the algae are circulated by pumps ensuring a more efficient distribution of available sunlight. Using such methods, crop outputs of 100 or more tons per acre can be produced. And these results can be obtained despite our lack of knowledge of how photosynthesis really works.

The disadvantages of algae as food are cost and taste. Some researchers estimate that fifty cents a pound is a reasonable estimate of product cost in the marketplace. And since they have a dark color and the strong aroma and taste of fish, there is some prejudice against their use on aesthetic grounds. Nevertheless, the powder has been added successfully to ice cream, soup, fish cakes, candy, cake, and soft drinks. In the long term, improvement in taste and reduction in cost could well add algae to the staple diet of human beings. And it is always possible, of course, that science will discover the secret of photosynthesis. It may then be possible to produce "pure" starches and proteins from carbon dioxide and water in efficient factories. Artificial flavorings could then be added to simulate more palatable items of food.

Why are wetlands important?

The coastal zones of the United States, which include estuaries, bays, tidal flats, marshlands, and sounds, contain an enormous variety and number of marine organisms. The basis for all animal life in coastal waters is an abundant plant growth—from mangroves to eelgrass and algae. They are supported by the natural mixing and flushing action of the tides and by the organic nutrients that flow from the adjacent land. These produce the rich bottoms and wetlands that are vital to marine life in coastal waters.

Estuaries have a slow mixing action caused by the seaward flow of fresh water and the landward flow of salt water from the ocean. This gradually changing salinity also helps account for the variety of species, and the large numbers of fish, shellfish, birds, and mammals found in coastal waters.

Many species of marine life, such as clams and oysters, spend their entire life cycles in the estuaries. Others, particularly shrimp, migrate from estuarine nursery areas to the sea to complete their life cycles. Still others, such as salmon and striped bass, pass through the estuaries to spawning grounds farther upstream, and the young reverse the process in returning to the sea. At least two-thirds of the animal population of the oceans either spend an essential part of their life cycle in estuarine waters, or depend heavily on species that do. Countless shorebirds and waterfowl are dependent on the plants and animals of the coastal zone. And all of this marine life has a vital stake in a stable system of coastal wetlands.

One only has to read the newspapers to discover how intense the competition is for use of land in our limited coastal regions. Ever larger ships require ever deeper channels. Mining and oil-drilling operations in coastal waters grow daily. Industrial and residential development compete to fill in vital wetlands for building sites, and airports and highways, with surrounding development patterns, gobble up additional land, much of it unnecessarily—for much industry, housing and transportation could be sited elsewhere. As a result, recreational areas—from beaches and surf to places for fishing, hunting, and pleasure-boating—become more congested as available lands diminish. And because over 90 percent of the U.S. fishery catch comes from coastal waters, it is clear that this industry has an important stake in preserving our marshes and wetlands.

The effect of pollution on coastal waters has received considerable attention. Just as detrimental is the physical alteration of submerged and adjacent coastal land—particularly the shallow marshes and wetlands. These changes include draining, dredging, and filling —and often destroy forever the essential food base for practically all marine life in the area. Unfortunately, these consequences are usually not apparent to the general public until after the permanent damage is done. Some 3 million waterfowl used to nest and feed in San Francisco Bay before a large part of it was gradually filled. The birds now number less than 600,000. In the Chesapeake Bay, oyster and crab catches are down and one fish species—the croaker —has all but disappeared in recent years. It is clear that changes for the worse are taking place in many irreplaceable estuaries.

47

To developers and landowners with little appreciation of the importance of estuaries, wetlands are extremely attractive for industrial and home construction. They cost little to dredge, fill, and bulkhead, and offer attractive building sites. Too often local governments encourage this construction, thereby allowing our natural wetlands to be nibbled away. The long-range costs of this kind of land use are borne, not just by the community, but by the people of the entire region.

Only 6 percent of our recreational shoreline is owned by government. Controls over development of the remaining wetlands are, for the most part, inadequate. Only a handful of states have meaningful statewide controls over changes that can be made to private coastal land or to contiguous dry lands. Unless this unfortunate state of affairs is corrected, our wetlands will continue to disappear, and with them much of the value—both aesthetic and economic— of our coastal waters.

Why do "shooting stars" burn up in the atmosphere?

It is a common misconception that meteorites or "shooting stars" are heated to incandescence by air friction. Scientists usually refer to this heating as *kinetic heating* or *aerodynamic heating*.

What happens is this. When an object moves through air, a very thin layer actually touching it remains stationary with respect to the object and is carried along with it. Next to this surface layer is the so-called boundary layer, in which each successive layer of air slips over the next. Somewhere between one-tenth of an inch and one inch from the surface layer the air is free from this slipping action.

The most important fact in this description is that air actually in contact with the surface has been accelerated from rest to the velocity of the object. In having this work done on it, the air is heated to a temperature that increases as the square of the velocity. This means that doubling the velocity of the meteorite increases the temperature rise by a factor of four.

For a speed of 18,000 mph, theory predicts a temperature rise of 58,300°F.: Actually, the temperature rise is reduced by such factors as heat conduction, friction, ionization of the air, radiation of heat,

48

and related corrections. It does point up, however, the great temperatures that can be developed by fast-moving objects in our atmosphere. At such temperatures meteorites become white hot, hence the term "shooting stars."

If a meteorite is small enough, or moving fast enough, all of its matter can be oxidized or burned away on the way down. Hence, it disappears from view before it reaches the ground.

Why is the air so clear in some deserts?

One important reason is the low moisture content of the air. Water vapor absorbs some of the light that passes through it, so dry regions tend to have clearer skies than humid regions. In dry, arid regions it is not uncommon to see mountains forty or more miles away.

A second reason for good visibility in deserts is the small number of solid or liquid particles, called *aerosols,* in the atmosphere. Part of the explanation is the almost complete lack of smoke-producing industries. Another contributing factor has to do with compactness of the soil and the size of the soil particles. The ground in many deserts is solid and compact because there is little construction, road building, or farming to tear up the soil. Despite the sparse vegetation, with only such plants as cactus and mesquite, the soil is held firmly together. Experts call such soil "desert pavement." In the Santa Cruz Valley of Arizona, winds greater than 30 to 40 mph are required to pick up and scatter soil particles. The rainfall there averages about 10 inches per year.

In more arid regions, such as as the Colorado Desert just west of Yuma, Arizona, the rainfall averages only 2 or 3 inches per year. Here there is no vegetation, and even light breezes cause the fine grains of sand to blow. In deserts made up of very fine sand, strong winds can lift particles to great altitudes.

The blowing of soil also occurs in any other region where the ground is dry and loosened by digging or plowing. With little vegetation, and a lack of moisture to bind together the grains of soil, even gentle winds can cause the particles to rise to altitudes of over two or three miles. They fall so slowly that they may remain in the atmosphere for weeks, obscuring our view of distant objects. Usually they remain there until rain or snow washes them back to the ground. The particle size most likely to be blown into the atmosphere is 0.004 inch in diameter, or somewhat larger than the diameter of a human hair.

Scientists estimate that the atmosphere contains about 10 million tons of solid pollutants. Because very little of this total is found over desert regions, the degree of visibility there is usually excellent. For that reason, many astronomical observatories are located in the arid regions of the world.

What is a volcano?

Scientists know that the inside of the earth is very hot—hot enough to melt rock. We need dig into the earth only a few thousand feet to notice an unmistakable warming trend. Mine shafts and oil wells, for example, are warmer than the surface above them.

Magma, or molten rock, collects in pools far below the earth's surface. Hot gases and magma force their way through cracks toward the surface where they build up tremendous pressure. At some places, this pressure blows a hole in the earth's surface and we have a volcano. When gases and magma shoot out, we say the volcano erupts.

Magma comes from a volcano as a hot liquid called *lava.* In some volcanoes it merely oozes through the opening, while in others it blasts forth along with rocks, cinders, steam and gases.

Some volcanoes are formed by slowly moving lava that flows onto the ground. There it cools off and freezes into rock. The lava piles up in the course of time and eventually a mountain is formed. Other, more prominent mountains are produced by material blown out of the ground. In such volcanoes, lava itself plays only a minor role in mountain building. Instead, cinders and volcanic ash are propelled from the interior of the volcano and pile up in the form of a cone. The slopes of these conical mountains are quite steep, in contrast to the more gentle slopes of mountains produced by flows of lava.

There have been a number of active volcanoes in the United

States. Lassen Peak in California is still an active volcano, rumbling a bit once in a while. Active volcanoes in Hawaii and Alaska still spurt forth on occasion. The Hawaiian Islands, which make up our fiftieth state, were actually formed by undersea volcanoes. The nine Azores Islands in the Atlantic Ocean were formed in the same way, by undersea volcanoes. All of these islands are merely the worn tops of great volcanoes. Even today volcanoes continue to erupt in Hawaii. Mauna Loa, on the island of Hawaii, is the world's largest active volcano.

Measurements of molten rock inside volcanic craters always yield a temperature close to 2,200°F. Using this figure, it is possible to estimate the depth from which such volcanic eruptions originate.

Most of the data about the temperatures inside the earth come from deep-well borings carried out around the world. All of these measurements indicate one important fact: the temperature of the rock increases steadily for increasing depth anywhere on earth. There are slight variations near the surface, of course, but at greater depths these variations disappear. The figure accepted by scientists is about 16°F. per thousand feet.

A simple calculation shows that the subsurface rock must reach the boiling temperature of water less than two miles beneath the surface. If there happen to be vertical cracks in the earth that reach that depth, groundwater would easily find its way down and begin to boil. Columns of water would then be ejected by the great pressure of steam to generate hot geysers, like the magnificent ones of Yellowstone National Park.

If the increase in temperature with depth continues at 16°F. per thousand feet through the outer layers of the crust, a temperature of 2,000°F. to 3,000°F. would be reached about thirty miles down. There seems to be little doubt that molten rock ejected by volcanoes originates at about that depth.

How does an atomic rocket engine work?

Any rocket works by ejecting a high-speed jet of gas in the direction opposite to that of its motion. But the gas does not have to be produced by burning a fuel. Any gaseous substance will do.

That is the basis of the atomic rocket engine. An atomic reactor can produce an enormous amount of energy, as everybody knows. But energy alone can't make a rocket move. Something has to be ejected to propel the rocket along. So an atomic engine must have three main parts: a tank holding something that can be ejected, an exhaust nozzle through which it is ejected, and an atomic reactor that generates the energy for ejecting the substance.

In current research, the substance to be ejected, called the *reaction mass,* is hydrogen carried as a liquid. It is passed through pipes in the reactor, where great heat changes it to a gas under high pressure. It is then ejected through the nozzle to provide the engine's thrust.

Because a rocket depends merely on ejecting something, another type of engine has come under study. It is called an *ion engine.* An ion differs from an ordinary atom in that it has been given an electric charge, which is a relatively simple scientific feat in this day and age. And ions can be accelerated to great speed by an electric field.

The principle of the ion engine is to make ions out of ordinary atoms or molecules, and then to speed them up in an electric field, which ejects them at very high velocity. Substances that are being studied for ion engines are mercury and cesium, both of which are quite heavy.

Ion engines do not work at all in the earth's atmosphere; they must be tested either in a large vacuum chamber or in earth orbit.

What causes clear-air turbulence in the atmosphere?

Every once in a while a pilot of a high-flying jet aircraft reports being shaken up badly by turbulence far away from clouds and storm conditions. Such turbulence—which strikes without warning and without visible cause—is called *clear-air turbulence,* or CAT.

Pilots and passengers have a deep respect for it. Under its influence, a plane can be thrown about so badly that a pilot has a hard time keeping it under control. In severe cases of CAT, people not held down by seat belts can be bounced against ceilings of cabins and injured.

Equally serious are the stresses to which clear-air turbulence subjects the plane. Wings, fuselage, and other surfaces are subjected to strong vibrations when the plane flies through such a turbulent region. The continuous back-and-forth bending of the metal structure may lead to "metal fatigue," which reduces the life of the plane. (Metal fatigue enables you to break a wire without using a wire cutter: merely flex the wire back and forth until it snaps.)

On a few occasions planes have suffered structural damage from severe CAT. In 1961 a B-52 crashed after an encounter with CAT. On another occasion a B-52 lost its vertical stabilizer when it encountered severe turbulence over the mountains of Colorado.

Scientists now know that CAT usually occurs near the jet stream, a fast narrow current of horizontal air that exists in the upper atmosphere. Since the jet stream flows through slower-moving air, it gives rise to abrupt changes in air velocity near its vertical and lateral boundaries.

Certain regions near the jet stream harbor a good deal of CAT. In these regions warm air overlies cold air, and "waves" are set off in the air similar to the ones we see on a pond when a gentle wind blows over it. These waves at the interface between warm and cold air are usually quite long—several hundred yards long, in fact. Sometimes when cirrus clouds form at the same altitude, we can actually see these waves. They show up as ripples on a sheet of cirrus clouds.

If atmospheric conditions are right, the waves (usually invisible) tend to grow and finally break up into small irregular eddies. These eddies of whirling air are experienced as clear-air turbulence and bumpiness when flown through by an airplane.

Why do Mexican jumping beans jump?

The secret behind the strange jumping of the Mexican jumping bean is a coiled caterpillar, or *larva,* of a certain gray moth. When the caterpillar decides to stretch a bit, it uncoils suddenly—like the

53

mainspring of a watch giving way. This abrupt motion within the bean causes it to tumble around and jump this way and that.

Jumping beans come from a plant that grows in the swamps of southern United States and Mexico. While the shrub is in bloom, the gray moth visits the plant and lays an egg in each flower. As the flower matures, it turns into a pod, which contains the jumping bean. Two of the three sections of the bean contain small black seeds; the third part often contains a gray moth's egg. As the beans mature, the egg inside grows into a caterpillar that makes jumping beans jump.

What is 24-karat gold?

In the jewelry trade, the term *karat* is a unit of fineness for gold equal to one twenty-fourth part of pure gold in an alloy. One karat, for example, means that an alloy is one twenty-fourth part pure gold. The term 24-karat gold refers to pure gold.

Twenty-four-karat gold is too soft a metal for normal use in rings and other jewelry, so gold is generally made harder by alloying it with copper or another metal. If a gold alloy has fourteen parts gold and 10 parts copper, we call it 14-karat gold, and so on.

The term *karat* is also used as a unit of weight for diamonds and other precious stones. In that sense it is equal to a weight of 200 milligrams (about seven thousandths of an ounce), and is usually spelled *carat*.

What do colloids have to do with cooking?

Every time a housewife whips up some flavorsome concoction in the kitchen, she is dealing with a bowl of what scientists would call *surface phenomena*. This is because the ability of various ingredients to mix, or stay mixed, is largely a property of their surfaces.

Although it may not be obvious at first glance, the smaller an object gets, the more surface it has for its weight. To illustrate, a chipmunk has about two square inches of skin per ounce, while an elephant has only about one-fiftieth as much. As a thing gets smaller and smaller, there comes a size where the surface takes precedence over its volume and becomes the controlling factor in determining its behavior.

If an orange drops into a bowl of water, it sinks. Even the larger pieces of orange in orange juice settle out in a relatively short time. But if the orange could be divided into small enough particles, its individual particles would not sink. They would be kept up by the ceaseless bombardment of moving water molecules—much as in a gigantic game of volleyball, in which a hundred balls are kept in the air at the same time. Extremely small particles have so much surface area—in relation to their infinitesimal weight—that they completely ignore gravity and are influenced instead by collisions with molecules. A substance of this kind is called a *colloid*. When the solid particles are too large for the liquid to support for long (ordinary orange juice), the result is a *suspension*. In a solution, the molecules of the liquid and solid mix completely, like sugar dissolved in tea.

Mayonnaise is a kind of colloid called an *emulsion*—a mixture of immiscible liquids. This culinary contradiction is made possible for the oil and vinegar of mayonnaise by egg yolk, which "glues" the two together. The egg yolk holds myriad microscopic oil globules in a colloidal state within the vinegar.

Gelatin is another food product that makes use of colloids. When powdered gelatin is mixed with hot water, it becomes a colloid. Upon cooling, it forms what is called a *gel*—a solid made up of microscopic gelatin particles bonded together by a network of fibers. Gels are also used to make capsule casings for many medical drugs.

The heating together of water and laundry starch produces a sticky liquid that—when dry—can stiffen shirt collars and other pieces of clothing. Chemists call this goo a *high-polymer colloid*. It is a colloid, rather than a solution, because of the giant size of the starch molecule, which consists of a long string of atoms.

Colloids and suspensions also occur in nature. Smoke is an airborne colloid that scientists call an *aerosol*. It is kept airborne by the supporting action of bombarding air molecules. In the case of a cloud or fog, water droplets form a suspension in the air. Both smoke and cloud appear white as a result of their tiny particle sizes. Because the particles vary widely in size, the sunlight that hits them scatters at random, producing all the colors of the spectrum. Seen together, they appear white.

Why are tides in the Bay of Fundy so great?

Ocean tides are caused by a combination of two kinds of forces—gravitational and centripetal. Both the moon and the sun contribute to the tides, the moon's effect being roughly twice that of the sun. Although the sun is much more massive than the moon, its much greater distance from the earth accounts for its lesser effect.

The effect of gravitational forces on the oceans is probably the easier to begin with. The following discussion will describe the effect of the moon on our tides, although the sun acts in much the same way. The force of gravitation between two objects depends not only on their masses, but also on the distance between them, being lesser as they move farther apart. So the part of the ocean directly under the moon experiences a greater gravitational attraction than the part on the opposite side of the earth.

In addition, the earth and moon are both spinning about each other—at a rate of about once a month. We usually say that the moon rotates about the earth, but that is not strictly true. The earth-moon system taken as a whole has a center of gravity located on the imaginary line between the two bodies. In the course of time, *both* the earth and moon revolve about that common center of gravity. This motion of the earth gives rise to centripetal forces that are similar to the forces you feel in going around a curve at high speed in a car. These two forces—gravitational and centripetal— give rise to the "ordinary" ocean tides, perhaps two or three feet in height.

Although the range of tides in the open ocean is hardly awesome in magnitude, much greater tides are found in certain bays and gulfs open to the ocean. The principle behind this effect is called

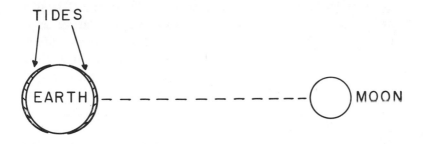

FIG. 5. The earth and moon revolve about each other, and the center of that motion—their combined center of gravity—is located on an imaginary line drawn between their centers. This motion, along with gravitational attraction, gives rise to the lunar tides.

resonance. To understand how resonance works, imagine a bay of rectangular shape and constant depth, much like a large bathtub. It's easy to see that an imaginary giant could make the water in this bay slosh back and forth like water in a basin. Once set in motion, the water would oscillate back and forth, much as a pendulum does, at some natural period or natural rate of oscillation.

Surprisingly, the same sort of thing can happen in a bay open to the ocean. Our bay has a characteristic period of oscillation depending upon its size and shape. But it communicates with the ocean, which is rising and falling about twice a day under the influence of the tides. The bay, therefore, is forced to oscillate at the same rate as the ocean tides. Each tide feeds energy from the ocean into the bay to set up the oscillation. This is like tapping a pendulum lightly each time it starts a downswing. If the tapping happens to coincide with the natural period of the pendulum, it soon swings widely back and forth—the process called *resonance*. If the tapping is done at the "wrong" rate, the pendulum hardly moves at all.

The same sort of thing happens to our bay. If its natural period is close to that of the ocean tides, a condition of resonance exists and an extremely great range of tides can take place. In other bays, where resonance does not exist, the tides are nominal in height.

The Bay of Fundy is well known for its great tides. It is 160 miles long, is straight sided, and has an extremely wide mouth. The tidal range at the mouth is large, but not unusual, about 9 feet or so at best. But a striking increase is noticed toward the head of the bay. About halfway up, at Saint John, the range reaches 25 feet. Near the end of the bay it reaches 51 feet. This tremendous amplification occurs because of resonance. When storms blow from the southwest, the tidal range, already enormous, can increase as much as 6 feet because of wind-blown water.

In contrast to the Bay of Fundy, tides at other places are quite moderate in range. At Kamaran, near the opening of the Red Sea to the ocean, the tides are about a foot in height. At Port Sudan near the center of the sea, they average less than an inch! And at Shadwan, near the closed end, they reach about 10 inches in height. The effect of resonance on Red Sea tides is clearly quite small.

What is the fourth state of matter?

Matter consists of tiny particles called *molecules.* Depending upon the distances between molecules, a substance can be solid, liquid, or gaseous. Hence the three states of matter that we normally think of.

During the past decade or so the rapid pace of science and technology has added a fourth state of matter—one that is neither solid, liquid, nor gas. The new member of the family is called *plasma.*

Plasma is primarily a cosmic material—the stuff of which stars like our sun are made. It is a form of matter created at extremely high temperatures, hence its presence in stars. At such temperatures, atoms are stripped of their electrons—tiny negatively charged particles that orbit the atom so fast that they constitute a solid "shell" around the atom's center, or nucleus. Such atoms, having lost one or more electrons, become positively charged particles called *ions.* A collection of ions, freely moving electrons, and atoms or molecules makes up a plasma.

A plasma is derived from gases, and any substance can be

changed into a gas if it is made hot enough. But a plasma behaves differently from an ordinary gas. At low temperatures the atoms of a gas are electrically neutral because the positive charges in the nucleus are cancelled by the equal negative charges of the orbiting electrons. But when an atom changes into an ion, the runaway electrons carry their negative charges away with them, leaving a remainder with a net positive charge. Such a gas—or plasma—will conduct an electric current that is sent into it.

The really important fact about all of this is that plasma, being electrically charged, responds to electric and magnetic forces. This gives scientists a way of controlling plasmas at the extremely high temperatures of interest today.

The reason for interest in reproducing starlike matter on earth has to do with our long-term need for energy. If plasmas can be controlled at temperatures of 100,000,000°F. and up, scientists will be able to generate energy by the nuclear fusion process. This is the combining rather than the splitting of atomic structures.

The more familiar plasmas on earth have much lower temperatures than those of the stars. Included are the aurora borealis, lightning flashes, electrical sparks, rocket engine exhausts, fluorescent lamps, and neon signs.

How long does it take a space vehicle to fly to another planet or star?

Strangely enough, there is an upper limit to the time it takes to reach another celestial body. It cannot take longer than 100 hours, for example, for an ordinary rocket ship to reach the moon, although the trip might be accomplished in less time.

To understand why this is so, imagine you have thrown a rock toward the moon. Obviously, if you don't throw it fast enough it will fall back to the earth and never reach the moon. But suppose you throw it just fast enough to do the job, about 7 miles per second—the *escape velocity*. It will slow down as it rises and will be going very slowly at the point where it leaves the earth's gravitational system and enters that of the moon. It will then start falling toward the moon with ever-increasing speed. Such a trip would take about 100 hours. Clearly, if you throw the stone with greater initial velocity the trip will take less than 100 hours. But it cannot exceed that elapsed time or it will never get there.

Scientists have calculated the maximum elapsed times for trips to the planets as shown in the accompanying table. (The only way to take longer is to take off deliberately at the wrong time so that an orbit around the sun is completed before a rendezvous is made with the planet.)

OPTIMUM TRAVEL TIMES TO THE MOON AND PLANETS

Moon	100 hours
Mercury	105.5 days
Venus	146 days
Mars	258 days
Jupiter	998 days
Saturn	6.0 years
Uranus	16.1 years
Neptune	30.8 years
Pluto	45.6 years

The shortest time for flying from the earth to any given planet is limited today by the amount of fuel a spacecraft can carry. Imagine three U.S. astronauts speeding on their way to the moon in an Apollo spacecraft. We know, of course, that they are merely "coasting." If fuel were no consideration, they could ignite their rockets and speed up their vehicle. This would shorten the elapsed time of their journey.

When the fuel capacity problem is solved, the minimum time required for such a trip will depend on the physical ability of the crew to withstand acceleration. Their vehicle would then speed up continually during the first part of the journey and slow down or decelerate during the latter part. Such journeys would require considerably less time than the nonpowered methods now in use. Only methods of powered flight are considered feasible for interstellar flight because of the great distance to the stars.

The nearest star to the earth, other than our own sun, is a small star named Proxima Centauri. It is some 25 trillion miles away—a distance so great that light waves coming from this "closest neighbor," traveling at 186,000 miles per second through space, require over four years to reach the earth. Of all the other stars in the universe, only a dozen or so are closer than 300 trillion miles away.

Most scientists agree that a spacecraft can never hope to reach the speed of light. So a round trip to Proxima Centauri will clearly take a good deal longer than eight years or so. But how much longer?

Scientists have calculated the time required for so-called 1-g round trips to points in outer space. These calculations assume, of course, that all of the problems of food and fuel have already been solved—an enormous task in itself. In any event, a 1-g trip means that a spaceship leaves Earth at a comfortable acceleration of 1-g, or 32 feet per second per second. This means that each second sees its speed increase by 32 feet per second. This may seem to be a simple enough requirement, but today's rockets can keep up this rate only for about twenty minutes. We will assume that our hypothetical 1-g rocketship can keep it up for years.

After traveling toward Proxima Centauri for over seven years, we would be speeding along at somewhat over half the speed of light, and would be halfway to our destination. But if we want to stop at Proxima Centauri, we must begin to decelerate—it takes precisely the same length of time—and distance—to slow down as it did to speed up. So a round trip to the nearest star, even if we assume unlimited power, would take about thirty years.

Before leaving this subject, we should probably mention a point of more than passing interest to our interstellar astronauts and their families. Upon their return to earth, the astronauts would find that, during their thirty-year space voyage, the earth and everything in it would have aged about 3,000 years! This fascinating result is based on the time-dilation effect, or "clock-paradox," discussed on page 145.

The task of traveling to a star, of course, far surpasses anything that can be accomplished or even programmed with present technology. In fact, a minority of scientists even refuse to accept the validity of the time-dilation effect. Nevertheless, these predictions —based on the Theory of Relativity—are mathematically sound, even if a bit spectacular.

How does the atmosphere help in satellite reentry?

The return to earth of a satellite or spacecraft is both a difficult and hazardous operation. The ideal method of landing would be to use braking rockets similar in size to those used during launch. These would provide power braking all the way down to the ground —like a motion picture of the blast-off played back in reverse. Unfortunately, power braking would mean putting a gigantic rocket in orbit simply in order to land the spaceship. A one-ton spaceship, in fact, would require a launch vehicle equal in weight to a large ocean liner!

All spacecraft to date, when landing on the earth, have used the atmosphere as a brake—so-called aerodynamic braking. This is much like a parachutist who goes up in a powered craft but makes an unpowered descent. Unfortunately, spacemen cannot use a simple parachute to land a spacecraft because of the enormous amount of heat developed when the craft enters the earth's atmosphere.

To grasp the magnitude of the problem, imagine a vehicle moving 18,000 miles per hour. Such a vehicle contains an enormous amount of kinetic energy—energy of motion. The laws of physics require that all of that energy must be converted to other forms of energy, such as heat, light, and sound, before the vehicle can come to rest. So ways had to be found to remove most of this heat and transfer it to the atmosphere. One of these methods is the radiation of energy from the vehicle into space. A heat shield at the front of the reentry vehicle reaches a temperature of several hundred degrees centigrade. At such high temperatures great amounts of energy are radiated into the atmosphere. The effect is similar to the heat you feel near a roaring fire, even though the intervening air is cool. Naturally, the "hot plate" must be thermally insulated from the crew compartment.

62

Another method of heat dissipation is called *ablation*. In essence, ablation is the burning off of part of the outside shell of the vehicle. The ablating surface absorbs a great deal of energy as its molecules are broken up by the heat of reentry.

A third method involves the transfer of heat to the surrounding atmosphere. This results in the vehicle leaving behind a trail of heated air. The heat transfer is accomplished in part when hot air from the surface of the vehicle is left behind by its motion. In addition, even more heat is dissipated by shock waves generated by the supersonic speed of the vehicle.

Such "drag-retarded" vehicles have a nearly flat front end, which is covered with an ablating substance that acts as a shield. The crew compartment is sheltered behind this shield, and some sort of "fin" area is provided behind it for aerodynamic stability. It would seem that this kind of reentry system will be with us for a long time because of its fuel economy and low cost. Landing rockets will be used only for landing on such bodies as the moon, which have no significant atmosphere.

What is matter?

Scientists define matter in many ways, and no one has yet come up with a definition that satisfies everybody. With that disclaimer in mind, here is an attempt to define the term *matter,* which is one of the most fundamental yet abstract concepts of modern science.

Matter is that which occupies space and has mass and energy. It will be helpful to discuss separately each of these qualities of matter.

Matter occupies space. This statement implies that there *are* such things as empty space and matter and that the latter occupies the former. In other words, matter and space do not exist merely in our imagination. A tangible world floats in the emptiness of space. Philosophers since Aristotle have argued about this distinction between the reality of matter and our sensory perceptions of it. But scientists are willing to accept the evidence and implications of their measurements of the world around them. These tell us that all objects occupy space and can be measured in three dimensions: length, width and depth. All objects have matter, and their dimensions define the space they occupy.

Matter has mass. One of nature's greatest mysteries is the fact that pieces of matter attract each other. This force of attraction is called gravity. We give the term *weight* to the pulling force by which the earth attracts an object. This pull is greater, the closer the object is to the center of the earth. If an object were removed many millions of miles from the earth, its weight would fall essentially to zero. Yet the object would still contain the same amount of matter. The term *mass* is used to describe the actual amount of matter in an object—an amount that is not affected by the place in space at which we happen to measure it. A baseball has the same mass here on earth at it has on the moon, even though its weight is six times greater on earth.

Mass can also be defined as a measure of *inertia.* Inertia is a "perverse" quality of matter that tends to oppose its state of rest or motion. If an object is at rest, inertia is the resistance it exerts to being set in motion. If it is moving, on the other hand, inertia opposes any change in speed or direction of that motion. The greater the mass of a body, the greater the inertia it exhibits.

Matter has energy. But what is energy? In science, definitions often lead in circles—especially when fundamental concepts are involved. Energy is even harder to define than matter, because we cannot see it. We can think of energy as something which generates a force that acts upon matter. Energy can exist in many forms— electrical, mechanical, chemical—and each form can be transformed into the others. For example, the water above Niagara Falls has a certain amount of *potential energy,* and in falling to the bottom this energy is converted to *kinetic energy*—energy of motion. Some of this energy is used to run electric generators which change it to electrical energy. This energy, in turn, is used in a multitude of ways. Some of it is converted to light energy and heat energy in lamp bulbs. Some of it runs electric motors and is changed again to kinetic energy. Some of it is used to produce chemicals from raw materials and shows up as chemical energy. In countless ways, these energy conversions parallel every facet of everyday life.

It was once thought that energy is merely a quality of matter. We now know that energy is really a thing in itself. The Theory of Relativity tells us that energy and mass can be converted one into the other. So both exist on an equal footing; the very matter of the universe can exist either as mass or energy.

We began by stating that matter contains energy and conclude by stating that matter is equivalent to energy. For the validity of that equivalence, we need look no further than to the awful power of nuclear weapons. Perhaps there is some slight consolation in knowing that such ideas have troubled the greatest minds of our time. Happily, the simpler concepts of matter and energy are usually sufficient for the great majority of everyday purposes.

Does water dowsing work?

Water witches, or *dowsers,* walk across a piece of land, usually holding an extended forked willow stick or other divining rod. Eventually a mysterious tug on the stick signifies the location of an underground "vein" of water. If drilling or digging fails to produce water, the dowser merely says, "You didn't go deep enough."

He is perfectly correct, of course. In most parts of the world, any hole dug deep enough will yield potable water—whether assisted by a forked willow stick or not. Even in Arizona, a region of low rainfall, drillers count on getting a dependable household supply from wells at several hundred feet.

Fresh water can be found—in reasonable quantity, at some depth—nearly everywhere in the world. The Sahara Desert itself rests on water: an estimated 150,000 cubic miles of it spreading underneath 2.5 million square miles of arid land area. Even the arid flats of Death Valley overlie quantities of groundwater. There are an estimated 100,000 cubic miles of water beneath the United States alone. In fact, almost all of the world's fresh water—2 million cubic miles of it—is inside the earth. This amounts to 97 percent of the world's total stock of fresh water, not counting the quantity (7 million cubic miles) tied up as ice in glaciers and ice caps. About half of the underground water is believed to be within a half mile of the surface and is therefore readily accessible.

Did Charybdis really exist?

According to the Homeric legend, a six-headed monster named Scylla lived in the Strait of Messina, between the Italian toe and the island of Sicily. On the opposite shore lurked the dangerous whirlpool Charybdis.

There are strong currents in the Strait of Messina, even though tides in the Mediterranean Sea are quite small. The currents are caused by the flow of water from east to west in the Mediterranean. Velocities in the strait can reach 4.5 miles per hour, and water flows turbulently through the strait to produce gentle whirlpools. One of these is Charybdis. It is certainly not a fearsome sight nowadays. Perhaps changing water depths or shore contours over the centuries have cut down on Charybdis' tendency toward rotational motion.

Why does a gas-filled balloon rise through the air?

A balloon filled with a light gas, such as helium or hydrogen, tends to rise—as every child knows. A law known as Archimedes' Principle explains why a balloon floats in the air. This principle is based on the fact that a fluid—such as water or air—exerts an upward or buoyant force upon a body placed in it. Archimedes' Principle tells us that when an object is placed in a fluid, the object is buoyed up by a force equal to the weight of fluid displaced by the object. This explains why your body "loses" weight when you step into a swimming pool.

A gas-filled balloon displaces air. This air weighs more than the gas-filled balloon. Thus, the air exerts a buoyant force upon the balloon, and the balloon rises and floats through the air.

What causes a cloudburst?

The maximum speed of falling of a raindrop in still air is about 17 miles per hour. Any tendency to fall faster causes the drop to break up, and the resulting droplets descend more slowly. The air is seldom motionless, however. If air currents rise at a speed of 17 miles per hour or greater, they prevent the rain from falling to the ground and the drops accumulate in the rain cloud. Then, if the air current stops suddenly, a vast accumulation of rain hurtles down in a short time and we have a cloudburst. On some occasions, downdrafts carry rain with them; this rain falls at speeds of 60 miles per hour or more, frequently causing torrential cloudbursts and severe local flooding.

Why do mosquitoes make sounds when they fly?

The sounds that insects make in flight are produced by the extremely high rate of flapping of their wings. Bees' wings reach a rate of 200 beats per second and mosquitoes reach nearly 300. The speedy motion sets up sound waves in the air at a frequency or rate equal to that of the flapping. This frequency is high enough to be audible as a buzzing sound.

How can insects flap their wings so fast? Scientists tell us that the muscles of insects are not too different from our own. If you try "flapping" your arm up and down, you will find it difficult to reach more than 5 or 6 flaps per second—a long way from 300!

Scientists believe that insects use a trick called *resonance* to get their wings moving so fast. To understand how this might work, imagine a pendulum swinging freely from its support. If you push it gently, it swings at a natural rate. It is said to be resonant. You need not push it on each swing. You can keep it going, in fact, by pushing it every fifth swing, or every eighth, or just about whenever you please. It still swings at the same resonant rate (or frequency) so long as your pushes are timed properly to coincide with its back-and-forth motion.

Mosquitoes seem to employ the same technique to flap their

wings. Each wing is connected by a joint to the thorax, or middle section, of the insect. By moving its muscles at a relatively slow rate, it sets up a vibratory motion in the walls of the thorax. This motion is transferred to the wings, which vibrate at their high natural rate, thereby generating the relatively high-pitched sounds we hear.

Does man have an internal "biological clock"?

Many plants and animals have highly developed biological clocks that help govern such diverse and important activities as the migration of birds and the blooming of flowers. To find his way as accurately as the whitethroat warbler, man needs a map, a compass, a sextant, and a chronometer. To wake up as promptly as a robin, he needs an alarm clock. Man does, nevertheless, have a biological clock of his own—even if it is rather poorly developed.

Human beings have a cycle of approximately 24 hours that parallels those of animals and plants. The term *circadian cycle* is often used to describe this daily periodicity. The word comes from the Latin *circa,* "about," and *dies,* "a day." Living things usually show differences in the length of their cycles: two similar bean seedlings may raise and lower their leaves in cycles of 23 and 25 hours respectively, so their clocks do not tick with great precision. Luckily, such clocks are "reset" each day by the sun, long before their errors can reach serious proportions. Otherwise a morning glory with a 25-hour clock would soon get out of step with the day, and flower at dusk instead of dawn.

The synchronizing effect of light was studied more than two centuries ago by John Hill, an English botanist. Hill reversed the normal day-night cycle by exposing peas to artificial light at night and keeping them in darkness by day. He found that their rhythmic movements quickly adjusted to the new schedule of "day" and "night." His revised lighting timetable had reset the biological clocks.

The chief circadian cycle in man is the daily rhythm of sleep and wakefulness. Most of the other daily human cycles, such as varia-

68

tions in hormones and body temperature, seem to stay in step with the sleep-waking cycle, and may be governed by it.

Like the clocks of the plants and animals, the human biological clock rarely runs precisely "on time." An English cave expert spent 105 days alone underground and found that he tended to fall asleep a little later every night. His internal "day" worked out to 24.7 hours on the average. A classic experiment along these lines was carried out in 1938, when two experimenters from the University of Chicago shut themselves up for 32 days in Mammoth Cave, Kentucky. The men tried to live on a 28-hour cycle, staying awake 19 hours and sleeping 9. Within a week, Bruce Richardson, then twenty-three years old, had readjusted his biological clock, but Nathaniel Kleitman, forty-three, could not make the change. His clock was too closely tied to the 24-hour cycle. Richardson's body temperature regularly hit a peak during waking hours, and a low while he slept. Kleitman's body clung stubbornly to its 24-hour cycle. As a result, he was often restless at night and sleepy and irritable during the day.

Under normal 24-hour conditions, the human clock is quite flexible, adapting easily to moderate change. On board ship, the cycle of body temperature keeps pace with the ship's passage through different time zones. It usually reaches a maximum at the same local time each day, even though the ship may slowly make its way halfway around the world where local afternoon time corresponds to predawn hours at the starting point.

With the advent of jet aircraft, the human clock has finally been defeated; it cannot readjust itself to today's jet speeds. In a flight from the United States to Europe, a tourist gets himself several hours out of step with the local daily rhythm of activities. Under these conditions most of us feel tense, tired, and irritable. On a short trip of several days or a week, a few individuals never do make the adjustment. Studies carried out by the United States Federal Aviation Agency show that these feelings are quite real: rapid travel across several time zones produces measurable changes of physiological and psychological processes. Volunteers were flown from the United States to Manila, a time difference of 10 hours. For 24 hours after arrival, none of them could concentrate well enough to add up a single column of numbers. In driving automobiles, their reaction time more than tripled. A similar experiment with north-south flights—in which the time difference was negligible—produced no functional impairments.

For most of us, it takes at least 24 hours for mental alertness to return after jetting across several time zones. In fact, the body's temperature cycle does not synchronize with the "new" time for another several days. For these reasons, the FAA advises tourists flying great distances east or west to relax for a day before taking on strenuous sightseeing activities. For the same reason, physicians recommend that people who must change from day-shift to night-shift work should do so only at intervals of several weeks. In that way, their bodies are not under the constant stress of trying to readjust their biological clocks.

How can ducks float?

Ducks are able to float even though—unlike wood—they are heavier than water. Their naturally oily feathers are normally repelled by water, and that forms a kind of feather boat upon which the duck floats. Chemical means, however, can be used to cause water to reverse its normal reaction to the duck. Application of a detergent—the same grease remover found in every kitchen—allows the duck's feathers to be "wetted." This causes the "feather boat" to leak, and it can no longer keep the duck afloat.

What causes the difference between ice, water, and steam?

Water is familiar to us as the liquid we drink, wash, and play in. At times it freezes into a slippery solid; at other times it boils off as a vapor or gas. The difference between these three states of water is the amount of *heat* they contain. Yet heat is not matter but a form of energy—the energy contained by the molecules of water.

In the solid state, ice contains the least amount of heat energy. The molecules of ice do not move about, but merely vibrate back and forth about fixed positions in the ice crystal. As heat is added to the ice the vibratory motion becomes more energetic, until the molecules break free of their fixed positions and begin to roll freely past one another. This is the liquid state that occurs at a melting temperature of 32°F. As more heat is added to the water, the molecules move past each other even more rapidly. Finally, at 212°F., they have enough energy to break the attractive bonds holding them together and the water is transformed into steam.

Steam, by the way, is an invisible gas. The "clouds of steam" we see coming from a boiling teapot are really clouds of tiny water droplets. If you watch them carefully, you will see that they soon evaporate and disappear as gaseous steam.

What is "radiation pollution"?

When most of us think of radiation, a vision of an atomic explosion usually leaps to mind with its mushroom cloud and terrifying aftermath of death and destruction. But in today's world, radiation has come to be more and more a by-product of our modern technology. At the present time, medical applications generate most of the existing man-made radiation. In the years ahead, nuclear power applications will generate additional radiation.

The exposure of people in the industrialized nations to a variety of man-made low-level radiation sources is on the increase. These include X rays, radioactive materials, and electronic devices for the home, office, and factory. This increase in both the number of sources and their dispersal among the general population has given rise to the term *radiation pollution*. Questions are now being raised by scientists and by the general public concerning the magnitude of the problem and the adequacy of existing radiation standards.

High levels of radiation are known to produce cancer and leukemia in human beings. Scientists have also demonstrated that at radiation doses of 100 rems or higher, the chances of getting cancer go up in proportion to the size of the dose. (The unit *rem* stands for "roentgen equivalent man," which depends on the amount of radiation absorbed by human tissue and the kind of radiation.) This evidence is based on studies of patients exposed to the atomic bomb explosions in Japan, and patients treated with high doses of radiation for medical purposes.

71

It is much more difficult to assess the potential danger of low-level radiation. It is not now possible, in fact, to measure the effects of very low doses—those comparable to the background radiation of our natural environment. This is because our biological response to radiation depends on myriad factors: the type, amount, and rate of radiation received; the location of the sources, whether external or internal; and whether the whole body or certain organs are irradiated.

One of the most serious risks of low-level radiation is the possibility of damage to or alteration of human genes. This danger, in fact, lies behind most of the recommended standards for radiation exposure. Human beings incur a natural mutation rate that is believed to result, at least in part, from natural background radiation. It is only reasonable to expect, then, that any man-made sources of radiation that increase the background radiation will cause an increase in the number of genes affected. The risk of such an increase in mutations is so real that all authorities argue for conservative radiation exposure practices.

The earth's natural background radiation comes from two major sources: one is cosmic radiation from outer space; the other is the natural abundance of radioactive isotopes found in water and mineral deposits. The total radiation from natural and man-made sources is shown in the following table.

AVERAGE ANNUAL DOSE OF RADIATION TO GENERAL POPULATION

Source	Dose (mrems)
Natural background	125.0
Diagnostic X ray	50.0
Therapeutic X ray	5.0
Radioisotopes	0.2
Occupational sources	0.2
Fallout from atmosphere	1.5
Miscellaneous (TV sets, luminous dials, etc.)	2.0
Total	183.9

Natural sources provide a yearly dose of 125 mrems. (One mrem is a millirem, or one-thousandth of a rem.) The medical use of radiation is now the largest man-made source of radiation, representing about 30 percent of the average yearly dose or about 94 percent of all man-made radiation to which the average person is exposed. An increasing awareness of this fact and its potential hazard has led to improvements in the application of radiation devices to medical purposes.

Past nuclear testing is responsible for about 3 percent of the man-made radiation that reaches the population. The major radioactive substances involved in this fallout are strontium 90 and cesium 137. Their half-lives, 28.0 and 30.0 years respectively, assure their presence in the environment for generations to come. In addition, the environment still contains a significant amount of tritium (an isotope of hydrogen) produced by weapons testing. Tritium has a half-life of 12.26 years.

A scientific committee of the United Nations reports that individuals who lived in the United States during the period of heaviest fallout in the 1950s and early 1960s will receive a total genetic fallout dose of about 110 millirems by the end of the century. This is just about equal to the dose man receives annually from natural background radiation. This "extra year" of exposure takes into account all sources of fallout, including radioactivity that may enter the body in food and water.

Nuclear power plants have caused considerable controversy in recent years. In 1969 they accounted for 1.4 percent of the nation's electric power; by 1980, according to the Atomic Energy Commission, this figure will reach about 25 percent; by the year 2000 the figure should reach 60 to 70 percent. With this substantial increase in nuclear power generation, environmental factors involved with the siting and operation of nuclear plants will merit careful study.

Nuclear energy production generates small amounts of radioactivity to which krypton 85 (half-life 10.76 years) and tritium are major contributors. They are released mainly from nuclear fuel-processing plants and to a much lesser extent from nuclear power plants. Measurements indicate that persons living near commercial nuclear power plants are typically exposed to radiation doses ranging from 1 to 10 millirems per year.

Because krypton 85 is long lasting, its quantity in the atmosphere is increasing. There is no evidence, however, that it can concentrate through the food chain. By the year 2000, the projected average yearly dose to the population from krypton 85 will be about 0.02 millirem. At that time, the estimated yearly dose of tritium will be one-tenth as great.

The potential hazard posed by a nuclear reactor is not an atomic explosion, but rather that excessive heating might melt the core and spill radioactive materials into the environment. This possibility is made highly remote, however, by an extensive program of safety. No radiation injuries have resulted from the operation of commercial power plants in the United States.

Another potential hazard of nuclear power generation is posed by the management of radioactive waste material. These are of two kinds: low-level and high-level wastes. Their disposal will become much more of a problem as their volume increases with our expanding use of radiation sources.

Low-level wastes are the gaseous, liquid, and solid wastes from nuclear facilities. They are packaged and shipped for storage to one of ten AEC owned or licensed burial sites. The sites were selected because their local underground conditions were very unlikely to allow radiation to escape. About 2 million cubic feet of low-level solid wastes are now buried at AEC sites. Reactors are permitted to release low levels of other radioactivity to the air and receiving waters.

High-level wastes consist mainly of used reactor fuel. After removal from the reactor, it is shipped in solid form to a reprocessing plant. During reprocessing, high-level liquid wastes are produced and stored in tanks at the plant. A process has recently been developed to change these liquids into solid form for permanent storage. About 80 million gallons of liquid wastes have accumulated over the years and are now being solidified. By the year 1980 commercial power plants will generate about 3.5 million gallons of high-level wastes. Upon solidification, this will amount to a volume of 35,000 cubic feet.

The standards applied to radiation hazards are the most comprehensive of any form of environmental pollution. Nevertheless, the effects of radiation are not fully understood, and disagreement exists over the adequacy of current standards. Experience has shown that actual exposures are small fractions of radiation protection standards, but—as new sources are developed—increased attention will have to be paid to the apportionment of radiation doses among all sources.

In spite of this conservatism, some scientists have questioned both the standards and the rationale behind their development. To answer the myriad questions concerning the establishment of appropriate radiation standards, the following steps appear necessary:

1. Continued research to discover the effects of low-level radiation doses.

2. Intensified research on the effects of radiation produced by such medical devices and consumer products as microwave ranges and TV sets.

3. Tight control over the release of radiation to the environment from nuclear power plants, underground nuclear testing, and the transportation, storage, and disposal of radioactive wastes.

Does sunlight cause skin cancer?

Geographical studies show that the southern states have a higher incidence of skin cancer than the northern states. It is also known that persons with outside occupations are more liable to get the disease on exposed parts of the body than persons who work indoors. It is quite easy, in fact, to show statistically that there seems to be a causal relation between solar radiation and skin cancer. Laboratory experiments with animals show that long exposure to ultraviolet radiation produces cancer.

This form of cancer is of greatest danger to people with light skins. Dark skin pigmentation apparently provides good protection.

At this point it might be helpful to take a look at the structure of human skin. The outside consists of a thin layer of horny cells, called the *corneum.* Below that lies another thin layer, the *Malpighian layer.* Together, these two form the *epidermis,* or outer skin. Below that is the *dermis,* or main skin layer, which contains nerves and small blood vessels.

Ultraviolet rays from the sun enter the dermis, where they cause chemical reactions to take place. Although the process is not completely understood, we do know that a noxious substance is produced that dilates the blood vessels and causes reddening of the skin or even blisters. This burn may be so severe that part of the skin is destroyed and peels.

Another chemical reaction produces *melanin,* a brown pigment whose presence causes tanning of the skin. This pigment settles in the epidermis and protects the inner skin from sunburn by ultraviolet rays.

No one knows, of course, why skin cancers develop in fair-skinned people as a result of repeated and prolonged exposure to sunlight. And it should be pointed out that ultraviolet radiation is only one cause of skin cancer. There are many skin cancers that do not appear to be related to solar radiation.

What are the tallest plants in the world?

If you guessed the redwood or sequoia trees of California, I'm afraid you will have to look elsewhere. The tallest plants in the world are found in the ocean, in the form of seaweed! Seaweeds over 600 feet tall have been found in the ocean near the southern tip of South America. This compares with heights of less than 400 feet for existing specimens of redwood or Australian eucalyptus trees. By way of comparison, the Statue of Liberty in New York harbor raises its torch only little more than 300 feet above the level of the water.

How do Polaroid sunglasses reduce glare?

We have all been momentarily blinded at one time or another by light from the sun reflected from some shiny, mirrorlike surface. Polaroid sunglasses have the unique ability to eliminate most of that glare. To understand how they work, it helps to keep in mind that light seems to travel in waves, or vibrations. When a light wave glances off a smooth, reflecting surface, it behaves like a flat skipping stone thrown swiftly across a calm pond or lake. If the stone happens to strike the water with its edge, it plunges in. If it happens to strike the water with its flat surface, it skips off.

Light behaves in much the same way. Imagine light waves glancing off a shiny horizontal surface. Before reaching the surface, the light consists of waves vibrating in all directions—up and down, left and right, and everything in between. After skipping off the shiny surface, however, most of the reflected light vibrates only in the left and right or horizontal direction. The light is said to be *horizontally polarized.* Since most glare-producing surfaces are horizontal, most annoying glare reaches our eyes with its light waves vibrating from side to side rather than up and down.

Polaroid lenses are made of a special material that is able to filter out much of the unwanted, horizontally polarized glare. To understand how, imagine two girls, each holding one end of a rope that passes through a picket fence. The only kind of motion the girls can impart to the rope is motion in the vertical direction. If they try to wiggle the rope horizontally, its motion is stopped by the vertical pickets. Neither can they swing the rope in a circle, as required for jumping rope.

Polaroid material is an optical counterpart of the picket fence, with its optical "pickets" set up in the vertical direction. It allows light with vertical vibrations to pass through, but blocks out most of the glare because glare waves vibrate horizontally.

The "pickets" in Polaroid material are nothing more than the molecules of which the material is made. The molecules are lined up during manufacture in such a way that they polarize light. In addition to Polaroid, certain natural minerals, such as tourmaline and Iceland spar, are able to polarize light.

What is the sun made of?

The sun is a vast, rotating sphere of extremely hot gas, mostly hydrogen and helium. Its mass is about 20 billion billion billion tons, or about 333,400 times that of the earth. Its diameter is about 800,000 miles, or some 100 times that of the earth.

The sun, like the earth, rotates about an axis through its north and south poles. Its period of rotation, however, is much longer than that of the earth. The sun rotates once in about 26 days near the solar equator, but it takes about 34 of our days for one rotation near the solar poles. The difference in rate of rotation between equator and poles is possible because the sun is not a solid object.

The sun generates its energy by nuclear reactions within its interior. These reactions convert hydrogen into helium, giving off a great amount of light and heat in the process. Although the sun is continually using up its hydrogen, there is no danger of its running out of it for many billions of years, so great is the quantity on hand. The temperature inside the sun where the nuclear reactions take place is thought to be in the neighborhood of 36,000,000°F. The temperature of the surface, however, is "only" 10,500°F.

Scientists believe that the sun has been radiating energy at substantially its present rate for about 5 billion years. Ultimately, the hydrogen supply will run out and the sun will have to enter a new and cooler phase of its existence.

Where did soil come from?

Soil is produced from rock by a natural process called *weathering*. One of the most important agents of this process is freezing water.

Water expands 9 percent when it freezes, and if freezing occurs in a crack of a rock, the force generated is great enough to split the strongest rock. Freezing water can exert a pressure of 30,000 pounds per square inch—equivalent to about 2,000 times atmospheric pressure! This far exceeds the tensile (or cohesive) strength of the strongest rock, which is only 3,500 pounds per square inch.

Weathering is most effective in cold climates where alternate freezing and thawing subject the rocks to repeated breaking forces. When the particles of rock are small enough, they become part of our soil.

Weathering is also produced by the collision and breaking of rock particles as they are transported by moving water, wind, or ice. This process is most important along streams, in deserts, and in glaciated areas.

Roots of the larger plants are also agents of weathering. Tree roots penetrate cracks of large boulders, causing the rock to split.

Animals, too, cause considerable weathering. Earthworms pass great amounts of soil through their digestive tracts, grinding mineral particles in their stomach. As many as a million earthworms may inhabit an acre of land, passing up to 18 tons of earth per year through their bodies! Other insects and animals transport unweathered minerals to the surface, where weathering is most effective.

The weathered soil is also subjected to chemical changes by the atmosphere. The elements sodium, calcium, magnesium, and potassium tend to be dissolved and carried to the ocean by streams. Silicon usually accumulates in the soil as clay or quartz. Iron and aluminum usually remain in the soil, and may become so concentrated that the soil can be mined as an ore of these metals.

By a combination of such processes, rocks—which originated deep in the earth—are continually pulverized to generate new surface soil. Mixed with this soil are the decayed remains of animals and plants. This organic matter is called *humus*.

The mineral particles in soil are classified by size as sand, silt, or clay. Sand particles are relatively large and can be seen easily with the unaided eye. Silt particles are very tiny, and particles of clay are microscopic.

Soil containing a mixture of sand, silt, clay, and a high percentage of humus is known as loam. Loam, usually a rich, dark soil that is neither too loose and sandy nor too fine and hard, is preferred by farmers for growing crops. Soils containing too much sand or clay, in contrast, are of less value in farming.

The rock that weathers to form soil is called *mantle rock*. It consists of boulders and loose rock particles that make up much of the earth's crust. The soil builds up in two layers: a layer of topsoil near the surface, and a layer of subsoil. Topsoil consists of sand, silt, clay, and humus while the underlying subsoil consists mostly of coarse rock particles. Beneath all of this is bedrock, a solid layer of the earth's crust.

Can loud music cause hearing loss?

Ear specialists warn that those of us who listen to loud music face the likelihood of ear damage and hearing impairment. To discover just how loud some music can be, two doctors measured sound levels in rock'n'roll establishments in San Francisco. Both were experts in otolaryngology at the University of California Medical Center. Dr. Charles P. Lebo and Dr. John A. Garrett found that the overall background sound level emanating from rock'n'roll establishments ranged around 100 decibels. A *decibel* is the unit used to express the level of intensity of sound. Peaks of 110 to 120 decibels were also recorded. Experts tell us that cumulative exposure to such high-level sounds is likely to produce ear damage. These sound levels approximate the intensity produced by a few riveting machines working simultaneously.

Listeners put up with such loud music because they want to "feel" the sounds. So electric guitars, electric chord organs, and other instruments have powerful amplifiers to generate high sound levels. In addition, there are usually microphones at each end of the stage to further amplify the music. The same dangerous sound levels can easily be generated in the home using powerful sound-amplifying systems.

The loudest sound levels normally encountered are on the flight decks of aircraft carriers, which produce 140 decibels. Some jet engines reach as high as 125 decibels.

Can the crew of a sailboat move it by blowing into the sails?

Oddly enough, the answer to this question is no. Even if it's a small sailboat with a large crew, it is not possible to move the boat by blowing into its sails. If it were to move, even a little bit, it would violate one of science's most cherished laws—the principle of conservation of momentum.

80

A complete discussion of this principle is well beyond the scope of this book, but perhaps we can gain an insight into the nature of momentum and of its principle of conservation. The dictionary defines momentum as "a property of a moving body that determines the length of time needed to bring it to rest when acted upon by a constant force." We can also think of momentum as that property of a running football fullback that makes him hard to stop. To get a feeling for this property, suppose you were a football coach. You have two candidates for the fullback position. Both run the hundred-yard dash in 10 seconds, but one weighs 200 pounds and the other weighs 175 pounds. If all other factors were equal, you would select the 200-pound player because he would be more difficult to stop. The scientist would say that his momentum at full speed is the greater of the two.

The momentum of a body depends both upon its velocity and upon its mass (the amount of matter it contains). If either goes up, the momentum goes up. (For those who are mathematically inclined, momentum is equal to the product of mass and velocity.)

When two or more objects interact in some way, by exerting force on one another for a period of time, the momentum of one body may be transferred to another. To illustrate, imagine a pool table that has been arranged for the start of a game. The cue ball darts forward into the neatly arranged pack of numbered balls. At the instant of impact, the momentum of the cue ball passes in part to each of the other balls, and all move off in various directions, at different speeds. According to the principle of conservation of momentum, the total momentum of all of the balls before collision is exactly equal to the total momentum of all the balls after the collision.

Here is a kind of constancy—or unchangeability—in nature. If we have a system made up of two or more bodies that interact for a time, we know that the total momentum before and after the interaction will remain the same.

This principle seems to be universally valid. If we measure the momenta of objects in a system before and after an interaction of the bodies, the change in momentum ought to be equal to zero. If it is not, we know that the system has been changed, by either the addition or loss of a body. This is the only way that the system's momentum could have changed.

Now let's apply the principle to the sailboat problem. The system consists of the boat, the crew, and the air they breathe. Before and after the blowing, the system consists of the same objects. The mass of the objects, therefore, is unchanged. And the principle of conservation of momentum tells us that the total momentum is unchanged. It follows then that the boat's velocity remains unchanged.

Was there ever a continent called Atlantis?

There is no scientific evidence that the continent of Atlantis ever existed during the time span of human life on earth.

Atlantis seems to have been invented in the fourth century B.C. by the Greek philosopher Plato as a mythical place in which to prove his political theories. He placed it beyond the Strait of Gibraltar in the Atlantic Ocean—a region unexplored by the ancient Greeks. After he had made his point, Plato abandoned Atlantis to its well-publicized watery end.

Later writers, however, have taken the tale seriously. Hundreds of articles and books have been written about the lost continent of Atlantis. Its inhabitants have been credited with inventing everything from submarines to atomic energy. Nevertheless, all of this seems to be little more than idle speculation. As far as we know, there never was an Atlantis.

What causes tornadoes?

The tornado is much smaller than the hurricane—a whirling vortex a few hundred yards in diameter instead of 200 miles or so for the larger storm—but it is far more ferocious when it does occur.

Like hurricanes, tornadoes are much more likely to happen in certain regions and at certain times of the year. The Midwest of the United States is the most active tornado region in the world.

When layers of hot, dry air aloft encounter warm, moist air from the Gulf of Mexico, and both contact a wedge of cold air flowing down from Canada, violent thunderstorms can occur. These storms form a line usually a hundred miles or so ahead of a cold front, and some of them give birth to tornadoes.

Although these ingredients of a tornado are well known, meteorologists still do not know much at all about the actual formation of tornado funnels or why only one thunderstorm in a hundred produces a funnel.

How does a fuse work?

Electric wiring in a building is designed to carry only a specified maximum amount of current. If we try to exceed that current by turning on too many appliances, or if there is a short circuit, a fuse "blows" to protect the overloaded electric wiring. If there were no fuse, the wiring would overheat and could conceivably start a fire.

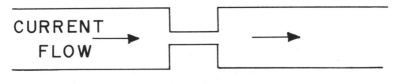

CURRENT FLOW

FUSE ELEMENT

FIG. 6. The principle of the electric fuse. If the current through the fuse is too great for any reason, the fuse gets hot in the narrow central region and melts away, thereby interrupting the operation of the electric circuit.

Fuses are nothing more than a strip of metal, having a low melting temperature, which is placed in the electric circuit along with the light bulbs or appliances. The fuse is designed to melt and open the circuit long before the wires have a chance to overheat. This break in the wire interrupts the current just as though the switch had been turned off. After a fuse blows, the circuit cannot be used again until the blown fuse is replaced by a new one.

What does an atom weigh?

Even though atoms are too tiny to be weighed individually, they do have a certain weight, and if we weigh enough of them their total weight can be measured. So chemists measure a large number of atoms and compute the individual weight of a single atom by dividing the total weight by the number of atoms.

Hydrogen is the lightest of the elements, and it takes 602,300,-000,000,000,000,000,000 (or 602.3 sextillion) of them to make up one gram of the gas! Since there are 28.35 grams in one ounce, one hydrogen atom weighs a trifling .000,000,000,000,000,000,000,-000,0586 ounce! Uranium, the heaviest natural element, weighs about 238 times as much as hydrogen. Some of the more common elements are given below, with their approximate weights relative to hydrogen: aluminum, 27.0; carbon, 12.0; copper, 63.5; gold, 197.0; helium, 4.0; iron, 56.0; lead, 207.0; mercury, 200.6; nitrogen, 14.0; oxygen, 16.0; silver, 108.0; and zinc, 65.0.

Why are astronauts weightless in a satellite?

To understand weightlessness, imagine an airplane flying parallel to the spherical surface of the earth. The craft and everything in it experiences a small centrifugal force because it is flying in a circle with a 4,000-mile radius. This is much like the force produced by whirling an object at the end of a string. As the plane's speed increases, so does the centrifugal force. When the speed is increased sufficiently, the outward force just balances the pull of gravity, and the craft is said to be a satellite in orbit. A person in such an orbiting vehicle also has his weight—the pull of gravity—balanced out by centrifugal force. For that reason his body has no tendency to fall toward the earth and cannot register any weight on a scale.

Weightlessness is also experienced by an object in a ballistic trajectory, one in which an object goes up and returns to earth without orbiting. A person in such a vehicle exerts no force against the floor or walls of the vehicle and merely floats along inside it. The term *free fall* is used to cover weightlessness both in orbit and in a ballistic trajectory.

How can an insect walk on walls and ceilings?

An insect, such as a fly or beetle, walks on all six legs. It supports itself on a sort of tripod consisting of a forward and rear leg on one side and a middle leg on the other, while it moves the other three legs forward. It then switches legs, supporting itself on the other "tripod" while the first three legs move forward.

Many insects can walk on walls and ceilings because most of those surfaces are relatively rough. They merely hold on to tiny, rough projections on the surface by means of claws at the ends of their limbs. Other insects are able to grab on to smooth surfaces by means of an adhesive organ called the *pulvillus*. This often takes the form of a hair-covered cushion or sucker located on an insect's foot. The hairs have soft, flattened ends. When pressed against a smooth surface, the flattened ends come in very close contact with the surface so that seizure or "adhesion" takes place. Thus, by the use of claws and pulvilli, many insects can crawl about at will, over walls and ceilings, seemingly defying the law of gravity!

How does soap work?

Certain liquids have a strong molecular attraction for many of the various substances they come in contact with. This attraction produces an important liquid phenomenon known as wetness.

If you drop a bit of mercury on a sheet of glass, the liquid will bead up into a ball—because its molecules are more strongly attracted to each other than to the glass. Water, on the contrary, will cling tenaciously to the glass, spreading over it and wetting it thoroughly. Scientists have discovered that the nuclei of the hydrogen atoms of water form a strong tie with the oxygen atoms in the silicon dioxide surface of the glass. It is this attraction that accounts for water's tendency to wet glass.

In order for water to wet glass, or any other substance for that matter, the surface must be clean. If it is covered with even minute amounts of oil or grease—which are usually present in particles of dust and dirt—water will demonstrate its natural aversion for these substances by refusing to wet the surface.

Fortunately, the structure of the soap molecule makes it possible for water to wet even grease and oil. One part of the soap molecule is attracted to the water molecule, and another part to the grease molecule. With a little rubbing or agitation, the grease and dirt are attracted off the surface to be cleaned and into the water, permitting them to be rinsed away at will. Without this simple property of soap, each of us would find it more difficult to present a clean face to the world.

Why are dark-colored automobiles warmer than light-colored ones?

Have you ever touched a dark-colored car that has stood in the hot sun for several hours? If so, you know how hot a dark object can become in bright sunlight. Similarly, a white or light-colored car stays remarkably cool under the same conditions. If you find that hard to believe, try the experiment yourself the next time you find yourself in a parking lot on a bright summer day. You will soon be convinced that your next car should be light in color, especially if you live in a warm, sunny region.

To understand what car colors have to do with temperature, it will help to understand why certain objects are dark while others are light. To begin with, imagine two cars parked in bright sunlight—one black, the other white. Both cars receive precisely the same amount of light. One of them appears black to us because it reflects practically none of the incident sunlight. Since very little light reaches our eyes from the car, we call it black. The other car reflects practically all of the incident light, so our eyes receive a great deal of light from the car.

At this point, we must consider the fact that sunlight is energy. The white car reflects practically all of the light energy that it receives from the sun, so the light energy can't accumulate and raise the temperature of the car. The black car, on the other hand, reflects very little of the light energy from the sun. This energy is absorbed by the car, where it accumulates, raising its temperature considerably higher than that of the white car.

The same explanation holds true for colored cars. The lighter the shade of paint, the cooler the car will be. This also explains why dark upholstery and dark clothes are much hotter in summer than light upholstery and light clothes.

From the scientist's point of view, the term *black body* has come to mean an ideal body that—if it existed—would absorb all and reflect none of the light falling on it. When illuminated, such a body would appear perfectly black and would be invisible except that its outline would be revealed by the obscuring of objects behind it.

The nearest thing to the ideal black body is the opening of a juglike cavity whose inside surface is black. When light enters the opening, it is almost completely trapped by multiple reflections from the inside walls of jug. Since practically all of the light is eventually absorbed, the opening appears intensely black.

Will the North Star always remain fixed at the North Pole?

The seemingly stable earth on which we live is a celestial illusion. To all appearances, our planet is stationed solidly in the heavens, while the rest of the universe glides slowly around it. Yet we know from the subtle proofs of science that the earth, drawing its moon along, is awhirl in space, and follows a complex path through the heavens.

Once each twenty-four hours, the earth rotates on its axis, spinning from west to east as it follows its path around the sun. These are the only two motions of the earth that have an important day-to-day effect on our lives. The earth's rotation gives us the cycle of day and night. The revolution about the sun, taking about 365¼ days, is the basis of our yearly calendar and is related to the earth's seasonal changes.

Superimposed on these primary motions of the earth are a number of others, which go on simultaneously. Once each 26,000 years or so, the tilted axis of the earth turns slowly around in a tight circle. This motion, called *precession,* is much like the wobbling of a spinning top as it slows down. The path of precession is not smooth, however, because the gravitational attraction of the sun and moon create a slight back-and-forth, nodding effect called *nutation.*

The precessional motion of the earth shifts its axis enough so that the axis does not always point toward the same North Star. In 3000 B.C., the star Alpha Draconis was the North Star, and Polaris is the North Star today. Alpha Cephei will be the North Star in the year 7500, and Vega will take over in 14,000. Furthermore, our own Pole Star, Polaris in Ursa Minor, is not exactly at the North Pole. It is actually about one degree off the pole. In fact, it is a fortunate historical accident that there does happen to be a rather bright star practically at this point in our time. Between 2000 B.C. and about A.D. 1000 there was no very bright star near the pole. There is no bright star today near the South Pole.

Returning to the motions of the earth, the earth and moon revolve about each other as both revolve about the sun. Thus the two bodies trace an intertwined pattern in their yearly trip around the sun. To visualize this motion, imagine two dancers spinning around each other as they circle the dance floor. Like each dancer, the earth follows a serpentine path around the sun.

The earth's orbit is not fixed around the sun. With each revolution, the earth begins its path in a position that is slightly counter-clockwise from that of the orbit of the previous year.

As a member of the solar system, the earth follows the sun in its motion through space. The sun is in constant motion, circling among billions of neighboring stars in the Milky Way galaxy. And the galaxy in turn is plunging along on its own journey into outer space.

Each of these eight motions takes place in concert with the others, producing a pathway through the heavens of brain-straining complexity. Man has accomplished a truly amazing feat in learning as much as he has about the earth's motion through space.

Are we running out of oil?

Periodically we are told that the world will soon have used up all of its petroleum stocks and our cars will stop forever. And periodically we find that new discoveries of enormous reserves have again pushed the day of reckoning far off into the future. But if and when we do run out of oil, chemists will merely start making gasoline out of coal. During World War II, German chemists developed two successful processes for doing just that. There is enough known coal in the United States to last thousands of years at the present rate of consumption, so it seems our cars will keep on running indefinitely.

What happens when we run out of coal? Perhaps then the car's internal combustion engine *will* be laid to rest. And with its passing, so, too, will petrochemical smog disappear from our cities.

What causes hurricanes?

A hurricane is a great vortex, or "whirlpool" in the air, perhaps 200 to 400 miles in diameter, which often forms over tropical oceans during the warmer months. Scientists are not sure of their cause, but they do know that hurricanes form only in regions having large-scale wind systems.

Whatever their cause, hurricanes unleash great fury on adjacent land areas. The winds of a hurricane pick up energy in passing over millions of square miles of open ocean. But the energy is released over a relatively small area covered by the storm. This energy gives the hurricane its fierce 150-mile-an-hour winds. So enormous is the energy liberated by an average hurricane that it could, if harnessed, supply all the electrical energy used in the United States during six months—an amount of energy equivalent to exploding ten atomic bombs per second! The great amount of energy released by a hurricane is accompanied by up to 40 billion tons of rain per day—enough to supply the fresh-water needs of the United States for two months.

Hurricanes are just as unpredictable as they are ferocious. If the winds aloft are very light and variable, meteorologists have little chance of predicting which way a hurricane will travel. This is because there is no clear understanding of the forces bearing on the gigantic vortex of air and energy. These forces include friction between the ocean or land and the winds, internal friction within the storm itself, and the release of huge amounts of energy as water vapor changes to rain in various portions of the storm.

Although scientists do not really understand such storms, they do hope to learn to modify them or redirect them away from large cities. Experiments have been begun in the "seeding" of hurricanes with silver iodide crystals and other substances. To date, such experiments have shown much promise but little practical success.

How fast do animals travel?

Most animals, especially wild ones, are not overly cooperative with zoologists interested in measuring their speed of travel, so the speed of all animals is not known. Nevertheless, with the help of modern scientific devices, some information is becoming available.

The horse, of course, is one animal that has been clocked for speed for many years. The speed of a fast racehorse with rider is about 45 to 50 miles per hour. This is over 20 miles per hour faster than the top speed of man (about 22 miles per hour), which is attained in the hundred-yard dash.

Although the horse is no slowpoke, it is far from the speediest of animals. Antelopes have been clocked at 60 miles per hour, some 10 miles per hour faster than the top speed of the horse. And the antelope is slower still than a well-known member of the feline family. No, not the cat, which is no faster than most dogs, but the beautiful and graceful cheetah. The cheetah holds the informal world's record among four-legged animals. Trained to hunt small game in India, the cheetah is believed to have a top speed somewhere between 70 and 80 miles per hour!

Although the greyhound is fast compared with other dogs, it cannot keep up with a horse. Neither, for that matter, can a wolf. The greyhound reaches a top speed almost twice that of a man, but still a few miles per hour slower than a race horse.

Although the elephant is thought of as a slow and lumbering animal, an angry bull elephant can easily catch up with the fleetest human being. And the fat, chunky wild boar also turns out to be a surprisingly good runner. Reaching 30 miles per hour, the boar is quite speedy enough to overtake fleeing people and injure them with his sharp tusks.

90

Although the horse can easily outdistance the camel in a short race, the camel's endurance shows up over long distances. Slow to start, the camel quickly settles down to a steady speed of 20 miles per hour, while the horse tapers off in speed after a relatively few miles. The camel then passes the horse with no difficulty at all.

During the old days of the western pony express, horses were changed every ten miles or so to cover the 1,980 miles between Missouri and California. The average speed for this trip for horse, rider, and mail was 11 miles per hour, a very respectable speed considering the terrain that was covered.

Near the bottom of the animal speed scale is the porcupine. Not needing high speed to escape predators, he ambles along at a modest 2 miles per hour. Slower yet is the lazy sloth. He burns up the track at a torrid 1 mile per hour! Though not a mammal, the snail must be cited for some sort of record. It almost takes a calendar to clock his speed. If you could get him to move in a straight line long enough to measure his "speed," you would find that he slithers along at a rate of about 2 feet per hour, or about 0.0004 miles per hour!

Although the whale is legless, lives in water, he, too, is a mammal, and not a slow one at that. The blue whale, a giant of the animal world, swims along at 15 miles per hour. The fastest whale is the sperm whale, which can reach a speed somewhat over 20 miles per hour. The streamlined swordfish is a speedster of the deep, reaching about 35 to 40 miles per hour. This is about twice as fast as the kangaroo, with his powerful hind legs.

A good human swimmer can reach a speed of about 4 miles per hour for a short distance. Although the salmon is far from the fastest fish, it can swim for long periods at twice that speed, or 8 miles per hour.

The fastest bird is aptly named the swift. Flapping its wings only 10 times per second, the swift attains a top speed of 200 miles per hour. Quite a bit slower are the vultures, which have been followed by airplanes in dives at 110 miles per hour. Ducks and geese normally fly at speeds between 55 and 60 miles per hour, although the canvasback duck can touch 100 miles per hour. The starling flies at about 50 miles per hour, and the robin at 35 miles per hour. The song sparrow is only half as fast, at 18 miles per hour. Most birds that have been clocked fly at speeds between 17 and 50 miles per hour.

Why do electric toaster wires get hot, and why do things expand when they get hot?

At high temperatures, most of the everyday things around us change into liquids and then into gases. Conversely, at lower temperatures, gases condense to form liquids, and liquids become solids. Clearly these changes in state are the result of temperature changes. But what is temperature and what are heat and cold?

Most of us have observed that heat is a form of energy. Wherever we notice that energy seems to be wasted, we detect a rise in temperature. In the ordinary incandescent lamp, to take one illustration, only a small part of the electrical energy is actually transformed into light; heat always shows up when the lamp is turned on. Or consider a rotating machine. Some of its kinetic energy—or energy of motion—is always converted to heat as a result of friction.

The nature of heat energy is buried deep within the very molecules of matter. In a solid substance, the atoms or molecules are located in relatively fixed positions with respect to one another. Nevertheless, they are able to move back and forth—or *vibrate*—slightly around their normal positions in the solid. The forces that act between the atoms can be thought of as elastic springs, which allow the atoms to oscillate in all directions around their positions of rest. Thus, the solid is not a truly rigid structure, but rather more like a bedspring seen in three dimensions. With that model of a molecule, it is easy to see what happens if we subject the structure to an exterior source of energy, such as a blow. The impact reverberates throughout the entire structure and the molecules begin to quiver as the "springs" vibrate. The same sort of thing happens within a molecule, and heat is a measure of the internal oscillations of the atomic system. These oscillations take place at a rate of about 10^{13} (1, followed by 13 zeroes) oscillations per second.

A mechanical blow is just one of many ways in which heat oscillations can be generated in matter. Imagine, for a moment, what happens when an electric current flows through the crystal structure of a metal. The current, of course, is a moving stream of electrons, and the atoms of the metal act as obstacles to the flow. The atoms are set into vibration by the countless impacts between electrons and atoms, and the metal heats up. In an electric toaster, enough current is used to heat the wires to a dull red glow. The wires then give off considerable electromagnetic radiation in the portion of the spectrum called heat or infrared radiation. You have only to place your hand near the toaster to feel the effect of these warming rays. Infrared rays are effective in warming other substances because their frequency, or rate of oscillation, is of the same order of magnitude as the natural frequency of oscillation of the atoms in solid things.

If a substance is heated to higher and higher temperatures, the oscillations of the atoms or molecules become greater and greater. The particles vibrate farther and farther from their positions of equilibrium. This explains, by the way, why most things expand when they get hot: they need more room in which to move. Finally, an atom may receive, by chance, enough energy to break the bonds holding it in place. It then moves a short distance until it collides with another particle of the substance, gives up some of its excess energy, and remains fixed in place for a time. So, when the temperature is raised, there is a diffusion of particles through the solid. At last a temperature is reached at which all of the particles begin to move about and the entire structure collapses. This is the melting point of the material, a temperature at which the kinetic or motional forces of the particles are as great as the binding forces trying to hold them together. The solid becomes a liquid—a random movement of particles whose relative positions are constantly changing.

The internal forces in a liquid are sufficient, nevertheless, to prevent most of the particles from evaporating from the surface. Of course, some of the particles on the surface can escape, or evaporate, if by chance they receive strong enough impulses from their neighbors to pop free. But relatively few escape until a temperature is reached at which another decisive change of state takes place—the boiling point. At this temperature all of the particles, on the average, have received enough energy to overcome the attractive forces of the other particles. They escape into the air and are transformed into a gas—a state of matter in which a substance is not confined to any given volume. Higher temperature still merely increases the average speed of the particles. The atmospheric pressure, or the pressure in an automobile tire, is merely a manifestation of the entire force with which the molecules strike the objects they meet. That is why the tire pressure rises as the temperature increases.

Where does water pollution come from?

The major sources of water pollution are industrial, municipal, and agricultural. About 300,000 water-using factories in the United States discharge almost four times as much wastes as all the sewered population of the nation. (This comparison is based on the amount of oxygen taken from the water in converting the wastes to harmless substances.) Furthermore, the output of industrial waste—some of which is toxic—is growing several times faster than the volume of sanitary sewage. About half of the industrial waste-water volume comes from four major industries: paper, organic chemicals, petroleum, and steel. Of all the industrial solid matter discharged into our watercourses, 37 percent comes from food processing; 18 percent, from paper manufacturing; 11 percent, from the chemical industry; and 24 percent, from steel making. The greatest volume of industrial wastes is discharged in the Northeast, the Ohio River, the Great Lakes, and the Gulf Coast.

Most industrial water can be cleaned up either by treatment or by improved manufacturing methods. In paper making, for example, the modern sulfate process generates only 7 percent of the wastes produced by the older sulfite process. Economical treatment processes are also available for most other industrial wastes. The total costs for waste-water cleanup are estimated to be well under 1 percent of the annual gross sales of all U.S. industry, although individual costs are much higher for some industries.

Small amounts of heavy metals, such as mercury, have become a particularly serious water pollution problem. Potentially dangerous levels of mercury have been found in some twenty states, resulting in the curtailment of sport and commercial fishing. The federal government has studied the sources of mercury discharge—mainly chemical plants—and has sought court action against a number of firms.

Another source of water pollution is waste heat from electric power-generating plants. Because the electric power industry must double every decade to meet consumer needs, we can expect thermal pollution to become a serious problem unless steps are taken to curb it. It is estimated that by 1980 cooling operations by the electric power industry will involve the equivalent of one-fifth of the total fresh-water runoff of the United States.

Many municipal waste-treatment plants handle commercial and industrial wastes in addition to domestic wastes from homes and apartments. On a nationwide average, about 55 percent of all municipal wastes comes from homes and commercial establishments and about 45 percent from industries. Less than one-third of the nation's population is served by a system of sewers and an adequate treatment plant, and about one-third has no sewer system at all. Some 5 percent have sewers without a treatment plant, and the remaining 32 percent have sewers but inadequate treatment plants. As you would expect, the greatest waste problems exist in areas with the heaviest concentration of people—particularly the Northeast.

Experts tell us that the municipal waste load will just about quadruple over the next fifty years. So, unless great strides are soon made in waste treatment, the pollution problem will continue to plague densely populated areas for decades to come.

Wastes from animal feedlots are a major source of agricultural pollution. Beef cattle, poultry, hogs, sheep, and horses, along with dairy farms, are the major sources of pollution from animal wastes.

In the United States today, the animal population produces an amount of waste equivalent to the wastes of 2 billion people! Fortunately, most of this waste never reaches the water. It is, nevertheless, an indication of the extent of the problem.

Agriculture also causes water pollution through the leaching of fertilizers into nearby bodies of water. Fertilizers contain nitrogen and phosphorus, two primary nutrients that feed algae in water. In some areas, particularly in the West, water leached from irrigated lands has caused the salt concentration in many rivers to exceed levels considered acceptable for most crops. In addition, runoff of rainwater often contains high levels of toxic pesticides.

The greatest volume of material entering our waterways is in the form of sediments carried by erosion. These sediments are at least 700 times greater than the total volume of sewage. In farming regions, agriculture increases land erosion up to nine times that allowed by natural cover; and construction increases the erosion rate a hundredfold or more.

In recent years, oil pollution has become a serious national and worldwide problem. It is estimated that 10,000 spills of oil and other hazardous substances annually pollute navigable waters in the United States. Most serious oil spills come from ships, but about one-third of the incidents involve pipelines, storage facilities, and terminals. In addition, gasoline service stations dispose of 350 million gallons of used oil each year, and much of it reaches our waterways.

Mine drainage is a significant source of water pollution in Appalachia, the Ohio Basin states, and in other mining regions. In Appalachia alone, over 10,000 miles of streams are polluted by acid mine drainage. Acid forms when water and air react with sulfur-bearing minerals in the mines, or in refuse piles, to form sulfuric acid and iron compounds. Coal mines idle for fifty years may still discharge large quantities of acid-bearing water. Mine drainage also contains copper, lead, zinc, and other metals toxic to aquatic life.

About 8 million watercraft of all descriptions ply the navigable waters of the United States. The sewage pollution from these vessels is equal to that from over half a million persons—comparable to the population of a city the size of San Diego. This pollution can be a major impediment to clean water in harbors and recreational areas of the nation. Additional pollution occurs when ships discharge bilge and ballast water heavy with oil and other wastes.

Water pollution arises from many sources to assail man's senses and hamper his activities. It is a serious threat to health; it greatly reduces recreational opportunities; it disturbs the aesthetic qualities of water; it cuts down on commercial and sport fishing; and it reduces the quality of water supplies for household and industrial use.

The nation seems to be on the threshold of a major attack on water pollution, but the problems are not simple ones to solve. In the long run, control of water pollution will require the expenditure of many billions of dollars as well as tighter enforcement of stricter regulations. It may also require changes in the products people consume and in the prices they have to pay for them. We will have to wait and see whether the nation is yet willing to make these sacrifices to achieve a clean environment.

How much does air weigh?

The easiest way of proving that air has weight is to compare the weight of a container, such as a gallon jug, before and after the air is pumped out of it. If you were to perform such an experiment, you would find that a gallon of cool air at sea level weighs about 5 grams, or about a fifth of an ounce.

You can convince yourself that air has weight by performing a couple of simple experiments. The first makes use of a water glass and a wash basin or pot full of water. If you turn the glass of water upside down under water and pull it upwards, the water doesn't descend in the glass so long as the rim remains under the water's surface. It is kept there by the weight of the atmosphere pushing down on the water's surface. A similar experiment involves placing a sheet of paper on a tumbler brimming over with water, after which you can turn it upside down without spilling the water. This

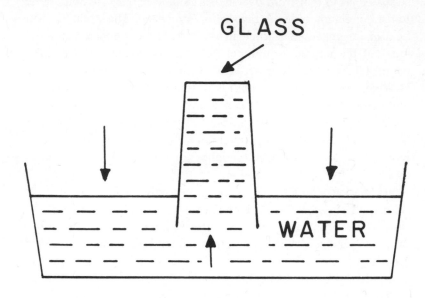

GLASS

WATER

FIG. 7. Water is kept in the glass by the weight of the atmosphere pushing down on the water's surface.

one takes a little practice, so you had better perfect your skill over a sink or out of doors before performing the trick in the living room! In both experiments, the pressure exerted by the atmosphere is more than sufficient to overcome the weight of the water tending to empty the glass, and the glass remains full.

Air pressure is caused by the weight of the overlying air in our atmosphere. At sea level the pressure is about 14.7 pounds per square inch. This is another way of saying that each square inch of a tabletop bears the weight of 14.7 pounds of air resting directly above it. Naturally, the pressure decreases at higher altitudes because there is less air to be found above the place of measurement. At 50,000 feet, for example, the atmospheric pressure is about a tenth of the pressure at sea level.

The weight of air may also depend on its temperature. If the pressure remains constant, a gallon of cool air weighs more than

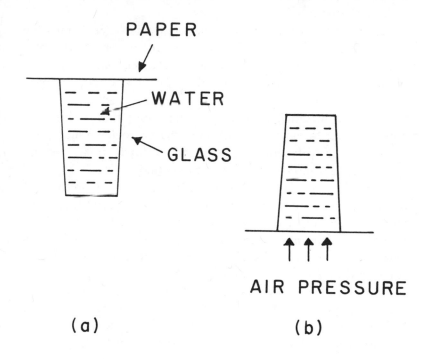

PAPER

WATER

GLASS

AIR PRESSURE

(a)   (b)

FIG. 8. A full glass of water (a) is covered with a sheet of paper after which it can be carefully turned upside down (b) without spilling. Atmospheric pressure produced by the weight of the air keeps the water in the glass.

a gallon of hot air. This is the reason that hot air rises up a chimney while cool air rushes in to take its place.

Can a computer learn from experience?

In 1962, a former checkers champion lost a game of checkers for the first time in eight years. His opponent was an IBM Model 7094 electronic computer. The computer won fairly, without coaching from the sidelines. But perhaps of greatest significance was the fact that the computer learned to play just as a human being learns

—from experience, observation, and a consideration of the probabilities involved.

The machine "looked ahead" some twenty moves and employed strategy worthy of a champion. And yet, the scientist who programmed the computer, Dr. Arthur L. Samuel, was not a great player himself. He could not and did not plan the winning strategy. The computer had been "taught" to look ahead, "consider" various moves and countermoves, and select the move that would most probably lead to victory. In addition, the computer remembered favorable and unfavorable moves and positions from previous games, avoiding those that had turned out poorly.

When the machine first learned to play, it was a pretty poor player—even a young child could beat it. But little by little it stored away on magnetic tape the sequences of moves that led to the capture of the opponent's men and to the "kinging" of its own men. In picking a move, it compared the existing board setup with patterns stored away in its memory and picked the move most likely to annoy the opponent. Because a roll of tape can remember a prodigious number of moves, the computer's play improved mightily with each game. After several thousand games the machine was able to beat good amateurs, including the man who taught it to play!

This, of course, was the reason the computer had been taught the game. Far from being a stunt, it showed how an intellectual pursuit can be reduced to computer science. It demonstrated and tested some of the methods by which a computer can be taught to learn from its own experience and assume ever more challenging tasks in the modern world.

How does cactus live in the desert?

It seldom rains in the desert, so desert plants must go months or even a year without water. The cactus is a common plant in the deserts of the American Southwest. Cacti survive long dry periods by storing water in their trunks. They obtain this water with the help of large root systems that lie close to the surface. These spreading roots quickly soak up moisture from even light rains.

Perhaps the most well-known desert plant is the saguaro cactus. It grows to a height of fifty feet, shooting forth a number of long arms that reach and bend here and there to form many strange shapes. Although ordinary plants have green leaves that synthesize food, the saguaro has no leaves at all. Instead it has a green shell, which does the job that leaves do. This shell is covered with a waxy material called resin, which helps prevent the loss of water to the parched air of the desert.

Strangely enough, too much rainfall can harm the saguaro cactus. If it gets too much water it cracks open and dies.

Why is it colder at the poles than at the equator?

All of the earth's heat comes from the sun. When the sun's rays strike the earth, some of the energy stays behind, and heats the earth, and the remainder is reflected back into space.

In a wide region around the earth's equator, between latitude 30 degrees north and 30 degrees south, the earth receives more energy from the sun during the year than it loses to space. Beyond these latitudes, the reverse is true.

For this reason, there is a net excess of solar heat in the equatorial tropics, and in the higher northern and southern latitudes, there is a net deficit of solar energy. This uneven heating would ordinarily cause the tropics to become hotter and hotter over the years, while the polar and temperate regions would become colder and colder. Luckily, some of the surplus energy is carried toward the poles by the winds and ocean currents.

The amount of energy transported by these means is enormous. On a typical day, the amount of energy crossing the 30th parallel of latitude is equivalent to 4 million "garden-variety" atomic bombs! Nevertheless, the movement of excess heat toward the poles only corrects partially for nature's uneven heating, and the poles remain colder than the tropics.

101

Do sunspots affect the weather?

Meteorologists have argued for decades as to whether there is any connection between sunspot activity and weather here on earth. At present, there is little evidence to support any such connection. But satellites are being used to make new observations of solar outbursts and of the radiation belts surrounding the earth. By this means, scientists hope to get closer to the answer.

A sunspot is a short-lived dark feature on the face of the sun. It is dark only by contrast, of course, being about 2,000°F. or 3,000°F. cooler than the 11,400-degree photosphere that surrounds it. Scientists suspect that this cooling may be caused by the strong magnetic fields that are always present in a sunspot.

Sunspots vary in size from small regions 200 to 300 miles in diameter to big spots about 30,000 miles across. Both the numbers and areas of sunspots vary in magnitude in a cycle of about eleven years.

Although sunspots may turn out to have no effect at all on the weather, they do affect long-distance radio communication here on earth. These disturbances, as well as increased auroral activity and fluctuations in the earth's magnetic field, are more frequent at the maximum phase of the sunspot cycle than at other times.

As to the origin of the sunspots, there is no generally accepted theory. Although scientists do know that the sun rotates on its axis much as the earth does, the rotation differs in that its speed at the sun's surface varies from place to place. It is as though New York City rotates from west to east faster than Miami and so might eventually catch up with it. Scientists believe that the sunspots are somehow related to this variable speed of rotation of the material that makes up the fluid sun. The exact mechanism, however, is still unknown.

How do fish orient themselves in schools?

With the help of advanced sonar systems, scientists have begun to learn a great deal about the schooling habits of fish. Have you ever noticed how schools of small fish near the seashore dart about almost as a unit in response to a disturbance? There is evidence that the fish use low-frequency sounds to orient themselves in schools.

All fish have ears that, although somewhat primitive, are similar in principle to human ears. Studies indicate that the hearing of fish is most sensitive at a frequency of about 500 cycles per second.

In addition to ears, many fish have a second sound-sensitive system, called a *lateral line*. This extends in a line along each side of the head and body of the fish. The lateral line consists of hairlike cells that project from the surface of the fish. Little is known as yet about the sensitivity and frequency range of the lateral line, but it seems to function at very low frequencies. Some scientists believe that the lateral line detects the turbulence produced by neighboring fish, thereby enabling each fish to align itself with the others.

The lateral line differs from the ordinary ear in that it is capable of accurately determining the direction as well as the magnitude of a disturbance. It is thought that fish use this sense organ to detect predators by the very-low-frequency disturbances they generate. Because the detection system is directional, the fish can also sense the angle at which the predator is approaching.

Why can some insects walk on water?

Some insects can walk on water because of the phenomenon of *surface tension*. This effect coats the surface of a liquid with a real but invisible elastic membrane that is composed of the liquid's own molecules. This membrane, or elastic layer, permits certain properly equipped bugs to glide effortlessly, and safely, across the surface with the ease and confidence of a skater on solid ice.

Surface tension stems from the fact that each molecule in most liquids—and particularly water—is like a small magnet, radiating attractive forces in all directions. These forces exist even though the molecules are in constant motion. So, to be completely satisfied, each molecule would "like" to be surrounded on all sides by its neighbors. But some of them, of course, must spend time on the surface of the liquid. These are exposed to air on one side, to which they have only slight molecular attraction. Thus the pull on these surface molecules is both downward, into the liquid, and sideways, toward their fellow surface molecules. The mutual attraction of the surface molecules is strong enough to form a powerful bond, as if they were all holding hands. This accounts for the invisible membrane produced by surface tension.

The water strider, like many other insects, is particularly well suited to foraging about on the surface of water. Its long hairy feet distribute its weight over a relatively large area of water, acting like aquatic snowshoes. But if the insect ever stood up on one foot, the weight concentration would pierce the surface membrane and the insect would probably get a dunking.

You can illustrate the principle of surface tension with a sewing needle and a saucer of water. With a little practice you can get the needle to float on water, seemingly defying the law of gravity.

How much gold is there in the world?

Because it is rare, beautiful, easily shaped, and free of tarnish, gold has always been man's most prized metal. The Egyptians, who were the first to mine it, called it the "royal metal." Medieval alchemists tried in vain to make it out of cheaper metals, a frustrated dream that did manage, nevertheless, to lead to important chemical discoveries. Man's lust for gold also helped launch the explorations that opened the New World to European influence. And men still regard gold as "global money," the most acceptable medium of international exchange.

Gold has been searched for so thoroughly that it can no longer be panned commercially from stream beds, or found in the form of giant nuggets in wagon ruts. Now men must dig deep for gold, some mines burrowing deeper than two miles into the earth, through solid rock.

When contrasted with all the time, energy, and lives spent in search of gold, the amount taken from the earth seems pitifully small. It has been estimated that if all of the gold unearthed since the discovery of America were melted down, it would produce only a fifty-foot cube. Its value, at today's official rate, would only amount to about $60 billion—a modest enough figure for all of the human effort and heartbreak it represents.

Why do cameras make negatives instead of positives?

Photographic film contains a material such as silver bromide as its active substance, a chemical that is sensitive to light. If a molecule of silver bromide in a film is exposed to light, it is quickly acted upon by the light energy and actually disintegrates. Metallic silver is a product of this chemical reaction, and because it is opaque, it appears dark when the film is held up to the light. Other parts of the film, not exposed to light, remain transparent. The result is a photographic negative—the parts exposed to light are dark and the remainder is light. Actually, the practical process of negative-making is more complicated than this simple description—which is just as well because otherwise all of our film would be much too insensitive, as we shall see.

Silver bromide can be broken down by chemical means as well as by light. Especially useful for this purpose are the so-called reducing agents—chemicals that offer hydrogen atoms for combination with other substances. These chemicals react with silver bromide only when the process of disintegration has already started. This is because it takes more energy to start a chemical reaction than to maintain it. This process—called *development*—takes place at first only in those grains of silver bromide that have already been exposed to light. All of the silver separates out in these grains. The microscopic grains not exposed to light remain transparent.

After development, the film is passed through a solution of sodium thiosulfate which removes the silver that had not previously been affected by the developer. Just the metallic silver is left behind, embedded in the carrier substance of the film. Only then can the film be examined in the light.

Although light produces an image in silver on the film, development brings about a great intensification of the chemical reaction.

Where only a single atom of silver had existed, there is now a whole black grain. The bigger the grain size, the greater the intensification caused by development. But grain size in good-quality film is kept quite small—much too small to be seen. Otherwise, when the image is enlarged, the grains—which are also enlarged—would become clearly visible. This would give an objectionable mottled effect to the photograph and definition would be poor. Where great enlargements are to be made, therefore, a fine-grain film must be used. Unfortunately, film sensitivity and fineness of grain are reciprocal qualities; one can be increased only at the expense of the other.

Why are insecticides harmful to lobsters, crabs and other crustaceans?

Lobsters, crabs, shrimps, and other crustaceans belong to the same primary division of the animal kingdom—the phylum Arthropoda—as do insects; so insecticide runoff from coastal farms and forestry operations can kill these valuable animals.

Insecticides have a double-edged efficiency that operates on nontarget as well as target organisms. Even in minute concentrations, many of these organic compounds can have disastrous effects. In one incident, heptachlor used in fire ant control programs washed into an estuary that produces 60 percent of South Carolina's shrimp catch. A devastating shrimp kill ensued.

The trend today is toward greater caution in the selection and use of insecticides. In that way, it is hoped that insect control can be achieved without imperiling other forms of life.

Why are transplanted hearts "rejected"?

The major unsolved problem in the heart transplant process is gaining improved understanding and control of the rejection process. After many surgical failures, the first successful heart transplant in an animal was achieved in 1959. Thereafter, it was confirmed that rejection of the graft could easily be detected by the electrocardiogram. As in all transplants, the obstacle to be overcome was the rejection of the graft.

After trial and error, drugs were found that could suppress the destructive rejection process, enabling dogs with transplanted hearts to live several years. But such drugs also reduce the body's defenses against other such "foreign" substances as disease germs and viruses. The drugs must be administered with great care so that virulent microbes are not able to overcome the weakened defenses of the body. Despite this side effect, however, the effectiveness of such drugs has been demonstrated in many human transplants.

A related field of research that offers great promise is bone marrow transplantation. Bone marrow is a vital tissue that generates red blood cells (for distribution of oxygen) and white blood cells (for combating infection). Marrow transplants do not involve major surgery, since the marrow can be administered intravenously.

Large doses of X ray or atomic radiation, certain drugs, and diseases such as leukemia can destroy bone marrow. This renders the patient vulnerable to fatal infection. Such patients might benefit from a successful bone marrow transplant.

Scientists have found that a prior marrow transplant enhances the acceptance of another transplanted organ. In animals, the marrow recipient will accept any other organ graft from the marrow donor without rejection. A successful bone marrow transplant would thus enable the recipient to receive a heart or kidney from the marrow donor without the need for continuous drug therapy, with its hazards and complications.

The real problem here is the difficulty of getting the body to accept the marrow transplant in the first place. Although they have been successfully carried out a number of times between identical twins, other tests between genetically unrelated human beings have not been successful. Advances are being made with animals, however, through the use of tissue-typing tests and drug therapy. Through such means, scientists hope to surmount the problems they have encountered in human marrow transplants.

What is meant by the "thrust" of a rocket?

In 1822 an English experimenter by the name of James Perkins built the first steam rocket. It consisted of a metal bottle or container partly filled with water and stoppered by a lead plug in its bottom. He placed his bottle-rocket on a briskly burning bonfire and moved back out of the way. The heat first changed the water into steam and then began to soften the lead plug. Finally the plug blew out and the metal bottle flew into the sky, trailing a jet of steam.

Before the plug came out, of course, the steam could not cause the bottle to move. Although the steam pressure was great, it was the same in all directions and its effects "cancelled out." But then the plug popped out and all that was changed. The steam still pushed against the top of the bottle with the same force as before. But there now was a hole where the plug had been and the steam could not exert any force at that point; it merely escaped into the atmosphere. So the steam's push on the top of the bottle was no longer counterbalanced by the equal downward push on the bottom. It is this force, or *thrust,* that made the bottle rise. Thrust is usually measured in units of pounds. In a given rocket, the higher the pressure the greater the velocity of the steam leaving the rocket, and the higher the thrust.

The black powder in firework rockets produces an exhaust velocity of about 2,500 feet per second, while modern rocket fuels give velocities of about 7,000 feet per second.

The largest of the U.S. rockets is the Saturn 5, with five rocket engines in its first stage. With its Apollo spacecraft payload, it stands 360 feet high. Each of the five engines has 1.5 million pounds of thrust, giving a total thrust of 7.5 million pounds. Most of the 3,000-ton weight of the Saturn rocket is fuel; the empty weight is "only" about 200 tons.

Where does cork come from?

That most useful material, cork, comes from the evergreen oak *Quercus suber,* from which it gets its name. The cork oak reaches a height of about thirty or forty feet and grows on the Mediterranean coasts of southern Europe and North Africa. About 90 percent of the world's cork supply comes from Spain, Portugal, Algeria, Morocco, and Tunisia. The cork oak has been introduced into the Americas and is now fairly widespread in California.

The first stripping of cork from the cork oak is made when the trees are fifteen to twenty years old. The first yield, called *virgin cork,* is rough and somewhat woody—rather poor stuff that is ground up and used for insulation products and for packing grapes. In later years, the outer layer becomes softer and more homogeneous. Successive cork strippings are made every ten years or so, the quality usually improving with each stripping. The trees are stripped between June and August and live to a useful age of 150 years, more or less.

Cork is buoyant, compressible, elastic and is a good insulator of heat and sound. It derives these properties from the great amount of trapped air within its cells. A one-inch cube of cork contains about 200 million air-filled cells. This means that about 50 percent of the volume of cork is made up of captive air. This gives cork a specific gravity of only 0.25—that is to say, a density only one-quarter that of water.

Until 1900 cork was used primarily to seal the countless bottles of excellent wine that abound in southern Europe. Nowadays cork is also used widely for insulation corkboard, sound isolation material, auto engine gaskets, beverage cap liners, life preservers, marine products, and floor and wall covering material.

How were the stars and planets formed?

According to the most widely accepted theories, stars and their planetary systems form from great swirling clouds of dust and gas in outer space. The gas and dust particles in such a cloud are always in motion, and all are influenced by a gravitational attraction emanating from the center of the cloud. Over millions or even billions of years the cloud contracts and the gravitational pull on outlying gas particles increases.

While this contraction is going on, some of the particles happen to shoot off into space and are lost. But others, arriving from outer space, are "captured" by the gravitational field and are forced into orbit around the cloud. Over eons of time, the entire cloud begins to assume a disk-shaped configuration—thick and dense near the center and thin at the edges. Finally, the contracting disk begins to rotate—slowly at first, then faster and faster, like an enormous pin-wheel in the sky. The initial rotation is a result of the motion of the particles of the disk. Then, as the disk's diameter decreases, the rotation speeds up just as an ice skater spins more rapidly when he pulls in his arms.

While this is going on, an observer might notice smaller whirls and eddies of dense gas beginning to form toward the outer regions of the disk. After millions of years, some of these eddies become centers of rotating mass themselves—not nearly as large as the huge disk itself, but significant nevertheless. These eddies become concentrated into *protoplanets,* while the main nucleus of the gas cloud becomes more and more dense as it continues to contract toward the center.

As the central nucleus of the cloud becomes more dense, it also becomes hotter, because as gas molecules are concentrated under ever increasing pressure, their temperature increases; this is similar to the heating up of a bicycle pump as you inflate a tire. At this point the main nucleus, or *protostar,* gets so hot that it begins to glow, as any hot body does. But it is not yet a star.

The force of compression continues to increase as more and more mass becomes concentrated at the center of the huge rotating disk. Its central temperature continues to grow, first to hundreds of thousands of degrees and then to millions of degrees Fahrenheit.

Then a remarkable thing begins to happen. Under these extreme temperatures and pressures, hydrogen atoms in the center of the protostar are taken apart, so to speak, and reassembled in a different way to produce an entirely different element, helium. And, strangely enough, the final mass of the helium atom is always a bit less than the combined mass of the hydrogen atoms that formed it. In each of these nuclear reactions a tiny bit of the hydrogen atoms' mass—about .7 percent—disappears as matter and is transformed into an enormous amount of energy. Some of this energy is in the form of heat, but much of it is given off as radiant energy—light waves and other forms of electromagnetic energy.

Once this nuclear activity is triggered within the protostar, both the temperature and pressure increase sharply within its core and an endless series of such reactions is begun. Scientists estimate that our own sun converts some 615 million tons of hydrogen gas into helium *every second.* Simultaneously, about 4.5 million tons of matter is converted into various forms of radiant energy.

A newly "ignited" star probably flares suddenly into Fourth-of-July brilliance from the dull red glow of its protostar days. As a new star it pours light and other forms of energy out in all directions into space. Its nuclear fire "burns" with a steady, reliable light until the hydrogen within the star is consumed. Depending upon the size of the star, that light may last anywhere from a few billion to over 100 billion years.

Many scientists believe that the planets of our solar system probably evolved from the smaller swirls of gas from which the sun formed. In time, these secondary concentrations of matter—too small to become stars themselves—condensed and cooled into solid matter. And all of them fell naturally into orbit about the central protostar that became our sun.

What is meant by "cryogenics"?

A biting wintry wind and a chilling layer of frost are the kind of things we usually associate with coldness. But even these manifestations of winter are much warmer than the "dry ice" in ice cream trucks. Dry ice, in fact, is the coldest thing ($-109.3°F.$) that most of us ever run into; yet dry ice is a virtual inferno in comparison with the extremely cold fluids achieved in the field of cryogenics (from the Greek *kryos,* "icy cold"; and the suffix *gen,* "producing"). This new science deals with the behavior of matter at fantastically low temperatures. Anything above $-200°F.$ is considered too "hot" to handle!

Cryogenics has managed to get down to within a few millionths of a degree of "absolute zero," the coldest possible temperature, where all atomic motion ceases. (Absolute zero is $-273.15°C.$ or $-459.67°F.$) At such fantastically low temperatures, the commonplace acts in unpredictable ways: electric currents, once begun, may circulate in "perpetual motion"; liquid helium defies gravity by creeping up the inner walls of a bottle and escaping down the outside; and flowers become so brittle that they crack into splinters and tiny fragments in the hand.

We have all read the old metaphor describing the atmosphere as an "ocean of air"; if the outdoor thermometer should ever drop to $-317.9°F.$, the metaphor would become a reality. At that temperature air changes into a pale blue liquid. Engulfed in such an extremely cold "ocean of air," all life would end. But in less overpowering quantities, liquid air becomes a major tool of cryogenics, and of our modern world.

The three main constituents of liquid air are nitrogen (78.09 percent), oxygen (20.95 percent), and argon (0.93 percent). In liquid form, these elements have many useful and extraordinary properties. Liquid oxygen, which is extremely active chemically, boils at $-297.4°F.$ and is produced today at an estimated rate of 1 ton per second. It is in great demand for converting pig iron into steel, and for blasting rockets into space. Liquid argon, chemically inactive, boils at $-302.6°F.$ and is used in electronics to grow the tiny crystals for transistor radios. Liquid nitrogen, rather inactive chemically, boils at $-320.5°F.$, and is an excellent refrigerant for food and living organs. It has been used for the indefinite storage of frozen blood. Some "cryobiologists" believe that it may some day be used to keep an entire living organism in frozen hibernation for years.

Liquid oxygen, commercially called LOX, was first manufactured in 1932 for use in the German V-2s that rained destruction on London in 1944. The V-2 worked much as modern rockets do. In the V-2, alcohol was burned with LOX to form a hot gas under pressure; the gas then escaped through a nozzle in the tail, producing a fiery jet that hurled the rocket into space. The German rocket engineers selected LOX because ordinary gaseous oxygen takes up too much space and requires impossibly large tanks.

Today's rockets use fuels other than alcohol—kerosene, for example—but most of them continue to rely on LOX for the oxidizer. In the future, rockets may use liquid hydrogen as a fuel (boiling point, $-422.9°F.$). Liquid hydrogen burns easily, and, with the

112

lowest atomic weight of all the elements, it generates the swiftest exhaust. When burned with LOX, the thrust is 40 percent greater than that of a kerosene-LOX engine. Although the resulting lightweight exhaust is nothing more than old-fashioned steam, it may well be used to propel manned expeditions to the planets.

In the temperature abyss near absolute zero, many metals, called *superconductors,* lose *all* resistance to the flow of electricity. If a wire made of such a metal is connected to a battery, the current grows stronger and stronger because there is no electrical resistance to impede it. If the voltage is then removed, the current can continue to flow through the circuit endlessly and without the slightest reduction in strength—an old dream of perpetual motion come true. It takes very little power to start such a current, and none at all to keep it going.

Although helium is named for the hottest place in the solar system (*helios* is Greek for "sun"), helium gas can be changed into the coldest of liquids. It changes from gas to liquid only upon reaching the fantastically low temperature of $-452°F$. At $-448°F.$, its behavior departs so radically from normal that scientists call it helium II. A weird trick of helium II is to flow as if nothing were impeding its motion, as in the creeping film mentioned earlier. Another is to make a metal magnet float in air. In a jar of liquid helium, a lead dish becomes a superconductor. When a small bar magnet is placed above it, the bar induces an electric current to flow in the dish. Because there is no resistance in the lead dish, the current turns the lead into a powerful electromagnet that repels the bar, keeping it hovering above the dish.

Liquid helium and other cryogenic fluids are produced in a *cryostat,* a machine for liquefying gases. First the gas is compressed, which heats it up. Then it is cooled by another, cooler substance. After that, it is allowed to expand, which cools it further. Gases can be used as coolants until the gas finally turns to a liquid. Then, by reducing the pressure of the vapor that exists over the liquid helium, the helium can be cooled to a few tenths of a degree above absolute zero. The extremely low temperatures mentioned earlier are achieved by making use of magnetic effects in the atoms.

Why doesn't the earth's atmosphere escape to outer space?

Strange as it may seem at first, the composition and very existence of the earth's atmosphere depends upon the strength of the force of gravity.

The earth has associated with it an *escape velocity,* a term we hear more and more often in this age of missiles and rockets. The escape velocity is the velocity an object must reach in order to escape into outer space. Given a great enough upward velocity, an object does indeed escape from the pull of the earth's gravitational field. This happens because the force of gravity falls off rapidly as an object rises above the earth's surface. At a height of 4,000 miles, for example, the pull of gravity is only one-quarter of the pull at the earth's surface.

But what has all of this to do with our atmosphere? The gas molecules in the air are always in motion, darting here and there at random. This motion is completely independent of the wind, and exists even when the air as a whole seems to be at rest. If a gas molecule's velocity happens to exceed the earth's escape velocity, it merely flies off into space and is lost forever. Fortunately, the earth's escape velocity, 6.95 miles per second, is great enough to retain the gases in its atmosphere.

Planets with extremely low escape velocities are not so fortunate. Mercury, with an escape velocity of only 2.6 miles per second, has lost most of any atmosphere it may have had in the past. Scientists believe that Mercury's atmosphere has a surface pressure of only three-thousandths that of the earth. Its atmosphere is extremely thin, and must consist of heavy, slow-moving gases. This is because lighter gases, such as hydrogen and helium, have greater velocities than heavier gases, such as carbon dioxide and nitrogen, and tend to escape more easily.

As for the earth, the prospects are reassuring. Only hydrogen, the lightest element, can escape at a rapid enough rate to affect its atmospheric abundance seriously. Helium can escape only very, very slowly, and the heavier gases hardly at all. We are going to have our atmosphere for a long, long time.

114

Why do ordinary sources of light get hot?

The light that illuminates the universe and all of space comes from the interior of molecules. The alternating electromagnetic fields we call light are generated when electric charges vibrate rapidly. We can see these fields, however, only if they vibrate within a certain limited range of frequencies. Among those which oscillate more rapidly than visible light are ultraviolet rays, which we cannot see but which—as part of sunlight—tan the skin. Those which oscillate more slowly than light are called *infrared rays*. We cannot see them either, but they make their presence known in another way—as radiant heat rays.

Electromagnetic radiation can be produced in molecules and atoms when negatively charged electrons jump from one energy level—or orbit—to another. In order to induce electrons to make such transitions it is necessary to supply them with extra energy. And the easiest way to do that is to raise the temperature.

Almost all of the familiar sources of light use thermally excited electrons. This is as true of the candle and gas flame as of the incandescent lamp. Unfortunately, such heat sources also produce thermal oscillations that are too low to be visible. Considerable heat, in fact, has to be applied in order to energize some of the electrons into the faster oscillations necessary for light. Thus, only a small part of the available energy is transformed into light; the greater part turns up as unwanted heat.

Through the use of the fluorescent lamp, scientists have found a way to produce light more efficiently than by conventional means. If a gas-filled tube is connected to an electric voltage so that the positive and negative terminals go to opposite ends of the tube, an ionization pulse is the result. (An *ion* is an atom or molecule that has acquired an electric charge.) A few ions are to be found in every gas. These speed toward one of the terminals in the tube, striking normal, uncharged gas molecules in their path. The impacts knock electrons out of the molecules, thereby producing negatively charged particles (the electrons) and positive ions (the molecules that have lost electrons). These, of course, immediately begin to rush toward the positive and negative terminals respectively. The process repeats over and over again until a dual avalanche of negative and positive charges takes place. The act of dislodging electrons from the molecules, and the subsequent joining together of electrons and ions in the tube, are merely the jumping of electrons from one energy level to another. So the fluorescent lamp emits radiation. Unfortunately, most of this radiation is in the form of invisible ultraviolet rays.

The ultraviolet rays generated in a fluorescent lamp are prevented from leaving by a coating inside the tube that absorbs them. This substance is carefully chosen so that its electrons can produce the smaller energy jumps that are needed to generate radiation in the visible oscillation range. Electrons in the coating absorb the high-energy ultraviolet rays and jump to a higher energy level with one bound. But they climb down from this higher level in smaller steps —giving off radiant energy with each step. And since the energy differences between these latter steps are smaller and correspond to the energy in visible light, the fluorescent coating absorbs invisible ultraviolet light energy and transforms it into visible light. Not only does this lamp transform a higher proportion of available energy into light, but the color of the light is closer to sunlight than that of the incandescent lamp.

Why do springs flow?

Whenever it rains, some of the water soaks into the earth, seeping downward until it reaches a nonporous layer of rock. Then it spreads out horizontally so that vast volumes under the surface of the earth become saturated with water. Only here and there, in a few rare caverns, does groundwater accumulate in well-defined underground pools or streams. There are no "veins" of water that must be reached by a successful well digger. A well is simply a hole dug down into the saturated region of the earth. Water flows into the well from the surrounding earth just as it will into any similar hole dug in the vicinity.

Layers near the surface of the earth are made up mostly of loose

116

porous material, principally sand, gravel, silt, and decaying vegetation. Beneath this material are porous rocks, such as sandstone and limestone. These, in turn, are underlaid by bedrock so compact that it is totally impermeable. Above this watertight layer lies the zone of saturated earth, a major water resource of the earth.

The top of the saturated zone is called the *water table*. The water reflecting at the bottom of a well is an exposed part of the water table. Around it, at the same level, the water table extends into the earth. The surface of lakes, ponds, and rivers are also evidences of the water table.

The level of the earth's water table varies from place to place. We know that some lakes are higher than others, and that rivers flow downhill. The water table, which connects all of these bodies of water, must also slope. Thus, the contours of the water table reflect in large measure the landscape above it; it is high in mountainous regions, and low in river valleys.

At certain places, the surface contour of the land falls off more sharply than the water table beneath it. So the land dips into the water table, as shown in the diagram, thereby exposing the saturated earth. Water flows out and we have a spring. If a large area of the land dips beneath the water table, a pond, lake, or swamp is the result. Across the lowest part of a valley, the water table may supply water to a river. In fact, the channel of a river or stream is

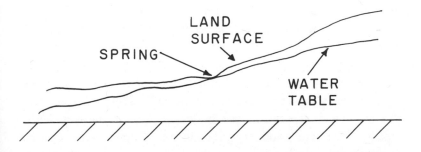

FIG. 9. The water table generally follows the contour of the land above it. A spring can occur when the land surface happens to dip below the water table.

117

often a continuous spring that feeds the flow of water even under sunlit skies when no rain is falling.

What are pulsars?

In August 1967, astronomers at Cambridge University made recordings of radio waves coming from a *pulsar,* a star that beats with a regular pulse. Then, in January 1969, astronomers at California's Lick Observatory took photographs of a pulsar in the Crab Nebula, and found that its light beats at the same rate as its radio pulses. The pictures established once and for all the existence of a new kind of star and opened up endless opportunities for imaginative research. In addition to providing prime scientific sport for decades to come, pulsars promise a new and deeper understanding of the universe.

At first, scientists suspected that pulsars were white dwarfs— "dying" end products of stellar development. There is now general agreement, however, that pulsars are small, rapidly spinning neutron stars that radiate energy in pulses of electromagnetic radiation. This radiation, which includes X rays, light, and radio waves, is generated by electrons in the magnetic field that the neutron star carries around with it.

Although neutron stars were discussed decades earlier on purely theoretical grounds, they were never detected in the sky, even with the most sophisticated equipment. But neutrons themselves are less illusive. Scientists know that neutrons are one of the building blocks of matter. They are found in the nuclei of all atoms except hydrogen. When generated outside the nucleus, they have a half-life of 11 minutes—which means that half of them decay in that length of time—each changing into a proton and fast-moving electron. But if a mass of neutrons as heavy as the sun were gathered together, their gravitational attraction would cram them together so tightly that they would not disintegrate. This compact mass of neutrons would be only 15 miles in diameter and its material would weigh 10 billion tons per cubic inch! The enormous gravitational

118

forces holding the star together would be so great that it could rotate as fast as 1,000 times per second without flying apart.

According to current theories, a neutron star comes into being when a star about one and one-half times as massive as the sun reaches old age. Instead of cooling off peacefully and becoming a white dwarf, the star's nuclear reactions go further, molding lighter elements into heavier ones and giving off energy in the process. The reactions come to an end only when the core of the star consists of iron and other elements of medium weight. These cannot enter into energy-producing nuclear reactions.

At this point, the temperature of the core begins to fall and there is a loss of gas pressure. Suddenly the core collapses and protons combine with electrons to form neutrons. In an instant, the massive core condenses into a tiny neutron star. The outer layers of the parent star also collapse, but these still contain some lighter elements capable of nuclear reactions. These explode in a kind of gigantic thermonuclear explosion, which blows the outer layers of the star into space, leaving only the neutron star, or pulsar, at the center. This is believed to be a *supernova explosion,* the most violent event that takes place in the heavens.

Scientists have also explained how a neutron star can generate pulses. At the instant of its creation it is rotating rapidly, enveloped in a magnetic field vastly more powerful than can be created on earth. Like the very neutrons of the star itself, both the rapid rotation and the powerful magnetic field are inherited from the much larger preexisting star. When the original star contracts, the rotation speeds up just as a spinning skater speeds up when he draws in his outstretched arms. Magnetism behaves similarly, increasing in proportion to the contraction. This rapidly spinning magnetic field reacts with charged particles near the star to send out electromagnetic radiation: X rays, light, heat, and radio waves. Furthermore, if the neutron star has some sort of irregularity on its surface, the magnetic field around it must have a corresponding distortion. This would cause the radiation to go forth in bursts— one for each rotation of the star.

Theory predicts that the speed of rotation of all neutron stars

119

should be slowing down, and measurements bear this out. Scientists have used this observation to help tie together the loose ends in connection with the Crab Nebula, a tangled patch of glowing filaments some 6,000 light-years away from the earth. During the early part of this century astronomers noticed that the Crab was expanding. At about the same time it was pointed out that Chinese astronomers had described a "guest star" that appeared brightly in the sky on July 4, 1054: Unrecorded by medieval Europeans, it was so bright it could be seen clearly in daytime. This was a supernova explosion that took place where we now see the Crab Nebula. Using the observed rate of expansion of the Crab, scientists concluded that it must have begun expanding some 900 years before, just when the Chinese "guest star" showed up. Astronomical studies of the Crab Nebula have also uncovered a neutron star at its center that gives off light and radio waves that pulsate at a rate of about 30 pulses per second. If it has always been slowing down steadily, the pulsar must have been spinning 50 times per second when it was born out of the supernova explosion of 1054. All of the facts fit together beautifully, leaving little doubt that the Crab pulsar is a dense neutron star that has been slowing down and losing energy ever since it was born.

Why do earthworms come to the surface when it rains?

Earthworms live in tunnels in the soil, and ordinarily the soil contains enough air for them to breathe. But when it rains, water floods their tunnels and they have to come to the surface for air.

An earthworm is a valuable member of the soil community. The soil gives it air, food, and shelter, and the earthworm, in turn, keeps the soil loose and arable. The tunnels of earthworms crisscross the upper regions of the soil, forming a network that protects them against temperature extremes and other hazards of surface life. They dig their tunnels by pushing the soil aside and by eating it. Scientists estimate that the soil brought to the surface each year by earthworms amounts to as much as 18 tons per acre.

How do mothballs work?

Mothballs are made of such substances as camphor, naphthalene, and paradichlorobenzene, which are obtained from wood, coal, or petroleum products. All of the substances used in mothballs are alike, however, in that they are highly volatile. This means that they readily change from the solid (or liquid) state into a gas, and mix with the air around them. The gases given off by modern mothballs are deadly to clothes moths and many other insects that attack wool and fur.

It is actually not the adult moth that damages clothing, but rather the offspring of the moth. The female clothes moth lays her eggs on clothing made of wool or fur. The eggs soon hatch out into tiny, wormlike creatures called *larvae,* which feed on the wool or fur. If the clothing is kept in a sealed plastic bag or other enclosure that contains mothballs, the gas permeates the clothing and forms a protective cloud around it. This gas kills the adult moth, the larvae, and even the unhatched eggs. In addition to balls, flakes, and crystals, the moth-killing substances are also packaged in the form of a liquid spray.

Why does a towel soak up water?

Most towels are made of cotton because of its excellent water-absorbing qualities. This ability to soak up and retain water depends on several properties of water and cotton.

Of prime importance is the great affinity water and cotton molecules have for each other. There are many places in the cotton molecule to which water molecules can adhere. But in order to adhere to these places, the water molecules must move up through the fibers to find an empty place, so to speak. This motion of water through the cotton takes place because of a property of water called *capillarity.*

Put some water in a glass, and you will notice that the water rises slightly up the sides. The water is attracted to the glass and adheres to the surface. Place a fine glass tube in the same water, and the water pulls itself up inside the tube in a kind of hand-over-hand action. As the water climbs up, the attraction of each surface water molecule to its neighbor tends to make the surface flatten out. This effect, called *surface tension,* enables the water at the sides of the tube to climb still higher. These alternate activities of climbing and flattening continue until the water reaches a height at which the weight of its column just balances the upward force of capillary action.

The smaller the bore of the tube, the greater the effect of capillarity. The word, in fact, derives from the Latin *capillaris,* "hair," which emphasizes the slenderness of the channel up which the water moves.

Capillary action attracts liquids into all sorts of tiny places, where they adhere and spread like ink into a blotter. The many fine cotton fibers in a towel offer a great number of such tiny spaces, and capillarity enables water to spread throughout the towel. Capillarity also enables melted wax to flow up the wick of a candle to keep the flame going. In nature, capillarity causes water to flow upward through the soil toward the roots of plants.

Unlike cotton, most man-made fibers are fast drying because they have little affinity for water. To offset this nonabsorbent quality, they are often combined with such natural fibers as cotton and wool in making fabrics for clothing.

Why does the distant highway seem to quiver on a hot day?

This everyday optical illusion is caused by an effect called refraction. On a hot day, air is heated by the pavement and rises quickly because hot air is lighter than colder air. As it rises, it mixes randomly with cooler air, which is descending to take its place. Thus, the air above the roadbed is in continual motion, warmer here and cooler there. As light passes through this moving collection of warm and cool air volumes, it is bent or refracted this way and that, constantly changing its course. When this light reaches our eyes, it seems to dance about in the course of time. This continually changing directivity of the arriving light gives rise to the quivering that we see.

What is meant by a "dying lake"?

One of the most serious consequences of water pollution is eutrophication—the "dying of lakes." Sooner or later, all lakes go through a natural cycle of eutrophication, but the process normally takes thousands of years. In the first stage, called the *oligotrophic,* lakes are quite deep and support only a relatively small amount of biological life. Lake Superior is a good example of an oligotrophic lake. In the course of time, sediments and plant nutrients flow into the lake from the surrounding land areas; the lake becomes shallower and more biologically productive. Lake Ontario is in this *mesotrophic* stage. As nutrients and sediments continue to enter the lake, large algal blooms grow, fish populations change, and the lake assumes undesirable characteristics. Lake Erie is now in this so-called *eutrophic* stage. Over long periods of time, the lake becomes a swamp and finally changes to dry land.

Pollution greatly accelerates the process of eutrophication by adding great quantities of nutrients to the water that feeds a lake—detergents, fertilizers, industrial wastes, and sewage. This is happening today to Lake Erie, as well as to many other lakes. Through pollution, therefore, man can now produce in decades the changes that would have taken thousands of years for nature to accomplish in our nation's lakes.

What causes cancer?

No one really knows what cancer is, whether it is one disease or many; nor do scientists know the essential difference between normal cells and cancer cells. Scientists can tell us, however, that cancer cells look different from their normal counterparts, they multiply faster, work differently, and respond differently to ordinary influences. In the words of Dr. Jonas Salk, we can think of a cancer cell "as a normal cell that has become bewitched."

How? There is no certain answer. But in recent years many researchers have come to believe that all cancer is caused by a change in DNA, the complex chemical in our cells that carries a code of all of our hereditary traits.

The cell is the basic unit of life, a densely occupied "factory" turning out a great variety of important body chemicals. But its most important task is producing new cells.

Most of our cells are constantly dying and being replaced by new and identical ones that they themselves make. The key chemical in this process is DNA (Deoxyribonucleic acid), which is the blueprint of our hereditary-bearing chromosomes. A new life begins when a sperm and egg cell join, each carrying a half-share of chromosomes. That cell divides, and redivides until the individual is complete. And each time each cell divides throughout life, there is a sharing of hereditary-ruling chromosomes.

Each DNA molecule consists of two long strands of atoms joined together at thousands of places along their lengths. It resembles nothing more than a long, twisted ladder with thousands of rungs. When a cell divides, this long molecule separates to generate a new double strand—a new DNA molecule duplicating precisely all of the old DNA's genetic information. There are 800,000 such DNA molecules in just one cell.

Using information encoded in the DNA molecule, each cell fabricates new proteins for the body, new structural materials, hormones, enzymes, hemoglobin for the blood, and most importantly, new DNA. Life, in essence, takes place in the cell, where complex compounds are constantly being built out of other compounds that the cell takes apart.

In a cancer cell, scientists suspect that the DNA has somehow been altered so that it gives the "wrong" commands in the cell-building process. Instead of saying "Make a normal cell," it seems to say, "Make an abnormal cell."

If this is true, there appear to be many possible ways in which DNA can be altered. Each chromosome contains about 20,000 DNA molecules and every human cell contains 46 chromosomes. The human body contains somewhere between 30 and 50 trillion cells. If an unfortunate change takes place somewhere in that vast amount of DNA, a cancer cell may develop, resulting in lawless, abnormal growth. Why? Again, no one knows. One of the confusing factors is the very multiplicity of apparent cancer causes. These include excess radiation, a wide variety of chemicals, cigarette smoke, certain viruses, and even atmospheric pollutants. Only one thing seems certain: cancer research is in the forefront of the current revolution in biology. We can only hope that this research will soon lead to a fuller understanding and cure for this major scourge of mankind.

How does a medicine dropper work?

A medicine dropper, a turkey baster, a suction cup, and a plunger or "plumber's helper" all work on the same basic principle —air pressure. When the rubber part of the medicine dropper is in its normal condition, air pressure is equal on all its surfaces, both inside and out. Squeezing it forces out much of the air; releasing it allows it to bounce back to its original shape. If, during these operations, the open tip happens to be located under the surface of a liquid, a partial vacuum (lower pressure) forms inside the dropper. The higher pressure outside forces some of the liquid up into the medicine dropper until the pressure difference is equalized.

The great power of atmospheric pressure was first demonstrated by Otto von Guericke, a German burgomaster and experimenter. He built a powerful vacuum pump capable of pumping most of the air out of virtually any container. With it he performed such wonders that he achieved the status of a miracle worker. In his vacuums, candles extinguished suddenly, sounds failed to travel, animals could not live, and grapes would not ferment.

One day in 1654 he combined science and showmanship in his most dramatic and celebrated demonstration. He had obtained two hollow bronze hemispheres, both about twenty inches in diameter. Their rims were carefully machined and polished so that they formed an airtight seal when brought together. He then pumped out the air and hitched a team of horses to each hemisphere. As the awestruck throng looked on, the horses strained with all their might to pull the hemispheres apart, but they were unsuccessful. The hemispheres were held together, as von Guericke assured the onlookers, solely by the pressure of the outside air. It is precisely this pressure that forces a liquid up into a medicine dropper.

Does the north magnetic pole move around?

The north magnetic pole, located near the Arctic islands off the northern coast of Canada, is gradually shifting. During the present century it has moved over 300 miles in a direction slightly west of north. At many other places on the earth, the compass needle has been known to shift direction considerably in an interval of only a few years.

Such changes are apparently related to variation of the earth's magnetism deep below its surface. Most geophysicists believe that such magnetic changes are caused by the gradual movement of electrically charged material within the earth.

How big are raindrops?

For centuries, men have wondered about the rain. What are raindrops? How big are they? Are they all the same size?

Only since the turn of this century have we begun to get the answers to such questions. And oddly enough, it was a farmer of Jericho, Vermont—Wilson Bentley—who first measured the size of raindrops. Bentley is best known today for the thousands of beautiful photographs he made of snowflakes. But that's another story, and now we're interested in raindrops.

Bentley's investigations showed that raindrops vary in size all the way from about one-quarter of an inch in diameter down to extremely small droplets, perhaps one-hundredth of an inch in diameter. His results have never been improved upon.

Just as interesting as his measurements, however, was his method of measurement. He let the rain fall for a second or two into a pan of fine, sifted flour. The flour was about one inch deep—deep enough to prevent the drops from hitting the bottom of the pan and splashing. Bentley found that each drop would produce a pellet of dough. He let the pellets dry and then measured their diameters.

126

But how did the know the relationship between the size of his dough pellet and the size of the raindrop that produced it? Perhaps the dough pellet was larger than its raindrop?

Bentley answered this question by producing artificial "raindrops" of known size with the help of a medicine dropper. He measured a drop's diameter just before it left the dropper. Then he let it fall about twenty-five or thirty feet into his pan of flour. In that way he could compare the size of his dough pellet with the size of the original raindrop. He did this for drops of different size from the smallest to the largest.

Bentley found that small drops, about one-twelfth of an inch in diameter, produced pellets of that same diameter. Quarter-inch raindrops, however, were flattened somewhat in impact, and produced flattened pellets whose longer diameter was about one-third greater than the diameter of the raindrop.

Another way to measure raindrop size involves the use of an old nylon stocking (60 gauge) and confectioners' sugar. Here's how it's done. Go to the five-and-ten and get a five- or six-inch embroidery hoop. Cut off a piece of the old nylon stocking and mount it tightly on the hoop and coat it with the sugar. Shake off any excess sugar and you're ready to go out and measure raindrops.

Wherever a raindrop passes through the nylon screen, it leaves a nice clear, sugar-free circle. These circles are about 25 or 30 percent larger than the drops that produced them.

Why do people talk loudly at a party?

If you try to hear a weak sound in the presence of another, unwanted sound, the hearing threshold for the desired sound becomes higher. Acoustic engineers say that the desired sound is *masked* by the unwanted sound.

Masking sounds may either be pure tones or noise, continuous or intermittent. People who live near airports are subjected to the masking noise of aircraft, which can be loud enough near runways to make conversation all but impossible. The same effect takes place in back yards that adjoin modern high-speed highways.

A well-known example of masking is the so-called party effect, which takes place when many people are assembled in a room, and all try to converse simultaneously. When the concentration of talkers reaches a critical level, the masking effect of the combined voices causes each individual to raise his voice until everyone is speaking as loud as possible in order to be heard. Hence the din at all large parties.

In general, a masking sound of a certain frequency (or pitch) is most effective in masking sounds having nearly the same frequency. To distinguish a wanted sound in the presence of masking sounds, a listener utilizes frequency differences, the directional characteristics of his ears, and the brain's ability to "filter" out unwanted kinds of sound. For that reason, it is easier to converse in the presence of music than in the presence of other competing voices.

Is there such a thing as a "sixth sense" or extrasensory perception in animals?

Perception that goes beyond the senses we know is called *extrasensory perception.* It has become a controversial issue, blurred considerably by many factors, including imprecise terminology. If we agree to define a sense organ as any organ that gives an animal information about his environment, there is really no such thing as extrasensory perception. But on the other hand, if we apply the term to perception by processes not yet known to us, then it may occur widely among living creatures. The important point, of course, is that nature demands complete objectivity before it will give up its secrets to scientists. Science is one field in which wishing will not make it so.

A sense organ that is completely alien to man is connected with the electric "battery" that nature has provided to some fishes. It has long been known, of course, that South America's electric eel can deliver stunning electric shocks in defending itself against its enemies, but only recently have scientists discovered that certain fish use electricity to locate prey and avoid obstacles. Such fish have as their "sixth sense" a high sensitivity to electric fields.

An example of this curious feature is found in the African freshwater fish *Gymnarchus niloticus,* which has a set of muscles in its tail that are no longer able to contract. Instead, they emit a stream of weak electric discharges, at a rate of about 300 per second. During each of the discharges, the tail momentarily assumes a negative charge with respect to the head of the fish. In this way, the fish sets up a pulsating electric field in the surrounding water, and it can sense disturbances in the field. The sense organs are near the head and consist of pores set in the otherwise insulating skin. The pores lead to sensory cells, which connect with the brain. Such fish have been trained to distinguish between nonconductors placed near them, such as glass and rubber, and identically shaped conducting objects. These diverse objects distort the electric field around the fish in different ways, and the fish can discern these differences.

Electric sense organs, of course, are merely one glimpse into the fascinating world of animal senses. Some marine animals can detect and respond to slight differences in salinity of water; bees find their way to the nectar in a flower by sensing differences in the humidity of the air; lizards find water the same way; and bats navigate unerringly in total darkness with the help of "sound" echoes that are outside the human range of hearing. The homing "instinct" in birds and the migration of fishes still baffle the scientist to a great extent. Some marine animals spawn only during spring tides or full moon tides or new moon tides; how they know which is which is still a mystery.

The method used by electric fishes to find their prey was not known a generation ago, so it was then a "sixth sense," or a kind of extrasensory perception. The term, of course, is of little importance and is not worth quarreling about. What is important is the valid research by which scientists seek to discover new and fascinating facts about the world and its amazing creatures.

What is paraffin wax made of?

Most of the new synthetic materials that chemistry has given us begin with nature's own building blocks, the small simple molecules called *monomers* that come from such sources as coal, oil, and natural gas. To build a new giant molecule, or *polymer,* chemists begin with one or more kinds of building blocks, changing them where necessary and attaching them to each other in long, well-defined chains. In effect, by using appropriate building blocks and controlling their arrangement in the polymer, chemists can get such desired qualities as strength, elasticity, durability, adhesion, and hardness.

In building synthetic polymers from small molecules, the chemist is really copying a natural process as old as life itself. Nature abounds with examples of the molecular chain. Methane, for example, provides the basic unit of structure of materials that range all the way from gaseous to liquid to solid.

The methane molecule is a hydrocarbon that is generated during the decomposition of organic matter. It contains 1 carbon atom surrounded by 4 hydrogen atoms. It is extremely inflammable and is often responsible for explosions in mines. The next larger hydrocarbon, ethane, has 2 carbon atoms and 6 hydrogen atoms. Ethane and methane constitute as much as 90 percent of natural gas. The addition of more carbon atoms, with their associated hydrogen atoms, produces heavier and longer molecules. The next member of the family, three-carbon propane, is used as bottled gas. The heaviest of the methane-family gases are the four-carbon butanes, used in cigarette lighters. A mixture of propane and butane can be changed to a liquid under pressure—the well-known liquefied petroleum fuel, or LP-gas.

When still more carbon atoms are added to the chain, liquids—such as five-carbon pentanes—are formed. Pentanes are used in anesthetics. The larger molecules in the series get progressively heavier. The heptanes (7 carbon atoms) and the octanes (8 carbon atoms) are often used to rate the antiknock quality of gasolines. The heaviest liquids are the seventeen-carbon heptadecanes, sometimes found in crude oil.

When 18 or more carbon atoms and their attendant hydrogen atoms are linked in the methane chain, they produce a series of solids called *petroleum waxes*. Those with up to 30 carbon atoms form the everyday paraffin waxes that are used to make candles, coat milk cartons, and seal jars of homemade jelly and jam. Other waxes are derived from the longer chains containing up to 70 carbon atoms.

Ordinary paraffin containing 30 carbon atoms is about as large a member of the methane series as is found in nature. But chemists have learned nature's trick well, and have stretched the series to include the important plastic polyethylene, a polymer containing as many as 200,000 carbons in its long chain. Polyethylene is used to make the wide variety of squeeze bottles that dispense everything from glue to shampoo. In addition to polyethylene, methane is used as the base for perhaps a hundred important products. These include Plexiglas, antifreeze, aerosol propellants, solvents, synthetic rubber, vinyl plastics, paints, acrylic fibers, and Teflon.

How does a pneumatic hammer work?

Driven by compressed air, a pneumatic hammer is powerful enough to break up the hardest concrete. When the operating lever is pressed, compressed air rushes in behind a piston, moving it forward at great speed. The piston strikes a pointed chipping tool, which transmits the blow to the pavement that is to be broken. Meanwhile, the return air valve reverses its position, allowing the compressed air to push against the forward end of the piston. This moves the piston back to its original position and the entire procedure repeats over and over again. The machine pounds away at the pavement with a machine-gun speed of 2,000 blows a minute.

How is fresh water made from seawater?

In 1958 the United States government decided to build an experimental desalting plant along the Gulf Coast. Some thirty cities applied for the installation, but Freeport, Texas—where even well water was salty—was selected. The plant cost $1,200,000 and provides 1 million gallons of fresh water per day, made from salt water drawn from the Gulf of Mexico. The plant turned out to be so efficient that the fresh water had too little salt in it, and towns-people complained that it tasted flat. So the distilled water was mixed with salty water from local wells to restore some of its taste. (In a similar plant operating in Aruba, in the Dutch West Indies, the taste of the water is improved by passing it through beds of broken coral.) Experts believe that plants producing 500 million gallons a day are entirely feasible and will be built in critical places within the next twenty years.

Freeport's desalination plant uses a process called *flash distillation,* in which the water is boiled off and the salt left behind. The vapor is then condensed to form pure, salt-free water. There are many other processes for removing salt from water. On the island of Symi, near Greece, each of the approximately 4,000 inhabitants gets about a gallon per day from a solar-distillation unit. This method, which is illustrated in the diagram, uses the sun's heat to

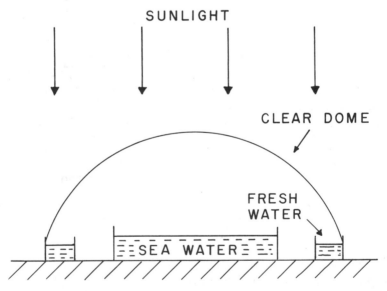

FIG. 10. The principle of solar distillation of seawater. Heat from the sun evaporates water from a central supply of seawater. Fresh water then condenses on the underside of the transparent dome and drips into collecting pans at the edges of the dome.

132

evaporate seawater. Fresh water then recondenses on the underside of the unit's transparent plastic dome. As the water accumulates, it trickles down the sloping dome and drips into collecting pans at the edges of the unit where it is drained out. The method is inexpensive, but the output is low: at best, it provides only about one-eighth of a gallon per day for each square foot of area.

Freezing is another promising method of desalting water. When salt water freezes, the salt is left behind in the liquid as pure ice forms at the surface. The ice is removed by scraping it off the top with a rotating blade, and the brine is drained away from the bottom of the tank. The ice, of course, melts to provide pure water. At Wrightsville Beach, North Carolina, a freezing desalination plant, built by the United States Office of Saline Water, produces 200,000 gallons of desalted water a day.

Another method, called *reverse osmosis,* removes salt from water by passing seawater through a synthetic membrane. In still another, called *hydration,* propane is added to the water, forming a solid compound of propane and water. The compound is separated from the brine and then heated, which releases the fresh water. Because of practical problems, neither of these methods is yet efficient enough for field use.

If the available water supply is not too salty, a process called *electrodialysis* becomes economically feasible. When salt dissolves in water, it breaks up into electrically charged particles, or *ions,* of sodium and chlorine. The essence of the process is to put the salt water into a container that has a positive terminal and a negative terminal. The positively charged sodium ions then move toward the negative terminal, and the negatively charged chlorine ions move toward the positive terminal. The center of the tank is then relatively free of ions and, hence, salt.

This method is too expensive, however, except where the salt problem is not great. In Webster, South Dakota, the local water was brackish but not nearly as salty as seawater. Webster built a plant based on electrodialysis that produces about 250,000 gallons of water per day.

133

Does the eating of sweets cause tooth decay?

If you were hoping for a negative answer, I'm afraid you are in for a disappointment. Dental research scientists tell us that sucrose (ordinary sugar) favors the conditions that lead to tooth decay and peridontal disease. The total amount of sugar eaten is less important, however, than the frequency of eating. A reasonable compromise, we are told, between total abstinence and indulgence is to eat all the sweets you want once a day—perhaps as a dessert after a well-balanced meal.

Sucrose is a dental problem child because it is the essential food for the "decay-causing bacteria" that we hear so much about in toothpaste commercials. What happens is this. When certain bacteria encounter sucrose in various foods and beverages, they produce gummy substances called *dextrans* which enable them to adhere tenaciously to the teeth. They grow and multiply rapidly into large colonies called *plaque*. Other bacteria take up residence in the plaque and change the sugars into acids. The acids, in turn, attack the tooth enamel and dissolve it away. The bacteria are then free to invade the underlying dentin and a serious cavity is under way.

These acid-generating bacteria start to work just a few seconds after any sugar enters the mouth. Once started, acid production usually continues for long periods of time. So tooth destruction takes place long after the time when sweets were actually in the mouth. This explains why frequent snacking on sweets is an invitation to tooth decay. This conclusion, by the way, has been fully backed up by controlled experiments on animals.

Plaque, the archenemy of the teeth, is also responsible for most forms of peridontal disease. This is a disease that attacks the gums and bone that support the teeth. It begins with an accumulation of plaque on the teeth, along the gum line. Chemical irritants produced by bacteria in the plaque cause gum irritation and bleeding. As time goes on the plaque bacteria closest to the tooth surface die, harden in minerals called *tartar* or *calculus,* which in turn is covered by a layer of living bacterial plaque. Somewhat later, the fibers that fasten the gums to the teeth are attacked and destroyed, thereby allowing the gums to separate from the teeth. This leaves pockets or spaces between gums and teeth that become filled with bacteria. Eventually, the disease attacks the bone that supports the teeth, causing them to become loose. In this condition, the teeth are relatively easy prey to various kinds of decay and infection. Although peridontal disease is usually thought of as a disease of adults, its early stages can also be observed in children. The most frequent sign is swollen gums that bleed easily.

Plaque is the more insidious because it is transparent and colorless. Only in very thick layers can it sometimes be seen as whitish mats.

Once a dentist has removed all plaque and tartar, most people can keep their teeth relatively free from plaque by regular oral care. This requires the removal of plaque from all tooth surfaces at least once a day, preferably at bedtime. For this purpose dentists recommend thorough brushing and the use of dental floss or tape. Water sprays and jets may also be of value to some people, but they should be used only under the guidance of the dentist.

There are hopeful indications that research may soon add to the arsenal against plaque. Studies with animals have shown that certain chemicals are quite effective in breaking down plaque and preventing tooth decay. In a series of experiments, a group of hamsters were given a sugar-containing diet designed to encourage tooth decay. Some of the animals were also given *dextranase,* a chemical that breaks down dextran—the sticky substance that enables bacteria to stick to teeth. In those animals given dextranase, plaque was eliminated, further plaque formation was halted, and cavity formation was reduced. In those animals not given the chemical, plaque formation and decay were rampant. Trials are now under way to see if dextranase will work on human beings. In addition, other enzymes, chemicals, and antibacterial agents are being studied for the same purpose.

While scientists continue to seek out more effective methods of preventing tooth decay, each of us should continue to rely heavily on the best tool available—the regular removal of plaque both at home and in the dentist's office.

How does an aerosol can work?

An aerosol is a suspension in a gas of innumerable tiny liquid or solid particles. A few everyday examples of natural aerosols are smoke, fog, and clouds. In today's modern world, our homes are filled with "aerosol cans," which dispense aerosols of everything from perfume and hair spray to furniture polish and paint.

A typical aerosol can contains a liquid and a gas under pressure. When the plunger on top of the can is pressed, the gas is allowed to escape to the atmosphere. In doing so, it speeds across the top of a fine tube that is partially immersed in the liquid. This causes some of the liquid to flow up through the tube and mix with the gas in the form of tiny droplets. The escaping gas thus carries with it a quantity of liquid in finely divided form.

It is also possible to dispense solid particles with an aerosol can. The finely divided powder is suspended in a volatile liquid in the can, along with the usual amount of compressed gas. When the spray is released, the liquid droplets carry the solid particles along with them. The liquid evaporates rapidly, leaving a fine layer of the solid powder on the sprayed surface.

Spray coming from an aerosol can is rather cool, because compressed gas gets colder when it expands. This is why spray insecticide sometimes freezes if the nozzle is held too close to the sprayed surface.

Do plants help the land conserve water?

The answer to this question is yes and no. The organic matter of decaying vegetation does help reduce the runoff after a rainstorm, so in that sense plants do help to slow the flow of water to the oceans. But plants are also great users, and wasters, of water.

The productivity of most of the world's farmland is at the mercy of weather and climate. In some places men pray for rain; in others they build dams and irrigation projects to supplement a marginal annual rainfall; in still others they must battle severe seasonal drought. Now scientists are attacking another paradoxical aspect of the problem: the fact that plants squander most of the water they do get.

Plants take in carbon dioxide from the air through tiny openings on the leaves called *stomata*. They need this gas for use in the food-producing process called *photosynthesis*. Unfortunately, a large part of the water that a plant's roots take in escapes through the open stomata. A field of corn, for example, gives off about ten times as much water as would evaporate from the same field bare of plants. In fact, about two-thirds of the world's rainfall is dissipated in this way, by transpiration from plants.

Researchers are now investigating ways of reducing this water loss from the leaves of plants. Chemicals are being studied that keep the stomata half closed—open wide enough to take in the necessary carbon dioxide, yet closed enough to save a significant part of the water they would normally lose. If a chemical is found that is suitable in all respects, it may one day be used as a spray to save crops during periods of severe drought.

What is the range of the human voice?

The range of the human voice extends from about 60 cycles per second at the low end, for a bass, to about 1,300 cycles for the highest note of a high soprano. This amounts to somewhat over four octaves, although the maximum range of any one voice rarely exceeds three octaves.

Many musical instruments have greater range than the human voice. The piano, for example, exceeds seven octaves, from about 27 cycles per second to 4,186 cycles per second. Some organs have an even greater range of frequencies.

137

Why doesn't a sparkler firework burn your hand?

At one time or another most of us have lit a common sparkler firework and allowed the shower of brilliant sparks to fall harmlessly on our hands. Although the sparks have a temperature of several thousand degrees, they produce practically no sensation whatever on the hand. This is because they contain so little matter that their heat capacity is negligibly small.

The same sort of thing takes place in our atmosphere at high altitudes. At 130 miles up, for example, the temperature of the air reaches 1,000°F. or higher. Yet satellites and space vehicles can fly continuously at this altitude without being warmed by the hot air. The explanation of this paradox, of course, is that the air at great altitudes is too thin to contain much heat; it cannot act as a thermal bath, warming a body immersed in it.

At sea level, the molecules that compose the air are so numerous and closely packed that they travel only a few millionths of an inch, on the average, before colliding with another molecule. But 130 miles up, a molecule must travel, not a few millionths of an inch, but something like a *mile* before colliding with another molecule. The molecules are just so few and far between that they are not able to impart a sensible amount of heat to a large object such as a space vehicle.

What are quasars?

Scientists know that the earth, besides receiving light from visible stars, is continually bathed in a flood of radio waves coming from tiny regions in the sky. These regions were originally called *radio stars* because they seemed to emit no visible light, only radio waves. Even to this day, only a fraction of these radio sources have been paired up with optically visible objects in the sky. The term *quasar* is a contraction of *quasi-stellar radio source,* and is applied to one class of radio-emitting objects.

In 1960 scientists made a puzzling discovery with the help of the 200-inch telescope at Mount Palomar. Searching one of the "blank" areas of the sky from which a strong radio signal was coming, they discovered its source: a dim and quite insignificant star. The star had been photographed before, but had never been studied carefully because it had always seemed so very "ordinary." In short order, many other humble-looking stars turned out to be powerful radio sources. Feeble as they seemed to be, these stars were in fact flooding space with unimaginably great amounts of invisible radio energy.

Puzzled, scientists began examining their light in detail with the help of a *spectroscope,* a device that breaks light up into its component colors or wavelengths. To their amazement, they found that the light from these stars was like that from no other known stars.

Then Maarten Schmidt, an astronomer at the California Institute of Technology, made an important discovery. He noticed that quasar starlight contains the telltale wavelengths given off by hydrogen but that these wavelengths have been mysteriously moved toward the red end of the light spectrum from their customary positions near the blue end. This *red shift,* as it is called, can only mean one thing: quasars must be fantastically distant from the earth—out near the fringe of visibility with the 200-inch telescope. Here was an amazing discovery; quasars at such remote distances from our galaxy must pour forth light and radio energy with fantastic brilliance— far greater than that of a hundred galaxies, each containing a hundred billion stars each! Quasars seem to be dim stars only because they are so incredibly far away.

In studying quasars, astronomers are not only investigating the brightest objects in the sky, but are probing farther into the remote past than has ever before been possible. Quasar light now entering our telescopes started on its way to us up to 10 billion years ago— perhaps before our own sun became a star. No one knows, of course, where these quasars are today or even if they still exist. Equally mystifying is their physical makeup. Scientists do not believe that any known type of star or quasi-galaxy could continue to radiate light and radio waves in such huge quantities in a stable fashion for billions of years.

But whatever they turn out to be, they are almost certainly

139

smaller and denser than galaxies, and much more unstable. It is possible their life span may be as low as a few million years, a mere trifle as astronomers reckon time.

How do computers compute?

There are two kinds of computers: analog and digital. Analog computers represent numbers by a physical quantity such as length, angle, or magnitude of electric voltage. The accuracy of analog computers is limited by the precision with which such physical quantities can be measured. Digital computers, on the other hand, represent numbers by separate things such as pebbles, or pulses, of electric current. A person counting on his fingers is really using the simplest of digital computers. Thus, the accuracy of a digital computer is not limited by the accuracy of measurement, but only by the number of digit-representing elements built into the machine. Digital computers are described in the following discussion because of their great importance in the fields of science, business, and industry.

A complete understanding of how digital computers work is beyond the scope of this book, but it is possible to describe the general principles involved. When you and I do a problem in arithmetic, such as addition or multiplication, we go through several steps:

1. We write down, or *store,* numbers as necessary.

2. We look them up (*retrieve* them) as they are needed for subsequent steps.

3. We *control* the entire operation by performing each step in the required order.

A computer also performs the operations of storage and retrieval of information, and control of each step in the operation.

Imagine for a moment the series of operations you might follow in doing the following simple addition:

$$\begin{array}{r} 45 \\ 87 \\ \hline 132 \end{array}$$

Instructions	Arithmetic

Step 1	Add the two units figures.	$7 + 5 = 12$
Step 2	Write the units figure of the above sum as the units figure of the answer.	$--2$ (answer)
Step 3	Carry the tens figures of the sum of step 1.	carry 1
Step 4	Add the carried figure to the two tens figures of the problem.	$1 + 4 + 8 = 13$
Step 5	Write the units figure of the sum of step 4 as the tens figure of the answer.	-32 (answer)
Step 6	Write the tens figure of the sum of step 4 as the hundreds figure of the answer.	132 (answer)

A computer follows much the same routine in solving its problems, no matter how complicated they may be. The instructions are stored in the *memory unit.* They are "read" by the *control unit,* which directs the *arithmetic unit* to do the steps specified. The result of each step is stored in the memory unit. When a previously stored number is called for, the control unit transfers the number from the memory unit to the arithmetic unit. Thus, three main functions are performed: storage and retrieval of instructions and numbers, processing of numbers by arithmetic, and control of these operations by a program of instructions.

The required program of instructions must be available before the computation begins. When we solve a problem in arithmetic or algebra, we may not always be aware that a program has been prepared in advance. Nevertheless, stored in our memory are the rules and algorithms used to solve typical problems. If we do happen to get stuck, we merely go to a book and refresh our memory. That's where we have it over the computer. When a computer gets stuck, all it can do is seek human help!

What causes deserts?

Most scientists define a desert as a place having less than 10 inches of rain each year, compared with 50 inches for a relatively moist region. Various parts of the earth are dry for different reasons. Some deserts just happen to be located in hot, dry parts of the earth. Winds in these places carry so little moisture that there is little chance of rain. Although cloudbursts occur occasionally in such areas, the water evaporates rapidly and the land soon becomes dry again. In other regions, mountains are responsible for the deserts. Winds pick up moisture over the ocean and carry rain clouds inland. There they come against a mountain range and are forced to rise. The increased altitude cools the clouds and they rain. The rain falls on the side of the mountains facing the sea and there is no rain for the far side—the desert side.

One of the world's great deserts is the Mojave in southeastern California. The temperature of the Mojave rises to over 100°F. each day of the summer, although the nights are usually cool.

Another famous desert extends from North Africa into Asia. In Africa it is called the Sahara, and a section in Asia is called the Gobi Desert. Other big deserts are found in Australia, South Africa, and South America.

The Sahara and Gobi are hot, dry, and sandy, fitting our usual picture of a desert. The winds blow the sand into hills or dunes as tall as a building. Other deserts are rocky flatlands or harsh, dry mountainous regions. And desert lands in Siberia are extremely cold, with raw, biting winds. But all have one thing in common: extremely low annual rainfall.

How do artificial gills work?

Fish can breathe under water by drawing in oxygen through their gills, membranes that filter dissolved gases from water. Today, with the help of a new man-made silicone rubber membrane, scientists have enabled birds and other animals to live and breathe under water in much the same way that fish do.

To do its job, the silicone membrane is sliced one-half thousandth of an inch thick and two sheets are laminated together. This ensures the absence of pinholes in the film. Then a box large enough to hold a bird or other small animal is completely covered with the film. All seams are sealed so that the cage is completely watertight. The cage can then be completely submerged in water without danger to the bird. The silicone film, just one thousandth of an inch thick, permits the passage of oxygen through its molecular structure for the bird to breathe.

Putting a canary safely under water requires an amount of film area corresponding to a one-cubic-foot cage. This film area provides enough oxygen to sustain the bird indefinitely. In a similar fashion, a silicone-enclosed human diver would require 260 square feet of film—equivalent to an eight-foot cube. Freed of clumsy air tanks and hoses, he could not only obtain oxygen from the sea, but could expel carbon dioxide gas in the same way.

Silicone rubber films, which are derived from ordinary sand and other minerals, have long been known to have gas-permeable properties. Only recently, however, have sufficiently thin films been sliced to permit life-sustaining amounts of oxygen to pass through.

How can seashells be found hundreds of feet above sea level?

Scientists believe that the outer shell of the earth, some 70 miles thick, consists of a relatively light but brittle crust. The underlying rocks become less brittle with increasing depth, until at a depth of 430 miles the material is quite flexible. So we can think of the earth as a brittle layer floating on a very viscous substance—much like a block of wood floating on a pool of thick molasses.

To understand what this has to do with seashells, imagine a rowboat floating on a pond. We know that the boat sinks to a lower depth when we step into it, and that it floats higher in the water when we get out of it. The boat falls or rises in response to the amount of weight in the boat. In much the same way, certain parts of the earth's surface sink, or *subside,* under the weight of accumulating sediments. In other places, the opposite effect takes place. The earth actually rises as dirt and rock are transported elsewhere. This process is called *isostacy.*

Land surveys in the delta region of the Mississippi River show that the surface is sinking about 8 feet per century. As sediment from the river settles on the delta, the increased weight causes a lowering of the land. (Of course, as the delta subsides, more sediment is deposited on the falling surface.)

Even more striking evidence of isostacy is related to the vertical movements of North America. During the last Ice Age, much of North America was covered with thousands of feet of ice. The enormous weight of this ice undoubtedly caused considerable subsidence or sinking of the land. Thus, many coastal regions sank under the surface of the ocean. Later, when the ice melted, the continent was relieved of the weight of the ice and rose to its normal position—just as our rowboat rose when we stepped out of it. In the vicinity of Lake Champlain and Montreal, many marine fossils including seashells and bones of seals and whales have been found hundreds of feet above sea level. They must have developed when the region was depressed below sea level by the weight of nearby glaciers. Later, because of the reduced weight, the ocean bottom with the fossils was lifted high above the sea to its present position. This movement is still taking place, as is testified by the many minor earthquakes in the region, which indicate that the earth's brittle crust is still shifting slightly.

Why do bridges freeze before road surfaces?

A wet bridge tends to freeze before the adjacent road surface because it is not in direct contact with the earth. When temperatures drop, both bridge and road give off heat to the cooling air. But the road is continually warmed by heat rising from deep below the ground. In most parts of the United States, the temperature of the earth about fifty feet below the surface remains constant throughout the year at about 50°F. This keeps the temperature of a road from falling too rapidly. A bridge, on the other hand, is quite well insulated from the earth. As the bridge's heat is lost, it cannot be replaced too easily from the reservoir of heat in the ground.

The same sort of thing accounts at times for the uneven melting of a new snowfall as the flakes begin to fall. Here and there twigs, shrubs, and leaves of grass are white with snow while roads are wet with melted snow. Once again, objects that are reasonably well insulated from the earth tend to lose their heat more quickly than those which are thermally bonded to the earth. For that reason, as the air temperature falls, the temperature of an insulated object drops rather quickly below freezing.

Do bears hibernate?

Body processes slow down considerably when an animal goes into hibernation. Breathing takes place as infrequently as once in five minutes and the heart beats only four or five times a minute. Body temperature of hibernating animals drops to as low as 45°F.

A few of the true hibernators are reptiles, amphibians, woodchucks, ground squirrels, various insects, some bats, and some mice. Bears, raccoons, and chipmunks are not true hibernators. They go into a prolonged winter sleep, but there is not much change in their body processes. Biologists refer to these animals as *light sleepers,* or *dozers.*

What is meant by the "clock paradox"?

According to Einstein's Theory of Relativity, time is a variable rather than a fixed quantity. The rate at which it flows depends upon how fast you are moving. This variability is much too small to be detected in everyday living, of course, but it assumes great importance at velocities within a few percent of the speed of light. In simplest terms, the faster you travel, the more slowly time passes for you.

An example will illustrate the implications of this odd behavior of time. Imagine a spaceship making a round trip between earth and a distant point in space. If it travels at 87 percent of the speed of light (580 million mph), everything inside seems to take twice as long as it should to an outside observer. At 99.5 percent of the speed of light, the time scale of the spaceship is slowed down by a factor of 10; at 99.99 percent, by a factor of 100.

As you can see, this time dilation effect increases enormously as one's speed approaches the speed of light. Yet scientists assure us that everything appears quite normal to astronauts aboard the spaceship; their clocks seem to them to run at the right speed, they get hungry at about the right times, and the universe appears just as it was before the trip began.

Most scientists interpret this effect to mean that men aboard a fast-moving spaceship *will age more slowly* than those left behind on earth. To illustrate, imagine a one-year space trip at 99.99 percent of the speed of light. Upon their return, the spacemen would find the earth 100 years older and all their friends and relatives dead. Impossible? Only a small minority of scientists and mathematicians refuse to accept a universe in which this sort of thing can happen.

Unexpected experimental observations now seem to confirm that a "slowing down of time" does indeed occur in our real world for objects moving fast enough. Scientists have long known that mysterious "cosmic rays"—tiny subatomic particles—are constantly bombarding the earth from outer space. These cosmic rays are known to be moving at speeds approaching the speed of light. They collide with gas molecules high up in the atmosphere, and in so doing produce a peculiar kind of subatomic particle called the *mu-meson*. Most of the mu-mesons immediately collide and react in turn with other molecules of atmospheric gas almost as fast as they are generated. Nevertheless, a few do reach the surface and have been detected by nuclear physicists.

Mu-mesons are known to be unstable. Even if they avoid collisions with other particles, they exist only for about 2 microseconds before changing spontaneously into a different kind of particle. And this is where the paradox comes into the story. Scientists know that it takes 20 microseconds for a mu-meson to travel from high in the atmosphere, where it is produced, to the ground, where it is detected. But how can a trip of 20 microseconds be made by a particle whose "lifetime" is only 2 microseconds?

Modern physics provides the answer. According to our measurements, the average lifetimes of the cosmic mu-mesons are about ten times as long as they "ought" to be. This means that their internal "clocks" or time scales are slowed down by a factor of 10. This tells us that they must be moving at about 99.5 percent of the speed of light, for at that speed the time rate of the mu-meson would be slowed down tenfold, as mentioned earlier. This speed is consistent with the known velocity of incoming cosmic rays.

From the point of view of a mu-meson, however, its lifetime is still a normal 2 microseconds, just as it ought to be. It reaches the earth's surface sooner than it should because it perceives our atmosphere as contracted or shrunken to one-tenth of the thickness that we measure for it on earth.

Here, then, is the paradox; a mu-meson ages only 2 microseconds in passing through the atmosphere, while earth-bound clocks tick off 20 microseconds. Nor is there any way to determine which measurement is correct. According to our observations, the mu-meson slows down; according to the mu-meson's measurements (assuming it can make measurements), our atmosphere is much shallower than we think it is. All that is really certain is that the mu-meson, traveling at great speed, does indeed survive a journey that takes ten times the average lifetime of a mu-meson to complete; yet, it does in fact make that trip in one mu-meson lifetime, with enough time left over for its presence to be detected! Impossible as it may seem, those are the facts.

All of this, then, is at least one piece of experimental evidence that can be explained only on the basis of Einstein's theory that the time scale of objects moving close to the speed of light does indeed slow down. Unbelievable as it may seem, this evidence of "time dilation" is merely one of a multitude of observations made over the past half century that tend to confirm Einstein's relativistic concept of the universe. During that period of time, the equations of relativity have withstood every test that the genius of man could devise, and literally billions of dollars' worth of engineering have been based upon them. Enormous accelerators that speed atomic particles almost to the speed of light would not work if Einstein's equations were not a true representation of the real world—at least, as true as can be measured. So, until a better explanation comes along, we will have to accept the fact that even perfect clocks run at different rates, depending upon their motion.

Is rust good for anything?

Rust is a chemical compound consisting of iron and oxygen, a substance we usually think of as an annoyance rather than as a useful tool of man. But, today, ordinary rust is helping to keep whole populations from starving. Iron rust or granulated iron oxide is a *catalyst*—a substance that assists or speeds up a chemical reaction between other chemical substances without entering into the reaction itself and without being changed in the least—that speeds up the reaction between nitrogen gas and hydrogen to make cheap ammonia gas (NH_3). Using this gas, chemists make great quantities of nitric acid and nitrate fertilizer.

Another catalyst, vanadium oxide, plays a key role in supporting dozens of industries. It is used to speed up the production of more than 10 million tons of sulfuric acid annually. This acid is a vital raw material in the metal and oil industries and in the manufacture of fertilizer, paint, synthetic fibers, coal products, and explosives.

How is cream separated from milk?

In the days before homogenized milk, it was common to see several inches of cream floating over the remaining skim milk at the top of a milk bottle. The separation came about because of gravity. Cream is lighter than milk and naturally floats to the surface. This separation is avoided for homogenized milk by reducing the size of the creamy fat globules so that they are extremely small and evenly distributed. This reduces the tendency for them to float to the surface.

From a practical point of view, however, commercial dairies cannot afford to wait for gravity to separate cream from skim milk.

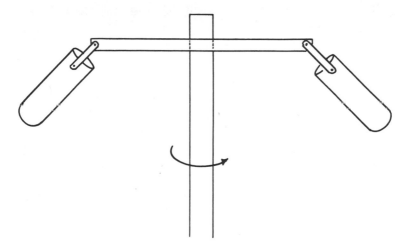

FIG. 11. The principle of the centrifuge—here, a cream separator. The rapidly spinning tubes generate a kind of artificial gravity that hastens the separation of cream and milk.

Instead, a kind of artificial gravity is produced in a *centrifuge,* which makes cream separate out much more rapidly than it would do if left to the action of gravity alone. As shown in the diagram, a simple centrifuge consists of a rotating bar, from the ends of which two tubes are suspended. Whole milk can be placed in these tubes. During rotation the tubes experience an outward force that makes them tilt in that direction. Such a force is called *centrifugal force.*

The magnitude of the effect generated in a centrifuge can be extremely great, and the following example will serve to illustrate just *how* great. Imagine a 1-pound weight spinning at 40 revolutions per second at a distance of 6 inches from the center of rotation. Under these conditions, the weight experiences a force that corresponds to a hanging weight (of gravity) equal to 1,000 pounds! Scientists say that it experiences 1,000 *g* because the effect on the object is the same as if it were placed in a gravitational field 1,000 times as great as the earth's.

It is common for laboratory centrifuges to generate 100,000 *g* on substances placed in them. In such a device, a 1-ounce sample would "weigh" over 3 tons! Any sediment in a liquid sample would "fall" much faster than would be possible without the help of a centrifuge.

This same effect, on a reduced scale, is used to give us a thrill on playland rides. The "scenic railway," "loop-the-loop," and countless other variations play on our ability to sense an apparent change in weight of our bodies. Such effects are produced by changing our direction of motion at a fairly rapid rate, just as happens to milk placed in a centrifuge.

Does a boomerang come back?

Well, yes and no. If you mean does a boomerang return after hitting what it is aimed at, the answer is no. The stories of Australian aborigines being able to throw a boomerang so that it will hit a target behind a tree and then return to the thrower are just not true. But boomerangs are remarkable nevertheless.

In the early part of its flight a boomerang's path is almost a straight line. It is supposed to hit the target during this part of its journey. If the boomerang were moving in a vacuum, it would continue to move in a straight line in accordance with Newton's First Law of Motion, which tells us that a moving object will continue to move in the same direction at the same speed unless it is acted upon by an external force.

Because of the air, however, a boomerang slows down in flight. It is so shaped that the air resistance is greater on one part than on the other, so its path becomes more and more curved as it slows down below a certain speed. Its curved path causes it to return more or less to its starting point, depending on the skill of the thrower and the shape of the boomerang.

A boomerang consists of a flattened, curved blade, quite flat on one side and more rounded on the other. Its ability to come back also seems to be related to a small twist in its structure. A skillful

Australian aborigine can make a boomerang describe first a large loop, then one or two smaller ones before it falls at his feet.

Boomerangs that return, called *play boomerangs,* are found only in certain restricted parts of Australia. There are other forms that do not come back to the thrower: heavy ones for fighting at close quarters, and lighter ones for hunting game at a distance. Weapons similar to the boomerang were also used in ancient Egypt, as well as by Hopi Indians in Arizona.

What is meant by "noise pollution"?

Noise has been defined as "sound without value," and most of us have noticed that the intensity, variety, and clamor of unwanted sounds have soared in recent years. For many city residents the din never ceases; for most of us, it too rarely diminishes. For this reason, noise has lately been added to the growing list of environmental pollutants that plague our lives.

Noise is greatest in urban areas, where three-fourths of the nation lives. The general din and roar of air and surface transportation, the hum of construction projects, the clatter of industrial machinery, all pound the ear in a continual assault. In the last decade, the extent and level of urban noise has risen significantly, as has the social awareness of noise and the discomfort it causes.

The most severe noise levels are usually encountered on the job. Excessive exposure to such noise for long periods is known to cause irreversible hearing loss. A government agency estimates that as many as 16 million American workers are now threatened with damage to their hearing.

There are many sources of noise pollution in addition to the work environment. A few are listed on the accompanying chart, which is adapted from a report of the U.S. Council on Environmental Quality, a governmental agency.

Traffic noise on a busy city street often reaches 90 decibels. We should explain here that the decibel is a logarithmic measure of sound, so linear comparisons of decibels cannot be made. For example, a noise intensity level of 90 decibels is ten times as great as

SOUND LEVELS AND HUMAN RESPONSE

Sound Source	Decibels	Response Criteria
	150	
Carrier deck jet operation	140	
		Painfully loud
	130	Upper limit of speech
Jet takeoff (200 feet)	120	intelligibility
Discotheque		
Auto horn (3 feet)		
Riveting machine	110	Upper limit of human voice
Jet takeoff (2000 feet)		
Shout (0.5 feet)	100	
N.Y. subway station		Very annoying
Heavy truck (50 feet)	90	Hearing damage (8 hours)
Pneumatic drill (50 feet)		
	80	Annoying
Freight train (50 feet)		
Freeway traffic (50 feet)	70	Telephone use difficult
		Intrusive
Air-conditioning unit (20 feet)	60	
Light auto traffic (50 feet)		
	50	Quiet
Living room		
Bedroom	40	
Library		
Soft whisper (15 feet)	30	Very quiet
Broadcasting studio	20	
	10	Just audible
	0	Threshold of hearing

one at 80 decibels, and a hundred times as great as one at 70 decibels. So a busy city street can be 1 million times louder than a very quiet room—one in which a soft whisper can be heard at 15 feet. Most scientists agree that steady exposure at 90 decibels or so can cause permanent hearing damage.

The worst offenders in the city are trucks, buses, motorcycles, and rail systems. For automotive vehicles at high speed, the tire noise predominates, while at slower speeds motor noise takes over. At expressway speeds a single tractor-trailer truck can generate over 90 decibels, while a line of trucks can produce 100 decibels or more.

Subway systems are inherently noisy because of the steel wheels rolling on steel rails. Ventilators to street level allow some of this noise to escape, but most of the noise is absorbed by the ground. For passengers locked in metal cars, the noise level reaches 100 decibels.

Commercial jets have created major noise problems in and around major airports. On takeoff, a four-engine jet generates about 115 to 120 decibels. As a result, over a third of the nation's major airports are involved with formal complaints and lawsuits about noise. It is estimated that 15 million people will soon be living near enough to airports to be subjected to intense aircraft noise.

Other sources of noise—rarely curbed by government—include jackhammers, garbage trucks, lawnmowers, discotheques, and juke-boxes. In the home, kitchen appliances and air-conditioners add to the din.

Scientists are able to predict, on a statistical basis, the risk of hearing loss for continuous types of noise—such as that in many factories. Unfortunately, more research is needed to predict the damage that may be caused by louder noise that is intermittent or discontinuous.

Noise is known to cause a constriction of the smaller arteries. This can lead to increased pulse and respiration rate. Some doctors even feel that continual exposure to loud noises can cause such chronic diseases as ulcers and hypertension.

Individual persons vary widely in their sensitivity to noise. A small percentage appears not to be bothered by noise, even loud noise. At the other extreme, a hypersensitive few are distressed even by low noise levels. It also appears that sensitivity to noise may vary widely from day to day.

The recognition that noise is an important environmental problem has arrived late in the United States, and little has been done toward noise abatement. In 1970 the federal government allocated only $34 million for noise-related programs. The lion's share of this amount—$31 million—was devoted to sonic boom and aircraft noise. This suggests that a more balanced research program, to deal with all sources of noise pollution, is needed.

Why do people grow old?

No one knows the answer to this question, of course, but scientists are beginning to search for the key to aging. Some scientists believe that the reasons human beings grow old may be hidden in the behavior of certain chemicals that the body produces and deposits in the blood. These chemicals are probably present in minute amounts, but over a lifetime they may react with tissues (which are made of proteins) in our body, causing them to harden or shrink. Long-term experiments are now under way in an attempt to detect any changes in blood composition that may take place in human beings. If one or more chemicals in the blood begin to change progressively with age, they may offer a key to the matter of aging.

It may turn out, of course, that the aging of living things may be caused by other factors, such as the normal radioactivity we encounter, or some cause as yet undreamed of. Only time and research will tell.

Why are golf balls dimpled?

In the early days of the game, golf balls were made as smooth as possible in order to reduce air friction, a logical approach indeed. Later it was noticed that old, scarred balls went farther than new, smooth balls. Oddly enough, this observation was no fluke. Experiments were performed on a golf course in which both dimpled balls and smooth balls were struck with identical swings. The dimpled balls were driven 230 yards in flight, while the smooth balls traveled only 50 yards in flight! Here is a result that is contrary to everything that intuition would lead us to expect. As usual, nature is full of surprises.

The science of fluid dynamics explains why a dimpled golf ball travels farther than a smooth one. The thin layer of air around a moving object is called a *boundary layer*. During the flight of a golf ball, the flow of air in this layer can be of two kinds: laminar or turbulent. *Laminar flow* is truly a steady flow in that each particle of air passing a given place on the ball arrives there with exactly the same speed and direction of flow as all of the particles that preceded it. In *turbulent flow,* on the other hand, there is a seemingly random and irregular fluctuation superimposed on the average downstream motion of the air. In this kind of flow there is a good deal of mixing of air in the region around the ball.

It turns out that for a blunt object, such as a driven golf ball, the total drag caused by air resistance is less when the flow is turbulent than when it is laminar. So to keep the drag low, it is necessary to make the boundary layer turbulent, and dimpling does the trick.

Scientists tell us, however, that just the opposite is true of slim, streamlined objects, such as airplane wings, which knife through the air. For these, the boundary layer flow must be maintained laminar for lowest drag. Such objects are made as smooth as possible.

How big is the universe?

Until very recent times, scientists believed that the Milky Way was the limit to the sky. The Milky Way is a vast collection of stars arranged in a roughly disk-shaped pattern with our sun located out near the edge. The pattern is a few thousand light-years thick and several times that large in diameter. (A light-year is the distance that light travels in a year, about 5,878,000,000,000 miles.) This makes the sky pretty big indeed!

Then, in the 1920s, an astronomer named E. P. Hubble was able to measure accurately the distance to a star that is 900,000 light-years away, far beyond the limits of the Milky Way. This star is part of another great galaxy of stars (the great nebula of Andromeda), which is quite similar to our own Milky Way. This means that the Milky Way is not a unique collection of stars. We know that there are many billions of similar galaxies, each containing many billions of stars. A group of galaxies called the *Hydra cluster* is estimated to be 1.1 billion light-years away. Other clusters contain thousands of galaxies, each with perhaps as many as 10 billion stars.

Scientists have a term, *metagalaxy,* which includes everything in the material universe: every planet, every star, every galaxy, and everything else that exists. Its diameter is greater than 10 billion light-years—how much greater we can only guess. Some scientists

155

even think it may have no beginning or end! Expressed in miles, the entire universe has a diameter of at least 60 thousand, million, million, million miles.

Where does all this end? Can there be no limit to the size of space? Up to the present time, scientists have no indication of a limit. As new telescopes and techniques are developed, astronomers discover new, fainter, and even more distant galaxies of stars. And the "edges" of observed space are just as densely populated with stars as are the "local" regions. How big is the universe? No one really knows.

Was twenty-four dollars a fair price to pay for Manhattan?

The *Encyclopaedia Britannica* tells us that Peter Minuit purchased Manhattan Island from the Indians in 1626 with pieces of bright cloth, beads, and trinkets valued at sixty guilders, or about twenty-four dollars. Of course, the dollar had not yet been invented in 1626, so there may be some question as to its exact value in those days. Nevertheless, there seems little doubt that the monetary consideration given the Indians was not overwhelming in terms of the guilder. This land deal, in fact, has often been represented as one of the greatest swindles of all time. The idea of Manhattan with all of its skyscrapers, having once sold for twenty-four dollars' worth of trinkets seems ludicrous. But was it really such a bad deal after all? We can find out with the help of compound interest tables.

If you deposit $100.00 in a bank at 5 percent interest, your investment is worth $105.00 at the end of one year. At the end of two years it is worth $110.25. Notice the "extra" 25 cents; in that small amount lies the magic of compound interest. During the second year, the interest is calculated on a principal of $105.00 instead of $100.00. Thus the amount of interest earned increases each year because it is calculated on successively larger amounts of principal. In the example given above, your bank account will double in about fourteen years, and will keep on doubling every fourteen years thereafter as long as you or your heirs continue to supervise the account.

Now let us see what this has to do with the Manhattan land deal. Suppose Peter Minuit, instead of going into real estate, had put his twenty-four dollars into bonds, mortgages, bank deposits and savings-and-loan-association accounts giving an average yield of 7 percent per annum. By now his investment would have grown to about $400 billion. At 8 percent it would now be worth about $13,000 billion. If he had gone into business with a return of 10 percent per annum, the initial investment would today have reached a value of about $7 million billion! The mind boggles at such enormous sums of money.

Was twenty-four dollars a fair price for Manhattan? It is hard to say. This admittedly superficial analysis merely indicates that the Dutch may not have been as shrewd at bargaining as it may seem on the surface.

Why are some people nearsighted or farsighted?

We can think of the eye as a small, spherical camera. Light passes through the lens and is focused on the *retina,* or light-sensitive layer on the back surface of the eye. When the lens functions properly, it can be focused equally well for near and far objects by muscles that change the curvature of the lens. Unfortunately, this adjustment is rarely perfect, and most of us are either a little nearsighted or farsighted.

In nearsightedness, light from a distant object is brought into focus in front of the retina, as in *a* in the sketch on page 158. The eye muscles are unable to focus the rays on the retina. For farsighted people, the reverse is true. The rays are focused too far behind the retina, as in *b*.

Nearsightedness (*myopia*) can be corrected by wearing spectacles that are a bit thinner in the center than at the edges. Farsightedness (*hyperopia*) can be corrected by lenses that are thicker at the center than at the edges.

Nearsighted eyes are so called because they can focus suitably only for objects relatively close to the eye. The reverse is true for farsighted eyes.

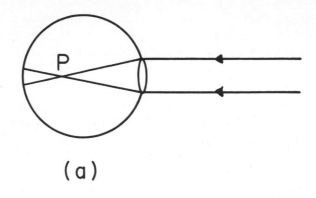

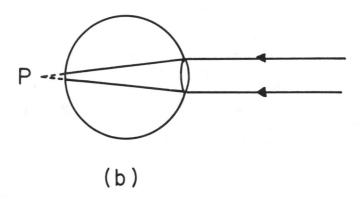

FIG. 12. In nearsighted eyes (*a*) the image is focused in front of the retina as at point *P*. In farsighted eyes the reverse is true, as in (*b*).

Why do deserts get so cold at night?

High temperature is a characteristic that most of us associate with desert regions. A temperature of 136.4°F. in the shade—one of the highest ever recorded—was measured at Aziza, in the Sahara

Desert. Summer temperatures of 120°F. are common in many deserts, and the temperature of the ground's surface often soars 50 degrees hotter than the air. Nevertheless, a blazing summer day can be followed by a drop in desert air temperature of 50 degrees or more. These extremes are caused by the ease with which desert regions absorb and radiate energy.

In the daytime, deserts absorb more solar energy than humid regions. In fact, of all the solar radiation striking the desert area, only 10 percent is deflected upward. This is accomplished by dust particles and clouds in the atmosphere. This means that 90 percent of the radiation heats the ground and lower air. In contrast, humid lands absorb only 40 percent of the solar heat. Twenty percent is deflected by clouds, 10 percent by dust particles in the air, and 30 percent by water surfaces and plant cover. Because deserts absorb more of the available heat than humid regions, they tend to get hotter during the daytime.

At night, deserts turn cold while humid lands remain warmer. This is due to the more rapid loss of heat by desert regions. After sundown, the desert gives up, or radiates, all of the day's accumulated heat. Of this amount, only 10 percent is deflected down again by dust particles in the air. The remaining 90 percent is lost. Humid climates, on the other hand, let only about 50 percent of the earth's heat get away. Some 20 percent is deflected downward by clouds, 10 percent by dust particles, and 20 percent is retained by land cover and water.

Because of the factors described above, deserts tend to have both hotter days and colder nights than similarly situated humid regions.

The desert's nighttime coolness is an important factor in the ability of desert animals to survive. To combat the hot, arid climate, nearly all birds and animals limit their activity to the cool hours of night, early morning, or evening. The desert may seem empty of animals during the scorching midday heat, but it jumps to life in the refreshing coolness of evening. As the sun nears the horizon, the reptiles are first to make their appearance, with lizards scurrying to gather a supper of insects that have begun moving about. Then the birds begin to forage—thrashers, wrens, quail, or flycatchers. Squirrels and jackrabbits also make their appearance, followed by the burrowing rodents. Then the bats emerge from dark desert caves, catching flying insects unerringly against a blue-black sky. Finally the owls and carnivores—which prey on rodents—become active, and the starry desert night is alive with the activity of the mammals, snakes, and a few of the night birds.

At sunrise, the sequence is reversed. Mammals retreat to their sheltered homes, lizards feed in the warming air, and birds retreat to their elevated perches. No animal can face the desert at its blazing worst, and all await the cool night that is sure to come.

What are the advantages of the metric system?

Do you ever get swamped in a sea of inches, feet, yards, and miles? Most of us have memorized the facts that there are 12 inches in a foot, 3 feet in a yard, and 5,280 feet in a mile. But how many yards are in a mile? If you don't know, you can divide 5,280 by 3, which gives 1,760 yards.

We can carry this a step further with *rods* and *furlongs*. Both rods and furlongs are used to measure length. A rod is 5½ yards long, while a furlong is 220 yards long. If you are interested, there are 40 rods in a furlong and 8 furlongs in a mile. Rods are often used to measure tracts of land, and furlongs are used to measure horse-racing tracks.

If you happen to be nautically minded, you know that water depth is often measured in a unit called the *fathom,* which is equal to 6 feet in length. To further complicate matters, there is the *nautical mile,* equal in length to 6076.115 feet.

It is really not too surprising that so many different units have come into use. Suppose you were going shopping for a living room rug. Would you prefer to think of it as 5 yards long by 4 yards wide, or $\frac{1}{352}$ mile long by $\frac{1}{440}$ mile wide? In either case the rug would be the same size, but the yards clearly have it. We have so many units because it is easiest to visualize a length when it is expressed as a number of convenient size.

Because there are so many units, it is often necessary to switch from one to another, a process that is complicated by the odd numbers that relate each unit with the others. To change from inches to rods, for example, you have to divide by 198. To go from rods to feet you multiply by 16½. These odd conversion numbers were arrived at quite by accident. An inch was originally the length of the thumb from tip to knuckle. The foot was, of course, the length of a foot, and the yard measured from the nose to the fingertips of the arm stretched out to the side. The rod was merely the length of a rod used to measure off distances, while the furlong, which comes from two old English words meaning "furrow" and "long," was the distance along a plowed furrow. One mile comes from the Latin word for "thousand." It was originally the distance covered by a marching soldier in a thousand paces. (The Roman pace was about 5 feet long, and represents the distance between successive places where the same foot came down while marching.)

Over the centuries, the various units were modified and standardized so that one unit would go into another unit with a convenient whole number wherever possible. Naturally, the various numbers used in converting units were all different and quite impossible for most of us to remember.

About 200 years ago, France had a system of measurements just about as cumbersome as ours. At the end of the French Revolution, a new measurement system was adopted based on a length called the *meter,* from a Latin word meaning to "measure." A meter is about 10 percent longer than our yard.

With the next step, the French broke with tradition and built the meter up by tens. To do this they borrowed prefixes from the Greek meaning "ten" (*deca*), "hundred" (*hecto*), and "thousand" (*kilo*). Thus 10 meters became a *decameter;* 100 meters, a *hectometer;* 1,000 meters, a *kilometer.*

The French were just as logical going in the other direction, to smaller distances. Here, they adapted prefixes from the Latin: one-tenth (*deci*), one-hundredth (*centi*), and one-thousandth (*milli*). Thus, a *decimeter* is a tenth of a meter; a *centimeter* is a hundredth of a meter; a *millimeter* is a thousandth of a meter.

Whether Greek or Latin, whether greater or smaller than a meter, each change in units takes place by tens. Because all of the units are based on the meter, this French system of measurement is called the *metric system*.

Changing units in the metric system is as simple as multiplying or dividing by ten. To change meters to kilometers, just multiply by 10 three times. To change from meters to millimeters, divide by 10 three times. Changing units becomes no more difficult than moving a decimal point in the number. Thus, 724 meters becomes 72.4 decameters, which is equal to 7.24 hectometers, which, finally, is equal to .724 kilometers. And that is much easier than changing yards to miles, as in the U.S. system.

Having conquered the measurement of distance, the inventors of the metric system turned to capacity and volume. In our system we measure capacity in such units as *pints, quarts, pecks,* and *bushels*. To complicate matters further, we use dry pints and quarts for solids such as berries, and liquid pints and quarts—which are different from the dry ones—for liquids such as milk and gasoline. If you don't know how many dry pints are in a peck (16), or liquid gills in a gallon (32), don't worry about it—you have plenty of company.

In the metric system our U.S. fluid ounces, gills, pints, and the rest are replaced by a standard cubic container that is one *decimeter* (one-tenth of a meter) on each side and has a volume of 1 cubic decimeter, or 1,000 cubic centimeters. This capacity is called a *liter*. As with the meter, the liter is increased to *decaliters, hectoliters,* and *kiloliters,* and decreased to *deciliters, centiliters,* and *milliliters*—always by factors of 10. To illustrate, 1 liter contains 1,000 cubic centimeters, as mentioned above. But 1 liter also contains 1,000 milliliters. So 1 cubic centimeter is equal to 1 milliliter.

The metric system has also been applied to the measurement of weight. In the U.S. system we have *drams, grains, scruples, ounces,*

162

pounds, and *tons*—both long and short. Some of these are *avoirdupois,* others are *troy,* still others are *apothecaries.* The same term, of course, may apply to a different weight depending on the particular system. A troy ounce is heavier than an avoirdupois ounce, while the opposite is true for the pound!

In the metric system, 1 milliliter of water weighs just one *gram.* Naturally, 10 grams is a *decagram,* 10 decagrams is a *hectogram,* and 10 hectograms is a *kilogram.* Going the other way are the *decigram* ($\frac{1}{10}$ gram), *centigram* ($\frac{1}{100}$ gram), and *milligram* ($\frac{1}{1000}$ gram). By mental arithmetic we can see that a kilogram is 1,000 grams, or 1,000,000 milligrams.

The metric system is so sound and logical that practically every nation in the world except the United States has definite plans toward converting to it. The United Kingdom has begun the process, which is expected to be completed by 1975.

American industry has usually opposed changing to the metric system because of the cost of replacing machinery and retraining employees. Nevertheless, U.S. scientists—along with scientists all over the world—use the metric system in every phase of their work.

The following table lists the more common units of the metric system along with the approximate U.S. equivalents.

Do sand dunes move?

A *dune* is a mound or hill of wind-blown sand. Dunes form in any location having an adequate supply of sand and enough average wind speed to move significant amounts of sand.

The site of a dune is determined by a decrease in wind velocity such as might be caused by a low bush or clump of grass. Dune locations can change, therefore, as natural or man-made obstacles to the wind change the pattern of wind velocity in a region. The same general principle covers the movement of falling or drifting snow, which explains the usefulness of snow fences. By inducing the snow to mound up away from roads and highways, they help reduce the problems of snow removal.

163

WEIGHTS AND MEASURES

Metric System

LENGTH

Unit	Abbreviation	Number of Meters	Approximate U.S. Equivalent
kilometer	km	1,000	0.62 mile
hectometer	hm	100	109.36 yards
decameter	dkm	10	32.81 feet
meter	m	1	39.37 inches
decimeter	dm	0.1	3.94 inches
centimeter	cm	0.01	0.39 inch
millimeter	mm	0.001	0.04 inch

AREA

Unit	Abbreviation	Number of Square Meters	Approximate U.S. Equivalent
square kilometer	sq km *or* km²	1,000,000	0.3861 square mile
hectare	ha	10,000	2.47 acres
square centimeter	sq cm *or* cm²	0.0001	0.155 square inch

CAPACITY

Unit	Abbreviation	Number of Liters	Cubic	Dry	Liquid
kiloliter	kl	1,000	1.31 cubic yards		
hectoliter	hl	100	3.53 cubic feet	2.84 bushels	
decaliter	dkl	10	0.35 cubic foot	1.14 pecks	2.64 gallons
liter	l	1	61.02 cubic inches	0.908 quart	1.057 quarts
deciliter	dl	0.10	6.1 cubic inches	0.18 pint	0.21 pint
centiliter	cl	0.01	0.6 cubic inch		0.338 fluid ounce
milliliter	ml	0.001	0.06 cubic inch		0.27 fluid dram

MASS AND WEIGHT

Unit	Abbreviation	Number of Grams	Dry
metric ton	MT or t	1,000,000	1.1 tons
kilogram	kg	1,000	2.2046 pounds
hectogram	hg	100	3.527 ounces
decagram	dkg	10	0.353 ounce
gram	g or gm	1	0.035 ounce
decigram	dg	0.10	1.543 grains
centigram	cg	0.01	0.154 grain
milligram	mg	0.001	0.015 grain

Extensive dunes occur mostly in deserts, or along the shores of lakes or the ocean. Most of them are a few tens of feet high. A number of dunes on the east shore of Lake Michigan are over 200 feet high. Others in southern Iran reach 700 feet above the surrounding desert.

Sand tends to accumulate in certain regions because the smaller and lighter particles of silt and clay are blown to other more distant places by the wind. The thickest layers of such material are found in western China, where material blown from the deserts of central Asia form deposits—called *loess*—over 200 feet thick. The term was first applied to similar deposits of wind-blown silt in the Rhine Valley. The fertile soil of the North American Midwest developed from a similar deposit up to fifty feet thick that accumulated in the region after the Ice Ages. Glaciers had ground up enormous quantities of fresh rock, and the resulting particles were carried downstream by the meltwater. This material was then carried by the wind and distributed over the region.

Does it rain more in the city than in the country?

Climatologists tell us, believe it or not, that an urban area is generally more foggy, cloudy, and rainy than its surrounding region. The burning of fuel in a city generates vast quantities of water vapor, and the various sources of heat cause the air to rise and mix, a condition necessary for cloud formation. Furthermore, dust particles generated by countless smokestacks act as nuclei around which water and fog droplets can form. According to Dr. Stanley Changnon, Jr., of the Illinois State Water Survey, Chicago received 7.53 inches more rain than surrounding areas between 1959 and 1968 —all because of the weather-making side effect of air pollution.

It is also true that the North Atlantic jet flyways are now more cloud-covered than in earlier, pre-jet days. This has been attributed to cloud-seeding by the vapor trails of jet aircraft.

On the average, cities have a temperature that is 0.9°F. to 1.4°F. higher than the surrounding countryside. The effect is even more pronounced in the winter, when the minimum temperature in a twenty-four-hour period may be 2°F. to 3°F. higher than that of surrounding areas. The following table summarizes temperature and other climatic changes produced by cities.

CLIMATIC CHANGES PRODUCED BY CITIES AS COMPARED WITH RURAL SURROUNDINGS

Temperature		
	Annual mean	0.9°F. to 1.4°F. higher
	Winter minimum	2°F. to 3°F. higher
Cloudiness		
	Clouds	5 to 10 percent more
	Fog, winter	100 percent more
	Fog, summer	30 percent more
Dust particles		10 times more
Wind speed		
	Annual mean	20 to 30 percent lower
	Extreme gusts	10 to 20 percent lower
Precipitation		5 to 10 percent more

Several factors combine to make the city warmer than the country. Heat generated by industry, home heating units, and air conditioning in the summer, all help raise the average city temperature. Buildings tend to obstruct the flow of air so that wind speeds are lower, thereby reducing heat loss from the city. In addition, the increased cloudiness, along with the tendency of buildings and pavements to retain heat, further reduces the loss of heat to the upper atmosphere.

The heat of the city contributes to increased rainfall by generating a "thermal mountain" over the city. This pushes the surrounding air up vertically over the city to colder levels, thereby helping to bring on rain. In addition, automobiles, industry, and home heating units all produce particulate materials. These tiny particles, which are carried up with the rising air, act as nuclei around which water vapor condenses to form drops or ice crystals. Air over Seattle, for example, has up to ten times as many condensation nuclei as air over adjacent areas.

Perhaps the most dramatic examples in which industrial pollution affects the weather are found not in cities, but rather in valleys, especially those where mountain walls tend to concentrate pollutants. A single wood pulp mill in Pennsylvania produces an enormous number of condensation nuclei. These sometimes cause enough fog to fill a valley several miles wide and twenty miles long. At times the billowing banks of fog spill over into adjacent valleys.

Scientists tell us that these atmospheric changes cannot be regarded as entirely local problems. Heat from the city, for example, escapes inevitably into surrounding areas. The combined thermal effects of many cities may eventually alter regional and global climates. Although scientists are pretty well agreed that inadvertent weather modification is surely occurring, not enough is yet known to predict all of its atmospheric consequences.

What do whales eat?

The size of whales defies our adjectives; "gigantic" or "elephantine" are hardly appropriate, for a large whale weighs more than two dozen elephants. In 1926 a blue whale was weighed—piece by piece—and its total weight added up to a staggering 135 tons. With a length of 89 feet, not large in those days, it was not possible to weigh it in one piece. The whale consisted, in part, of 62 tons of meat and 28 tons of blubber affixed to a 25-ton skeleton.

To support its enormous body, a whale must consume food by the ton. Sperm whales prey primarily on squid, and killer whales feed on seals, fish, and porpoises. But most of the other kinds of whales have a most remarkable diet, along with an unusual apparatus with which to eat it.

Our largest animals, it turns out, enjoy a diet of some of the tinier creatures of the ocean—shrimplike crustaceans called *krill*.

168

These crustaceans proliferate into enormous banks of krill in plankton-rich regions of the ocean. Whales cruise through these regions of plentiful food, eating krill by the truckload. Indeed, "harvesting" —rather than eating—is a more appropriate word to describe the dinner hour of the krill-eaters (called *baleen whales*).

The mouth of the baleen whale—large enough to hold a good-sized truck—contains a hanging curtain edged with hairy fringes. The curtain is made of a bony, flexible material that provided the "whalebone" for Victorian corsets and hoop skirts. In feeding, the baleen whale takes in a mouthful of water, which can amount to sixty or eighty gallons, and partly closes its mouth. Using its three-ton tongue, it then squeezes the water out through its sievelike baleen curtain, leaving the krill inside the mouth to be swallowed.

Unfortunately, many of the larger kinds of whale are on the verge of extinction because of excessive kills by the whaling industry. Since 1900, the world's whaling fleets have killed almost 2 million whales and have just about whaled themselves out of business. Species by species the great whales have been brought to the verge of extinction. In the 1930s there were enough blue whales— the largest creature ever to inhabit the earth—to furnish whalers with a catch of 30,000 per year. But modern whaling methods have decimated the whale population. In 1966 only 20 blue whales were caught. Today scientists believe there are only 1,000 or so left— not enough, they fear, to ensure that the species will survive. The story is repeated over and over again for other species: the finback whale, the humpback whale, the sei whale, the sperm whale. After centuries of hunting, and a decade or two of blind greed, very few whales are left.

Why does rubber stretch?

Rubber is a giant molecule, or *polymer,* consisting of between 1,000 and 5,000 isoprene molecules. Isoprene, from the rubber tree, is a simple compound made up of 5 carbon atoms and 8 hydrogen atoms. A catalyst in the rubber tree transforms the isoprene molecules so they can join end to end until thousands of units are assembled into individual rubber molecules.

Scientists have discovered that the properties of rubber depend as much on the irregular structure of the rubber molecule as on its great size. The molecule chains are coiled in a random manner, much like a tangled plate of spaghetti. It is this irregular, or *amorphous,* structure that gives rubber and similar materials their resilience. When you stretch a piece of rubber, the coiled spaghetti-like molecules tend to untangle and straighten out. When the tension is released, the strands coil back up into their former tangled state.

When rubber is stretched, its molecular structure changes enough to affect its physical properties. The coiled molecules straighten out into uniform parallel layers, and they no longer retain the structure of soft resilient substances. Instead, they achieve the orderly atomic arrangement of crystalline solids such as the metals. This, in turn, imparts to stretched rubber the strength and rigidity that the crystalline structure gives to solids.

Rubber's ability to change back and forth between the amorphous and crystalline states helps make it so useful. In the automobile tire, for example, this transition occurs continuously as the wheel rotates 10 times per second or more. The lower part of the tire bears the car's weight at any instant, and is therefore stretched and strengthened because its molecules approach the structure of a solid. As the wheel rotates, the tension is removed from the first part and it resumes its resilient state, well suited to absorb road shocks.

The first all-purpose synthetic that was able economically to replace natural rubber in automobiles is an artificial polymer called Buna S. It consists of a giant molecule made up of alternate molecules of butadiene, a gas, and styrene, used to make the plastic polystyrene. Like natural rubber, Buna S contains thousands of its two constituent molecules, each of which can be obtained from petroleum or coal. Synthetic rubber now accounts for three-fourths of the United States rubber production, and for one-third of all rubber used in the world.

How does molten lava form?

Most common rocks melt at temperatures in the range of 800°C. to 1,300°C. Molten rock within the earth is called *magma*. When magma breaks through the earth's surface and flows out over the land, it is called *lava*.

Rock expands as it melts, so that magma often is lighter (or less dense) than the rock that surrounds it. This causes it to float toward the surface. Magma formed deep in the earth at high pressure can squirt upward into a site of lower pressure, such as a fracture in the rock near the surface. In this way, magma makes its way upward toward the surface.

A few decades ago geologists believed that magma was merely the remnant of the once molten state of our planet. They know today, however, that the earth has been solid near the surface for at least 4 billion years. It seems unlikely that magma has been molten all of that time. They also know from the study of earthquakes (and their sound waves through the earth), that there are no large liquid zones in the earth within 1,800 miles of the surface. This leads many scientists to believe that magma must form in relatively small pockets near the earth's surface.

Temperature measurements in deep mines and wells show an average rise in temperature of about 1.6°F. to 1.8°F. for each 100 feet of depth (called the *geothermal gradient*). The heat can be explained, for the most part, from the nuclear decay of radioactive elements within the rocks. At that rate of increase in temperature, a depth of 23 miles would be hot enough to melt the most stubborn rocks. Yet we know that the earth is quite solid at that depth. What could prevent the expected melting?

Scientists believe that the great pressures within the earth prevent melting, despite the normal geothermal gradient. Some additional source of heat must be found to explain the local pockets of magma.

We do know that rocks deep in the earth sometimes break along lines called *faults*. The friction of rocks rubbing together along a fault might generate enough heat to melt adjacent rocks. This theory

171

is supported by the observation that volcanoes and lava flows often occur along fault lines. Of course, it's also possible that the magma may have formed elsewhere and was simply injected into a low pressure region near the fracture. Geologists still do not understand magma adequately, in part because man cannot descend deep into the earth to study it.

Why do we sometimes give off sparks when we touch metal objects?

Every substance contains negatively charged *electrons* and positively charged *protons*. Normally the atoms of the substance contain equal amounts of negative and positive charge and the substance is said to be electrically neutral. For that reason, the charges tend to remain stationary.

At times, however, a substance can be made to gain or lose electrons. This happens on a dry day when we walk across a thick rug or slide across an automobile seat. It takes a dry day, because humidity in the air lets any extra, unbalanced charge leak off an object almost as quickly as it generated. An object that has picked up "too many" electrons has a negative charge, and one with "too few" electrons has a positive charge.

When an electrical insulator becomes charged, the charge tends to remain anchored in the spot where it was developed. Poor insulators, however—like you and me—let the charge leak to other places. When an electrically charged person comes close to a good conductor, such as a piece of metal, a spark of electricity shoots across the gap to get rid of the excess charge. It is these "personal sparks" that startle us when we least expect it.

Unlike, or opposite, charges attract each other while like charges repel each other. To comprehend the magnitude of these forces, imagine a small cube of aluminum, 1 centimeter long on each side (about four-tenths of an inch). Aluminum has 13 positive charges (protons) in its nucleus, and thirteen negative charges (electrons) around the nucleus. The number of electrons or protons in the cube amounts to 7.8×10^{23} or 780,000,000,000,000,000,000,000! Now imagine that we could remove all of the electrons from the cube and place them at a point 1 meter—about a yard—away. Only positive charges are now left in the cube, and the electrons are all negatively charged. The force of attraction between the two groups of charges would be 32 million, million, million pounds! To help visualize the enormity of such a force, consider that it is equal to the weight of a steel cube 76 miles high. Luckily for us, only a relatively few electrons are involved in generating our "personal sparks."

Are leaded gasolines dangerous to health?

A small amount of the compound *lead tetraethyl* greatly improves the antiknock quality, or *octane rating,* of a gasoline. In recent years, however, an awareness of the problems of environmental contamination by the automobile has caused great concern. Lead, like most of the heavy metals, is a poison when ingested above trace amounts. It is estimated that about one-half ounce of lead finds its way into the atmosphere for each tankful of gasoline burned. Most of this is in the form of tiny particles of lead compounds that eventually fall to the ground in rain or snow to pollute the soil. Scientists feel that this continually increasing amount of lead in the soil cannot help but be dangerous. The lead may eventually move into the food chains of plants, animals, and the human population.

Fortunately, there are ways of improving the octane rating of gasoline without the use of lead. During the 1930s petroleum refiners discovered a variety of catalysts, such as aluminum chloride and sulfuric acid, which promote the reforming or restructuring of low-octane gasoline into higher-octane gasoline. The process may be slightly more expensive, but that seems a small price to pay for environmental purity.

Do athletes perform best "on an empty stomach"?

The accepted concept among coaches seems to be that athletes do best if they avoid eating just before engaging in strenuous exercise. The theory seems to be that the body just can't supply enough blood at the same time both to the digestive system and to the heavily taxed muscles. And the idea seems a reasonable one.

Recent experiments at the University of Iowa have now cast some doubt on the validity of the "empty stomach" concept. Athletes were given meals at various intervals before a number of athletic events, such as sprinting, running, and swimming. The events included the fifty-yard and hundred-yard dashes, and the half-mile and two-mile runs. The swimming events were free style, and included distances from a hundred yards to one mile. Each athlete's performance was clocked on many occasions for various time intervals between eating and the performance of the event.

The test meal was breakfast cereal, milk, toast, butter, and sugar. Each meal provided about 500 calories of food energy.

The results showed that eating a cereal and milk meal had no effect on the time required to perform the running and swimming events. Furthermore, there were no unpleasant aftereffects following the physical exertion.

Although this experiment is far from conclusive, it implies that moderate eating before exercise may not be as objectionable as was once thought.

Why does yeast make bread rise?

The term *yeast* refers to a class of minute fungi that are of great value to man because of their ability to cause certain foods to ferment. These foods, called *carbohydrates,* consist of compounds of carbon, hydrogen, and oxygen. Yeast cells can feed on carbohydrates and change such compounds into ethyl alcohol and carbon dioxide.

Yeast is used to produce wine from grape juice, cider from apple juice, beer from barley, and many other alcoholic beverages from various grains and vegetables.

In bread making, yeast is mixed with the flour and other ingredients. The yeast first converts some of the starch in the flour to a

174

sugar called *glucose,* then to alcohol and the gas carbon dioxide. As the gas accumulates, it forms bubbles within the dough, thereby increasing its volume. We say the dough has "risen." The dough is then kneaded to break up the larger gas bubbles and usually allowed to rise again, after which it is baked. The many small holes present in risen bread are merely the places where tiny carbon dioxide bubbles had formed.

Perhaps you're wondering about the alcohol in bread. You don't get tipsy on a few slices of bread because the heat of baking drives off all the alcohol. Various strains of the same kind of yeast, *Saccharomyces cerevisiae,* are used both in baking and in wine making.

While we are on the subject of wine making, there is always enough wild yeast with the grapes to carry on the fermentation process. But modern wine makers usually add a small amount of sulfur dioxide gas to the grape juice to retard the growth of unwanted wild yeasts and bacteria. The desired yeast, which is adapted to the gas, is then added to produce fermentation.

Wines can be spoiled by wild yeasts and bacteria. If too much air is present in the bottle, species of Acetobacter may oxidize the alcohol of table wines to vinegar. To minimize this risk, open wine should be stored in smaller full bottles rather than in large half-empty bottles containing a great deal of air.

Yeasts can also make trouble for us by spoiling fruits and vegetables. Their growth can be discouraged, however, by keeping fruits and vegetables in cool, dry places, where yeasts find it difficult to grow.

No one really knows when the practice of using yeast in bread began. It may well have started as a happy accident. Many kinds of wild yeast are found in nature, carried about the air. It is not unlikely that the first leavened bread came about when wild yeast happened to fall into a prehistoric baker's dough. From that beginning, it would only have been necessary to keep a handful of the unbaked dough on hand to be mixed with the next batch of new dough. In this way, a desirable strain of wild yeast might have been "domesticated" and propagated right down to the present day.

How empty is "empty" space?

Although outer space comes closer to being a perfect vacuum than anything we can produce on earth, it is far from completely empty. If we could remove from space the stars, planets, comets, and other heavenly bodies, a cubic inch of space would still contain about 400 free electrons, 400 hydrogen atoms, and 10 light flashes, or *photons*. In addition, each cubic yard would contain about 6 atoms of other matter, mostly sodium and potassium. To this we would have to add a sprinkling of such other atoms as calcium and titanium. Finally, we would find a tiny speck of dust in every quintillion cubic yards of the space between the stars.

How do glaciers move?

It's natural to think of ice as a solid, so at first it may seem strange that a huge mass of ice, such as a glacier, can move slowly down a valley. A large mass of ice will flow plastically—much like cold molasses—when it receives a gentle push, but it will break if a force is applied to it suddenly. Taffy is another substance with similar behavior; it breaks when a force is applied quickly, yet bends when deformed slowly.

In a region where snow accumulates faster than it can be eliminated by melting or evaporation, it gradually builds up to great depths. After the snow field reaches a depth of 100 feet, the snow at the bottom is changed to solid ice by the pressure from above. When the thickness reaches 250 feet, the ice at the bottom becomes plastic and begins to flow down the slope. At the moment the ice begins to move, a glacier is born. Glaciers move at speeds from a few inches to a few hundred feet per day. A glacier will flow from the center of accumulation until it reaches an area warm enough to evaporate or melt the ice.

Glaciers are found in many parts of the world. The Antarctic Ice Sheet consists of many glaciers covering 5 million square miles. An ice sheet in Greenland covers 637,000 square miles. In the United States, 41 active glacial areas are to be found in Colorado,

Wyoming, Montana, Idaho, Utah, Nevada, California, Oregon, and Washington. Many others are to be found in Alaska. Hubbard Glacier in Alaska extends 75 miles to the sea, where chunks break off to form icebergs.

Because of the cold climate, glaciers often extend down to sea level in polar regions. At lower and warmer latitudes glaciers do not exist at low elevations. Near the equator in eastern Africa, they can be found only at elevations above 16,000 feet, where glaciers are found on Mount Kenya and Mount Kilimanjaro.

If all glaciers were to melt, the sea level would rise about 200 feet. This would flood many of the world's major cities and much of its farmland. During the past century the world's climate has been getting slightly warmer, so scientists have begun to wonder if all glaciers will eventually melt. Nearly all known glaciers are currently diminishing in size.

Does smog affect the weather?

There is a growing awareness of the deadly effects of smog on our civilization. Here we are concerned with a different aspect of the smog problem—its effect on weather and climate.

Scientific studies have shown a conspicuous increase in the number of foggy days per year in areas subject to smog. Londoners, for example, have so long tolerated conditions of fog that they probably do not connect it with air pollution. The fog comes about because smog, in addition to cutting down on visibility, also reduces the amount of sunlight reaching the earth. To illustrate, on smoggy days late in 1966, Phoenix, Arizona received only half its normal share of solar radiation. Studies of European cities show that the intensity of solar rays reaching the earth are reduced by as much as 36 percent by an overhanging canopy of smog. This reduction amounts to about one-fourth of all the heat that normally reaches the ground. Scientists believe that a heat deficit of that magnitude would have a significant cooling effect on the area. There seems little doubt, then, that smog does play a role in shaping the weather.

No other living things can match the visual acuity of birds. A vulture soaring a mile high, carefully searching for carrion, a hawk patiently cruising across the meadows in search of rodents, a loon diligently searching for an underwater meal—all have extraordinary eyesight, considerably keener than man's.

Birds have extremely large eyes compared with mammals, perhaps as a prerequisite of flight. The exposed cornea, the only part we see, is small in comparison with the huge eyeball behind it. In most birds, in fact, the eyes are larger than the brain. The eye of an eagle or owl may be as large as a man's, while the ostrich has eyeballs almost as large as tennis balls.

Hawks see better than man because the retinas of their eyes are more densely packed with light-sensitive cells—as many as 1.5 million at their more sensitive points. The corresponding place in the human eye has only 200,000 such cells. This gives the hawk an improvement factor of almost 8 over man. Thus, a sparrow hawk in search of food brings to bear eyes that are eight times more acute than man's.

Birds can also see with great clarity at close range. A warbler, for example, must be constantly on the alert for danger in the form of a distant hawk, yet it can quickly focus its eyes on a minute insect egg an inch from its beak. It does this with the help of strong muscles that squeeze the normally rather flat lens into a more spherical shape for close-up vision.

Birds have still another visual advantage over mammals. Their eyes are placed further back on the head than ours, which gives each eye a large field of view to the side. Have you ever noticed a robin cock his head as he stops suddenly on the lawn? He is not listening for a worm, as many think; he is merely bringing the area of most acute vision to bear on that side, to search out the area for the movement of a worm.

Vision to the side is *monocular,* because only one of the bird's eyes is put to use. But straight ahead, where both eyes can see the same object, the images overlap and birds see with *binocular* vision,

178

as we do. Optically speaking, birds have the best of both worlds—monocular and binocular. Songbirds like the white-crowned sparrow feed on seeds and insects, so they need some depth perception in the forward direction, which is afforded by binocular vision. At the same time, they must be able to see far to the side to avoid predators. The woodcock is a bird that needs little binocular vision in front because it feeds by probing in the mud for unseen worms with its long bill. Its real need is to avoid danger from behind or above while its bill is deep in the soil. For this reason, its eyes are a bit higher and farther back than those of most birds. This gives it binocular vision to the rear and above, as well as in front. It can literally see from the back of its head, and its visible world is the entire hemisphere above the ground. The duck's vision is just as complete, as you may have suspected if you ever tried to sneak up on one.

Owls, with eyes placed in front of the face like those of man, have primarily binocular vision, with little vision to the side. Binocular sight is also important to hawks and some of the other birds that hunt lively prey. To see to the side or rear, they have to turn their heads, just as we do.

What time is it when the full moon is directly overhead?

You can often get a rough idea of the time of day or night by noticing the position of the full moon. A glance at the diagram on page 180 will show how it's done.

First of all, the sun must be at your back, so to speak, in order for you to see a completely illuminated hemisphere of the moon. Except for the moments of dawn or dusk, this means that you are on the dark, or nighttime, side of the earth. If the full moon is directly overhead, you are located at point *A* in the diagram. The time at that location is midnight—midway between the rising and setting sun. If you see the full moon on the eastern horizon, the time is about 6:00 P.M.; on the western horizon the time is about 6:00 A.M. For intermediate times of day, you can estimate the hour by noticing the angle of the moon in the sky.

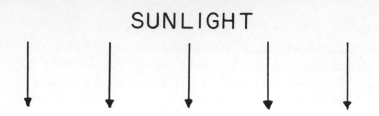

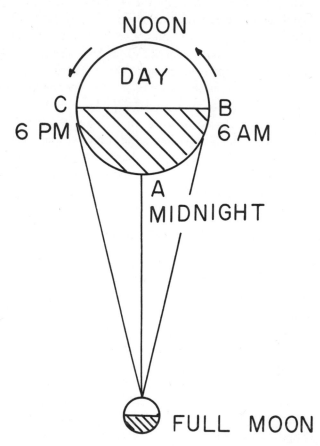

FIG. 13. If the full moon is directly overhead, the time is midnight and you are located at point A.

180

What is smoke?

When we burn fuel, such as wood, oil, or coal, the fuel—or most of it—combines with oxygen in the air to form gases that escape into the atmosphere. But most of the burning we do is far from perfect, so tiny particles of unburned fuel escape up the chimney in the form of smoke. In addition, most fuels contain a small amount of various substances that do not burn. Most of this material, which we call *ash,* stays behind after the fire burns out. Some of it, however, is carried aloft by the hot gases of the fire and adds to the volume of smoke produced.

How low a temperature has been reached in the laboratory?

Scientists tell us that temperature is the measure of the atomic order, or disorder, in a substance. When you heat things, for instance, the arrangement of the atoms becomes more and more disordered, while if you cool them down sufficiently, you increase the atomic order. Scientists are interested in achieving low temperatures because the increased atomic order lets their instruments "see" more details standing out. Roughly speaking, they can see more because the atoms are not jiggling around so much. So high temperatures mean atomic disorder, and low temperatures mean order.

If the temperature of a substance is made hotter and hotter, the atomic disorder increases indefinitely. There doesn't seem to be a limit to how hot something can get. At the other end, there is a limit to how cold it can be. Scientists call this temperature *absolute zero,* the temperature at which the atoms would reach a state of perfect order and would be "perfectly arranged" with respect to each other.

The Absolute Temperature Scale starts at the bottom, at absolute zero, and goes on up—as far as we know—without any upper limit. Absolute zero turns out to be -273.15 degrees on the Centigrade scale or -459.72 degrees on the Fahrenheit. For convenience, scientists often use the Kelvin scale, on which absolute zero is fixed at $0°$ Kelvin.

The coldest temperature that can be reached conveniently in a suitably equipped laboratory is about 0.003° Kelvin, or about three-thousandths of a degree above absolute zero. But temperatures have been reached which are only a few *millionths* of a degree above absolute zero.

It is natural to wonder whether we can go any lower in temperature, and if so, whether there is any point in doing it. Low temperature physicists know from theoretical considerations that they can go as far along the road to absolute zero as they choose to go. So we can be sure they will continue to probe the depths of temperature as long as there is further information to wrest from the atom.

What causes smog?

Every day, many thousands of tons of air pollution pour into the air of each of our great cities. Fortunately, this aerial sewage is usually free to mix with clean air up to great heights. It becomes so thinned out or diluted in the process that it almost disappears. The winds complete the job, pushing the polluted air away from the city, where it mixes with additional volumes of air and finally disappears.

On certain occasions, nature conspires to prevent the mixing of clean air with air pollutants and to retard their movement away from the city. The pollutants build up to great concentrations and smog covers the city. Thus smog is the result of an alliance between a more or less constant daily dose of atmospheric contamination (about 10,000 tons per day for Los Angeles) and an unpredictable amount of natural ventilation by the weather.

It was originally believed that most of our smog came from such sources as industrial and refinery chimneys, burning dumps, and backyard incinerators. In the city of Los Angeles, with the most difficult smog problem in the nation, such visible sources were the first to be attacked. Dumps and incinerators have been completely eliminated, and no visible smoke belches forth from chimneys. But you still see plenty of smog.

Chemists know that fumes given off during combustion are

usually invisible, even if the burning is incomplete. They have since discovered, however, that such invisible fumes often react and combine with each other in the presence of sunlight, to produce the eye irritation and reduced visibility that is so characteristic of smog.

The worst causes of smog are really the millions of automobiles that drive endlessly through our cities. This is true even for those cars whose exhaust gases appear "clean" and "invisible." Taken collectively, automobiles in Los Angeles produce several times more air pollution than all of the industrial activities put together. And at present, no clear solution appears on our smoggy horizon.

How was smallpox vaccination discovered?

Long before the advent of wonder drugs and scientific medicine, it was known that certain diseases could be caught only once in a lifetime. Doctors knew, for example, that if a person recovered from smallpox, he would never get smallpox again. In some Eastern countries, smallpox matter was deliberately injected into the body. They had devised a method to weaken the smallpox virus so that the injected person received only a mild case of the disease. Unfortunately, the method was not foolproof; many people did not recover from the injection.

The farmers of Gloucestershire, England, knew that anyone who had suffered from a mild disease called *cowpox* would never get smallpox. Cowpox, as its name implies, is a disease of cows that can be passed on to human beings.

Dr. Edward Jenner, a country physician, became interested in the apparent immunity to smallpox afforded by cowpox. He made careful studies and noticed that people who had had cowpox did not contract smallpox, even though they came in contact with smallpox patients. Later, he inserted some smallpox fluid into the arms of these people and they still did not contract the disease. Finally, he inoculated a healthy eight-year-old boy, Jimmy Phipps, with cowpox virus and the boy got cowpox. He then injected some smallpox matter into the boy with no ill effects at all.

Jenner published his results in 1796 and received, at first, a storm of abuse. Many people objected to his tampering with nature. Others rushed to claim credit for the discovery. Still others, through faulty vaccination technique, mixed in some smallpox matter and killed rather than protected the patients.

When the furor subsided, Jenner was recognized throughout the world for his great contribution to humanity. He was knighted by his own country and rewarded with 20,000 pounds sterling. A disease that had killed 60 million people in the previous century had finally been brought under control.

Why does milk turn sour?

The souring of milk is caused entirely by the growth of bacteria in it. If milk is boiled to kill the bacteria, and sealed in an airtight jar, it will not turn sour in any length of time or in any weather.

Bacteria are tiny, microscopic plants. Like all plants, they grow faster in warm temperatures than at cold temperatures. That helps explain why milk sours faster at room temperature than in the refrigerator.

The substance in milk that gives it its sour taste is *lactic acid,* which is produced by certain bacteria in a process called *fermentation.* The substance from which it is fermented is called *lactose,* a kind of sugar present in milk. Lactic acid is actually a wholesome food, and if good, clean milk turns sour, it is none the worse for it. Cottage cheese and many other food products are made from sour milk.

When will Halley's comet return?

The paths of comets and other heavenly bodies can be predicted mathematically. Using such methods, Edmund Halley predicted that the great comet of 1682 would return in 75 years. And the same comet has retraced its path every 75 years or so thereafter. The orbit of Halley's comet takes it close to the sun at one end and far out near the orbit of the planet Pluto at the other end. The comet last visited the earth in 1910, and is scheduled to pass by again in 1985.

184

How deep is the ocean?

The depth of the ocean varies even more widely than the land varies in height. A spot near the island of Guam in the Pacific Ocean measures 5,269 fathoms, or just 66 feet less than 6 miles. (A fathom equals 6 feet.) Another place 40 miles northeast of Mindanao, in the Philippine Islands, measures 5,144 fathoms. In 1951 the British vessel H.M.S. *Challenger* found a depth of 5,940 fathoms in the Mariana Deep. In the Atlantic, the Nores Deep, north of the West Indies, measures 4,562 fathoms. In the Indian Ocean, the Warton Deep, south of the East Indies, reaches a depth of 3,828 fathoms.

The average depth of the ocean is somewhere between 2 and 3 miles. This is considerably greater than the average height of land above sea level. The greatest ocean depths measure about a mile more than the peaks of our tallest mountains. A trip from the top of the highest mountain to the bottom of the greatest depth in the sea would mean covering a vertical distance of over 12 miles. On a globe the size of an orange, that distance would be represented by a scratch only four-thousandths of an inch in depth. So the earth is really a pretty smooth sphere.

The ocean depth was originally measured, or *sounded,* by lowering a weight on the end of a fine wire until the weight hit bottom. Today, ocean soundings are made more simply and accurately by means of sound waves. A sounding instrument aboard ship sends a short burst of sound energy down toward the sea bottom. Some of the energy is reflected from the bottom and picked up by a receiver on the ship. The device measures the elapsed time for the round trip in millionths of a second. And because sound travels at a known velocity (about 5,000 feet per second in seawater), it's a simple matter to calculate the ocean depth at the ship's location.

How high is the sky?

Unfortunately, this question is one that has no simple answer. From a legal point of view, many countries claim jurisdiction over vehicles passing through their airspace. This implies that a nation's sovereignty ends at the top of the atmosphere. But millions of words have been written in an attempt to define just where that place may be.

From a scientific point of view, the atmosphere has no clear-cut end; as it goes higher and higher, it gradually thins out into the partial—but not perfect—vacuum of outer space. For every 3.5 miles of altitude, the air pressure and density are approximately halved.

Men have little difficulty adapting to life and work at altitudes up to 3 or 4 miles. But 6-mile-high Mount Everest is beyond the limit of human life as we know it. For most activities beyond 5 miles, men must get oxygen from special breathing equipment.

Although unprotected man cannot live at an altitude of, let us say, 10 miles, a satellite at that low altitude would not last very long. Air resistance would quickly slow it down and it would fall to earth. Even 100 miles is not high enough to establish a long-lived or permanent orbit for a satellite. In fact, 100 miles is just about the altitude at which atmospheric drag begins to let up sufficiently to permit satellites to orbit, even on a short-term basis. At an altitude of 1,000 miles, however, the air is so thin that a satellite can stay up indefinitely.

How high is the sky? Perhaps a figure of 100 miles is a good choice. At that height, atmospheric pressure and density are only about a billionth of what they are at ground level. Below that height, prolonged free orbital flight is not possible because of atmospheric drag. Above that height satellites can stay in orbit long enough to perform useful tasks over and over again as they circle the earth. So for practical—if not legal—purposes, 100 miles up may be regarded as the "top" of the atmosphere and the beginning of interplanetary space.

Why do birds sing?

The songs that some birds sing are so elaborate that they play on the ears like phrases of beautiful music. The thrushes, for example, are perhaps the most gifted of the singing birds. Others, like Henslow's sparrow, emit something more like a hiccup than an aria. But practically all bird songs have the same meaning: first of all, a declaration to other males of the species, proclaiming territorial rights and warning intruders away; and secondarily, an invitation to available prospective mates proclaiming the singer's maleness—if he is still uncommitted.

Singing usually becomes more frequent and aggressive when another male is nearby. Should an intruder encroach upon a singer's territorial rights by crossing the unmarked border, the interloper is attacked. Usually, however, the tough talk of a bird song is sharp enough warning to send him on his way.

If a poorly stuffed male of the same species is planted in a singing male's domain, it is attacked over and over again. A mirror sometimes provokes the same aggressive behavior. But a robin will not attack a sparrow or wren or cardinal. It resents only other robins.

Experiments in England with a little robin redbreast showed that it was the red breast of its adversary that makes it "see red." Even a tuft of the red breast feathers on a wire was attacked wildly. In America, the red "epaulets" of the red-winged blackbird puff out when it threatens an opponent. It appears that adornments and prominent color patterns evoke belligerency in other males, while attracting females that may be ready to mate. Scientists suggest that aggression and defense of property have helped bring bird song and plumage to its high level of evolution—and it is these features that give birds much of their glamour.

Stuffed females also elicit an appropriate reaction on the part of males. As long as she is identifiable as a female of the species, the deluded male showers her with affection.

Singing also seems to play a part in strengthening the bond between a pair of birds during the short nesting season. The term "emotional song" is sometimes used to describe these forms of singing that do not seem connected with territory—the whisper songs of autumn and occasional winter singing.

Singing is most apparent in the early hours, tapering off by midday. Some birds, such as the thrushes, are most persistent just before dusk. The record for perseverance seems to belong to the red-eyed vireo of eastern North America's woodlands. He has been called the "preacher bird" by some. One of these birds repeated his refrain 22,197 times between dawn and dusk—a record likely to stand for some time.

It is probably no accident of nature that modestly colored birds are among the best singers. Brightly colored birds tend to rely on their bold plumage to advertise their presence, while drab, commonplace birds of the meadows and plains use their voices. Blending so unobtrusively into the landscape, they must fly high above their territory to make their rights known. The skylark, for example, proclaims his domain while in flight above it, showering down an endless torrent of song.

Some singing is innate, while other bird songs are learned. Some birds sing the right song when they reach the proper age, even though they were raised artificially from the egg, without a chance to hear their own kind. But other—perhaps more gifted—singers, such as nightingales and mockingbirds, learn their songs from older birds, even though they may have had an innate song of their own as youngsters. It appears that mimicry of this sort varies from region to region. The starling, introduced into New England from Great Britain, often mimics the wood pewee and meadowlark. Yet it never sings these songs in the land of its origin. And mockingbirds specialize in the songs of their particular locality, these being quite different across the continent.

How was nylon invented?

In 1928 the Du Pont chemical company decided to invest in pure research in the field of *polymers,* or giant molecules. Wallace Hume Carothers, a thirty-two-year-old chemist, was placed in charge of a team of highly skilled chemists that soon embarked on a new type of long-range research with no expectation of immediate practical results. Over the next decade, the team laid the groundwork for the field of *polymerization*—the building of giant molecules.

One process they studied is called *condensation polymerization,*

188

by which two small organic molecules link together and form a new larger molecule, giving water off in the process. The team tried thousands of chemical combinations in an attempt to find a useful synthetic fiber. Artificial silk and rayon, which had been produced for decades, were not true synthetics because they depended for their essential properties on the cellulose obtained from living plants. Then, in 1934, Carothers squeezed a hypodermic needle to produce the first truly practical synthetic fiber, nylon.

Nylon is a product of two organic substances, called *hexamethylenediamene* and *adipic acid,* which are derived from coal, air, and water. During manufacture, a pair of these molecules gives off 2 hydrogen atoms and 1 oxygen atom in the form of a water molecule. They then join together in the region vacated by the water molecule to form a longer nylon chain. The process is repeated some 1,700 times to produce the giant nylon molecule.

By the time nylon went into production, the company had spent about $20 million on research and development, but the money was well spent. Nylon is still the most useful synthetic fiber, accounting for $500 million in sales every year. First used in artificial "silk" stockings, nylon went to war in 1941. During the war enough nylon was manufactured to make 4 million parachutes, and enough tent fabric to cover Manhattan Island.

In addition to nylon, the booming brood of new synthetics includes Mylar, a transparent plastic film of great strength and dimensional stability; Dacron, a fiber useful for clothing; Surlyn, an improved version of polyethylene for see-through containers, and Corfam, a leather substitute porous enough for shoes.

Orlon is an example of success derived from failure. Orlon was originally intended for use outdoors. When it was discovered that the fiber tends to deteriorate with prolonged exposure, Orlon was turned to use in clothing. The acrylic fibers have a permanent crimp, which keeps the fibers separated and gives them a characteristic wool-like bulk and feel. This separation produces the lightness desired in sweaters and blankets, and the high strength of Orlon provides resistance to wrinkling.

The seemingly endless flow of synthetic materials shows no signs of diminishing. Scientists are hard at work on paints that will never chip or peel, preservatives that can keep food fresh for years without freezing, and oil that can be sealed into the automobile engine and never replaced.

Why do jet aircraft sometimes produce contrails?

A *contrail* is merely a long slender cloud that man learned how to make quite by accident. Almost everyone has seen contrails at one time or another. They show up high in the sky, trailing behind the airplane that generates them.

The exhaust of an airplane contains a variety of gases. One of these is water vapor, which tends to increase the relative humidity of the air. The exhaust also contains heat, which tends to lower the relative humidity. When air temperatures are extremely low, the former effect overcomes the latter until the air behind the engines becomes saturated with water vapor. All of this takes place rapidly, and the water vapor condenses into the tiny water droplets that we see as a cloud.

If you have not already guessed it, the term *contrail* comes from "condensation trail." In order for contrails to form, the airplane must fly through extremely cold air, below −20°F. So contrails are usually found behind jet airplanes flying at high altitudes where the air is quite cold. If an airplane has only one engine, it generates only one contrail. Multiengine aircraft produce an equal number of parallel contrails.

Although a contrail consists initially of tiny water droplets, these rapidly freeze to produce a thin ribbon of ice crystals. The duration of the contrail depends on the relative humidity of the air in which it is formed. If the relative humidity is low—as often happens—the contrail disappears fairly rapidly as dry air mixes with it. When this condition exists, the contrail may be very short in length. If the relative humidity of the air is quite high, contrails may last for several minutes and stretch for many tens of miles across the sky. Sometimes, when the air is very humid, contrails can persist indefinitely and even spread out horizontally. In some instances, they have triggered the formation of a layer of cirrus clouds wide enough to cover most of the sky.

What is steel?

Pure iron, called *wrought iron,* is not too strong. But with a small amount of carbon added, a strong iron-carbon alloy called *steel* is formed. This discovery was made—probably by accident—around the 13th or 12th century B.C. in eastern Asia Minor. The surface of an iron weapon might have picked up enough carbon from a charcoal fire to do the trick. In any event, it was noticed at that time that steel is harder than the best bronze, holds a sharp edge better, and makes better tools of war. The first army to be well equipped with quantities of steel weapons was the Assyrian. By 900 B.C. their superior weapons enabled them to build a great empire, and the Bronze Age gave way to the Iron Age.

In spite of its early start, steel making had to wait until 1856 for a method to produce it cheaply enough and in sufficient quantity for our current needs. The man who devised this method was Henry Bessemer (1813–1898).

In those days, iron was produced in the form of *cast iron,* too rich in carbon and, therefore, much too brittle for many applications. True, the carbon could be removed to form wrought iron, but this form was relatively soft and the process expensive.

Bessemer solved the problem by sending a blast of air through the molten cast iron. Oxygen from the air combined with the carbon to produce a gas that left the furnace, taking the unwanted carbon with it. By stopping the air blast at the right time, Bessemer obtained steel.

In subsequent years, other elements were added to ordinary steel to produce new steels having desired properties: manganese for hardness; chromium and nickel for stainless steel; and cobalt and tungsten for magnetic steels. Of all the metals, steel continues to be the most important to the world's economy.

191

Man is confronted today with the unhappy possibility that one of his proudest achievements—the development of pesticides—may well diminish the quality of life everywhere. There is no question, of course, that pesticides are of enormous benefit to man. They have helped produce food, protect health, and modify the environment to meet aesthetic and recreational needs. Yet, subtly and invisibly, pesticides have created problems of still undetermined magnitude. They have killed fish, shellfish, and birds, and have caused cancers in animals. Each year they kill between 100 and 200 human beings. Most of this mortality results from certain highly toxic pesticides, including sodium arsenite and parathion. There is still little knowledge of the impact on human beings of DDT and other persistent chlorinated hydrocarbon insecticides. Nevertheless, because of tests on animals, some scientists believe that DDT poses a significant threat to human beings. Tests show that Americans carry an average 8 parts per million of DDT in their body fat. Workmen who handle DDT may have several hundred parts per million and still show no harmful effects. Nevertheless, 200 million Americans are undergoing lifelong exposure to pesticides, such as DDT, and our knowledge of what is happening to them is fragmentary at best. While there may be no reason to predict a national disaster, there is even less cause for complacency.

A number of alternatives to the use of dangerous pesticides are now being studied. An obvious choice is the use of degradable pesticides, which disappear from the environment after a reasonable length of time.

Nonchemical methods of pest control are also being investigated. Some involve the use of parasites and predators. One example is the use of a species of weevil to combat Klamath weed in California pastures. It is risky, however, to introduce pest-killing animals to new areas: the mongoose was introduced to several Caribbean islands to control rats, and the mongoose itself soon became a pest.

The use of various pathogens, such as viruses, bacteria, and fungi, has had some success, but the trouble here is the danger they pose to human health. Perhaps one of the safest and most effective control measures is the selective breeding of resistant species of plants. This method now controls the Hessian fly, a serious pest of wheat.

Control of the screwworm fly by releasing a great number of males that were sterilized by irradiation has been dramatically successful. This technique—or the use of chemical sterilizing compounds—seems limited at the present time to certain pests. Unfortunately, such methods are more expensive than the use of pesticides.

About 80 percent of all pesticides manufactured today are used to control fewer than 100 species of pest organisms. So the development of nonchemical approaches would significantly reduce the use of pesticides.

Why is radiation used in treating cancer?

When high energy radiation encounters a molecule, it disrupts the electrical structure holding the molecule together. Several of its electrons may be knocked out of the molecule completely, or the molecule may even break up into fragments. In either event, the material is no longer the same chemical substance that it was before being irradiated.

When water within a living cell is irradiated, some of the water molecules are disrupted as described above. The resulting particles act as chemical vandals, destroying the normal operation of the cell. Scientists have found a way to make therapeutic use of this procedure. This is done by selecting a kind of radiation that is more harmful to the malignant or diseased cells than to the surrounding healthy ones.

In a related application, radiation can also disrupt the electrons in the bonds of the DNA molecules of chromosomes. These contain the genetic information in the cell and, therefore, its hereditary properties. In this way, radiation has been used to induce mutation in the laboratory.

193

Why do trees stop growing at the timberline?

Cold, drought, and wind are the chief deterrents to the growth of high-mountain plant life, and they have their most dramatic effect on trees. For lack of moisture and frost-free growing time, dense groves of pine and fir thin out at the greater heights into isolated specimens that are deformed by the fierce prevailing winds. Over two miles high, in the temperate zone, trees are gnarled or shrublike, some growing huddled over or even prostrate. Many survive the icy cold of winter only because they are protected by a thick blanket of snow.

Perhaps the first thing one notices in the Rocky Mountains is that broad-leaved trees tend to stick to the valleys and leave the mountainside to pines and fir. Up to about 9,500 feet in the Colorado Rockies, the mountains are covered by dense stands of Douglas fir. Above it are forests of spruce and subalpine fir. These two trees seem to help each other survive the harsh wintry environment. Spruce is long lived but a slow grower, lending stability to the forest. Fir, though shorter lived, casts many seeds and grows rapidly into a grove. This is important on mountain heights where groves greatly reduce the forces of the wind. Individual trees thus tend to protect each other from the wind, and are less likely to be blown down than single isolated trees.

At greater heights, the trees dwindle into wind-stunted, ground-hugging vegetation called *Krummholz,* a German word for "crooked wood." This is where trees make their last stand against the inhospitable mountain elements. This so-called timberline marks the beginning of what is called *tundra.*

To illustrate how truly fierce this environment really is, alpine ecologists from the University of Colorado spent ten years observing the growth of high-mountain plants. They found that a typical seedling of the cushion plant put out only two tiny leaves a year and grew only one-third of an inch in that entire ten-year period! At the timberline, winds blow throughout the year, sometimes at speeds of 100 miles per hour, and blinding snowstorms can occur in any season. Winter is eight months long and the "warm" season is only about two or three months long. It is little wonder that trees give way to smaller plants that can better withstand the rigors of high-mountain life.

How fast does a satellite travel?

There is a minimum speed that a satellite must have to stay in orbit. For a relatively low orbit, say 100 miles above the earth, that speed is 4.86 miles per second. At a distance of 1,000 miles, the orbital speed is 4.39 miles per second, and at 15,000 miles, it is 2.24 miles per second. Our natural moon, at a distance of some 240,000 miles, needs to move only 0.6 miles per second to stay in orbit. It can be seen that the required orbital velocity becomes smaller as the distance from the earth increases.

This doesn't mean, of course, that it is a simple matter to put a satellite in a distant orbit. It requires a greater amount of fuel, overall, to put a satellite in a more distant orbit than in a closer one.

At higher altitudes, a satellite takes more time to complete each orbit. This orbital period is about 88 minutes for a low orbit, and about a month for the moon. The following table gives the satellite velocity and the number of orbits per day achieved by a satellite for certain selected heights. At a height of 22,242 miles, in orbit over the equator, a satellite completes just 1 orbit per day and remains fixed over the same place on the earth's surface. Such "stationary" satellites are useful for communication purposes.

SATELLITE ORBIT DATA

Height (in miles)	Velocity (miles/sec.)	Number of Orbits per Day
163	4.82	16
547	4.61	14
1,036	4.38	12
1,682	4.12	10
2,588	3.82	8
3,973	3.47	6
6,436	3.03	4
12,545	2.41	2
22,242	1.91	1

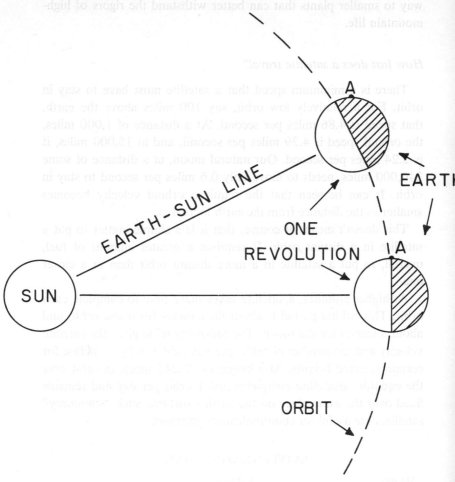

FIG. 14. As shown above, the earth completes one 360-degree turn (between the points marked A in the diagram) in a little less than twenty-four hours. The earth turns somewhat more than one revolution in twenty-four hours.

As mentioned above, a stationary satellite is one which remains above a fixed point on the earth's surface at all times. Actually, the period of a stationary satellite is not exactly 24 hours. To understand why this is so, we must understand the difference between

196

solar time and star time. It is commonly supposed that the earth completes 1 turn on its axis in 24 hours. But that isn't quite true. What it actually does in 24 hours is to make one rotation with respect to an imaginary line joining the earth and the sun. But that line revolves once per year around the sun just as the earth does.

By referring to the accompanying illustration, we can see how this yearly progression affects the period of a stationary satellite. Imagine that the earth is in the lower position in the diagram, and that a stationary satellite is located exactly above point *A*. The upper position of the earth represents its position after one complete turn of 360 degrees. Notice that the earth has not yet returned to the same relative position with respect to the sun. Point *A* has not yet reached the sunny side of the earth.

The time required for the earth to make one turn is actually 23 hours, 56 minutes, and 3 seconds, a period of time called a *sidereal day*. So a stationary satellite must complete one 360-degree turn in precisely that length of time, not 24 hours. Otherwise, the satellite would appear to move through the constellations of the Zodiac once each year as does the sun.

Other curious satellites are called *Trojan satellites;* the positions of these satellites are either 60 degrees behind or ahead of the earth in the same orbit as the earth. These satellites would each be about 93 million miles from both the earth and the sun. A line between each satellite and the earth would make an unchanging angle of 60 degrees with the earth-sun line. The satellites would be relatively stable against small perturbing forces.

Why are Teflon-covered cooking utensils easy to clean?

Teflon is a giant man-made molecule consisting of a chain of tens of thousands of smaller molecules of tetrafluoroethylene. The latter is a small molecule consisting of 2 carbon atoms and 4 fluorine atoms.

Teflon has gained great popularity as a frying-pan coating because food will not stick to it. This property comes from the fact that fluorine atoms, once bonded to the carbon atoms, are so happy with the arrangement that they repel almost all other substances. Teflon, in fact, is more inert and stable than any other natural or man-made resin. The fluorine atoms are so tightly bonded to the carbon atoms, and the latter to one another, that it is just about impossible to break their bonds so they can link up with the atoms of other materials. Because of this characteristic, Teflon will not combine with oxygen or support life; it is immune to attack from fungi or molds; no known acid will dissolve it; it does not melt until the temperature reaches 620°F.; and it is so slippery that fabrics of Teflon have been used, experimentally, in place of ice on skating rinks.

By modifying the Teflon molecule somewhat, chemists have given it other amazing properties. In one process, the Teflon molecule is made sticky on one end only. This sticky end reacts with fiber molecules of fabric and therefore sticks to them. But the other end is just as slippery as ever, so it resists combining either with the fiber, or with oil or water. Thus this new form of Teflon has a sticky side that adheres to a surface it is protecting, and a slippery side that wards off oil and water. It is marketed under such trade names as Zepel and Scotchgard for use as a water- and stain-proof coating on raincoats and other fabrics.

A way was also found to produce Teflon in spray form, thus making it economically feasible to put the material to consumer use. As most housewives know, Teflon is an ideal nonstick coating for pots, pans, and other cooking utensils, and for irons as well.

How fast does the earth travel?

The earth is about 93 million miles from the sun, about which it revolves once each year. This works out to a staggering 66,500 miles per hour, or 1,110 miles per minute. Although we normally think of the earth as a stationary body, it really moves through space at an enormous speed.

Superimposed on this velocity is the speed at which the earth rotates on its axis. This speed varies from zero at the poles to slightly over 1,000 miles per hour at the equator.

It was this great speed that for centuries kept astronomers from believing that the earth revolves about the sun. If the earth were moving so fast, they argued, objects would fly off a table and nothing would remain still. We know today that such objects are kept on earth by gravitational attraction and that they and the earth move at precisely the same speed around the sun. They merely appear to be stationary while the whole system moves at great speed.

The same sort of thing happens to people and objects aboard a jet airplane in flight. Passengers calmly eat their dinners, and everything stays nicely in place, even though plane and contents are racing along at 600 miles per hour or more.

What causes the wind?

Wind is caused by variations in air pressure from place to place on the earth's surface. The average atmospheric pressure at sea level is about 14.7 pounds per square inch, but it is not uncommon to find pressure variations as great as 1 percent or so on regional weather maps. Pressure differences of this magnitude produce forces that tend to move masses of air from high pressure regions to regions of lower pressure. We call these air movements *winds.*

Winds are also affected by the earth's rotation. As cool air moves toward the equator, for example, its path is deflected toward the west by the earth's motion underneath it. This is known as the *Coriolis effect,* and it produces the well-known "trade winds." These winds blow quite steadily from the northwest in the Northern Hemisphere and from the southeast south of the equator.

The Coriolis effect also causes the air to rotate around both the high and low pressure regions that we see on weather maps, rather than directly from high to low. In the Northern Hemisphere, the wind direction is always such that, when you look downwind, low pressure is on your left. As a consequence, winds blow in a clockwise direction around a high pressure center, and counterclockwise around a low. In the Southern Hemisphere, low pressure is to your right as you look downwind, and winds blow clockwise around a low pressure area.

Aside from the Coriolis effect, the earth's rotation also gives rise to prevailing winds—or lack of winds, as in the equatorial doldrums. In the Temperate Zone, which includes most of the United States, there are the prevailing westerlies. Farther north are the polar easterlies.

Does snow protect plants and animals?

Most of us automatically associate snow with cold. Actually, snow turns out to be an effective insulator of plants and animals in cold, mountainous regions where many living things depend upon it for protection from the elements. Although the temperature near the top of a deep snowbank may fall far below zero, the temperature on the ground underneath rarely falls very far below freezing. In addition, a snowbank acts as a temperature regulator, keeping the ground at nearly the same temperature, in spite of the extreme gyrations of temperature experienced at the surface.

High in the Rockies, in the month of June, research scientists made several test borings through a twelve-foot drift. At the bottom they found a tiny snow buttercup just in the process of opening its exquisite yellow buds. The ability of delicate mountain flowers to bloom under such adverse conditions is a marvel of mountain ecology made possible by a protective blanket of snow.

To mountain plants, such as the snow buttercup, snow is a protection, not a hazard. Their tiny cells are full of dissolved nutrients that resist freezing, just as an automobile's antifreeze does. In addition, their metabolism generates a small but apparently sufficient amount of heat to start the plant growing. This growth is in response to some natural triggering process that tells the plant that spring has arrived. Scientists wish they knew how the plant accomplishes this feat, deep in the dark under the snow.

Animals also make use of snow for warmth and protection. Even in high mountains, small animals remain remarkably active in cold weather. Rodents, the most common of mountain animals, are a bustle of activity throughout the winter. Like mountain plants, they find protection under the snow. There it never gets so cold that they cannot function comfortably. One icy winter day, research biologists discovered some lively meadow voles living under a deep

200

snowdrift. Down in their labyrinthine homes, under the protective layer of snow they managed to live and prosper mightily. They could only be kept out of their homes for short periods of time, however, or they would begin to freeze in the subzero weather.

Why does iron rust?

This question was answered about 200 years ago by a great French chemist, Antoine Lavoisier, often called the father of modern chemistry. Lavoisier discovered that iron rust is a compound consisting of two chemical elements, iron and oxygen.

Lavoisier polished a piece of iron until it was bright and clean, and completely free of rust. After weighing it with great precision, he placed the iron sample on a window sill where it would be acted upon by humid air. Each day, as the rust accumulated, he found that the piece of iron grew heavier. He concluded that iron grows heavier as it rusts and showed that this increase in weight was caused by an equal amount of life-giving oxygen taken by the iron from the air. The compound of iron and oxygen is called iron oxide.

Lavoisier also went a step further. He showed that, when a substance burns, it does so by a chemical combination of the combustible substance with oxygen. Without oxygen, in other words, iron cannot rust, and ordinary burning cannot take place. Somewhat later, Lavoisier showed that water, H_2O, consists of two gases in chemical combination—2 atoms of hydrogen bound chemically to 1 atom of oxygen.

With these discoveries, Lavoisier laid the cornerstone of modern inorganic chemistry—the branch of chemistry concerned primarily with nonliving matter, or the chemistry that is not dependent on the key element, carbon.

Why does water rise from root to plant?

Water enters the root hairs of a plant by a kind of diffusion called *osmosis,* a fundamental natural process that goes on in almost all living things. Through this process, water molecules are able to pass through living membranes even though the membrane will not pass drops of water. This seeming paradox is a result of the structure of the molecules in the membrane. A plant's membrane seems completely watertight—no pores are evident, even with the aid of a high-powered microscope. Yet there are tiny openings in the membrane, openings that are too small to be seen with an optical microscope.

A membrane, like all substances, is made up of molecules. And no matter how closely packed they are, there are always spaces between these molecules. The spaces are large enough to allow water molecules to pass through, but too small to allow water droplets to pass through. The open spaces, in fact, are too small even to allow larger molecules—such as glucose, a plant sugar—to get through. And this is the basis by which water diffuses into root hairs without letting plant juices out.

The diffusion of water into a root arises from the random movements of the water molecules, their incessant jiggling as they collide with each other and other molecules. Thus, they tend always to spread out from a region where they are closely packed into other regions of smaller concentrations. This also explains why a lump of sugar will eventually sweeten a cup of tea or coffee even though it is not stirred. Thus a membrane acts like a kind of sieve. Water passes through rapidly, while somewhat larger molecules that may be dissolved in the water, such as minerals, move through much more slowly. So the membrane holds most of the minerals on one side while letting the water pass through.

This *diffusion,* or sieve action, builds up a considerable pressure within the root system of the plant, a result of the greater concentration of water outside the plant than within the root, where minerals are present in the fluid. The water molecules flow into the plant, therefore, where their concentration is lower. This osmotic flow continues, theoretically, until the concentrations of water are the same on both sides of the membrane. Osmotic pressures as high as 273 atmospheres have been obtained in the laboratory through the use of special membranes. In plants scientists estimate that osmotic pressure is great enough to raise a column of water as high as 66 feet through the trunk of a tree.

But what, you may ask, of the giant Douglas firs of the Pacific Northwest, which tower 400 feet? No one knows for sure how water reaches the top of these tall trees. The best current theory is based on an unexpected property of water, its great *tensile strength,* or resistance to being pulled apart. It is easy enough to break a drop of water into smaller ones, but the task gets more difficult for columns of water. In fact, the hydrogen bonds that link water molecules together are so powerful that a column of water is as strong in some ways as a metal chain. Experiments have demonstrated, for example, that pure water enclosed in a fine airtight tube can withstand a pull of 5,000 pounds per square inch before breaking. The tensile strength of sap is somewhat less, about 3,000 pounds per square inch. But even that figure is enough to permit a slender column of sap, held within one of the fiber tubes of a tree, to be lifted several thousand feet—higher than the highest tree.

Despite the great tensile strength of sap, something must still do the lifting if the column is ever to reach the top of the tree. It is thought that *transpiration* supplies that lift. When water evaporates, or transpires, from a leaf of a tree, it lowers the concentration of water in the cells of the leaf. The cells replace the lost moisture by attracting water molecules from the liquid column in the fiber tube. This transfer of water molecules puts the column of sap under tension, as though a hand had grabbed the top of the column and pulled it up. Since the sap columns extend all the way from leaf to root, the pulling at the top moves all the way down, raising the sap a molecule at a time.

Scientists are not completely happy with this theory, however. What happens, for example, if the column of water breaks? Wouldn't that disrupt the sap-lifting process? It is hard to believe that such breaks wouldn't occur as the tree sways in a high wind. So the theory still remains a largely speculative one.

Can astrology predict the future?

For a long time, man believed that all heavenly bodies revolved about the earth. In medieval times he believed that man was the only purpose of creation—the center of the universe and of all living things.

Man also applied the motions of the heavenly bodies to his own personal magic. The notion that the planets and stars control our lives has existed in most civilizations as far back as written records exist. From the days of ancient Babylon until the end of the Renaissance, astrology was considered a major science. Great scientists like Galileo, Tycho Brahe, and Kepler were expected to make up horoscopes for their wealthy patrons. Even today over $125 million are spent each year on astrological literature and services in the United States alone.

Today's scientists consider astrology to be a pseudoscience, founded upon superstition, and the elimination of superstition is one of the goals of real science. For that reason, astrology cannot be expected to predict the future with any more certainty than the laws of chance would allow.

How does a camera make a picture?

Many substances are altered by light, some to a greater degree than others. Photography is made possible by that phenomenon.

To understand how picture making works, imagine a light-tight

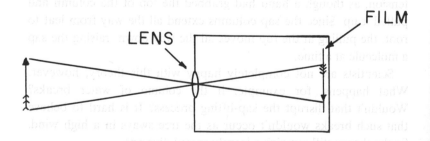

FIG. 15.   A simplified diagram of a camera.

box with a lens at one end and a piece of photographic film at the other. When properly focused, as shown in the diagram, the camera lens projects an image of the scene it "sees" upon the light-sensitive film in the camera. You can demonstrate this principle to yourself quite easily with the help of an ordinary unloaded camera. Merely open the back and place a small sheet of wax paper in the place normally occupied by film. Aim the camera out a window toward a brightly illuminated scene, and click the shutter. While the shutter is open, you will see a bright, upside-down image of the outdoor scene. If the camera has a "time" or "bulb" shutter setting, you can observe the scene at length.

Many light-sensitive chemicals have been used to make photographic film, but the most common are the *silver halides: silver chloride, silver bromide,* and *silver iodide.* When these compounds are exposed to light, a chemical change takes place; some of the silver in the compound is changed to metallic silver. As it happens, the amount of silver metal formed in a given place on the film depends upon the amount of light striking that place. The more light, the more silver.

Even so, the light striking the film produces only a so-called latent image, an image so faint that it cannot be seen. The latent or invisible image is then reinforced, or developed, in a suitable chemical bath. This process of development causes additional silver atoms to be released from the silver halide. Once again, the greatest amount of silver is produced in areas of greatest exposure. The amount of silver, in fact, depends directly upon the amount of light striking the film at that place. Development of the film releases tens of millions of silver atoms for every one initially released by the light.

The process described above produces what is called a *negative* —a kind of reversed image in which light and dark areas are just the opposite of corresponding areas in the original scene. But the whole business is corrected by printing a positive picture. This is done quite simply by putting the reversed image in contact with a sheet of light-sensitive paper to make a new "re-reversed" picture.

Can a human being be frozen and revived years later?

Biologists have performed experiments in which the heart of an embryo chicken is so carefully removed that it continues beating normally. It is then carefully cooled to −190°C., the temperature of liquid air. It can presumably be stored there indefinitely. After a time, the embryo heart is warmed up to room temperature, where it begins beating again with no sign of damage from its remarkable experience.

No scientists are suggesting, naturally enough, that this fantastic process can be attempted with anything as complex as an entire human being, but perhaps there will be a day when an adventurous person can arrange to "hibernate" for a decade or century and then be revived to observe how the world has changed.

Of more immediate interest, low temperatures can be used to slow down enormously the rate of chemical and physical processes going on in living things. If a surgeon wishes to perform a heart operation that will take some time, he can have the patient cooled down so that the activity of the brain is very much below normal. The brain then requires a relatively small amount of fresh blood, and it is much safer for the surgeon to operate on the heart. Presumably, the various chemical reactions taking place in the brain have been slowed down. Consequently, the brain's demand for oxygen from the bloodstream has been reduced. The temperature reductions for these operations can be relatively small, ranging up to 10°F. or 15°F.

There is also a drop in body temperature associated with hibernating animals. Here, the temperature drop can be appreciable, and the animal may cool down until its body temperature is only slightly above the freezing point of water, 32°F.

Where did the American Indians come from?

The first human beings did not make their home in America. Although scientists have searched North America for fossils of prehistoric men such as the Java man or the Neanderthal man, none have been found. It's now clear, as more and more fossil ape-men are turning up in Africa, Asia, and Europe, that human life originated in the Old World and only in the Old World.

Then where did the American Indians come from?

Most scientists are convinced that the American Indians walked from Siberia to Alaska over dry land. During the Ice Age, enormous amounts of water were locked up in the form of ice, and the ocean level was 200 or 300 feet lower than it is today. The low level of the sea would have been sufficient to dry up the Bering Strait between Alaska and Siberia, producing a high and dry land bridge some fifty-six miles long between the east cape of Siberia and Cape Prince of Wales, Alaska.

Mammoth and bison of the same species are found frozen in the permafrost of both Siberia and the Yukon Valley. This proves that late Ice Age animals walked across the isthmus in both directions. No doubt the first Americans followed them across, hunting as they came, without ever realizing that they were colonizing a vast new continent.

Evidence of this passage from Siberia to Alaska by the earliest American Indians has been found in the Alaska muck pits, a layer that has been frozen ever since the Ice Age. Here archaeologists have found flint spears and fire hearths frozen in the muck close to skeletons and bones of Ice Age animals. The trail of typical stone lance heads leads up the Yukon Valley and down what was then an ice-free corridor, to the plains of Canada. From there the trail continues along the Great Plains and into New Mexico.

Perhaps someday a miner or scientist will unearth the actual body of one of these early Americans, preserved in frozen earth. But even without that evidence, there is little doubt that the first Americans came across the Bering Isthmus in search of Ice Age animals.

How are weather forecasts made?

Weather forecasting, as every weatherman will admit, is far from an exact science. Even so, today's short-range forecasts are 80 percent accurate, leaving only about 20 percent of misses to worry about. This batting average is really quite good, considering the magnitude of the task.

Modern meteorologists are divided on two opposing methods of weather forecasting: the *statistical* method, and *numerical* weather prediction. Most forecasting today uses the statistical approach. In this method, the meteorologist compares present weather conditions with those that have prevailed in the past. He then bases his current predictions on what happened in the past under similar weather conditions. We might define statistical weather forecasting as the prediction of weather by a set of rules derived from the statistics of past weather behavior. This method considers present weather conditions, and refers to records of atmospheric behavior under similar conditions in the past. The forecast is then made by a more or less learned extrapolation of present conditions several hours into the future.

The factors considered by meteorologists include visibility, type of cloud cover, barometric pressure, changes in barometric pressure —whether rising, falling, or steady—humidity, cloud height, wind speed, and direction, and temperature at the ground and at various elevations. Some of these factors can be determined merely by visual observation. Others require such sophisticated instruments as radar-tracked radiosondes and weather satellites.

Meteorologists also have a number of "rules of thumb" to help in prediction. One of these tells us that the weather will probably continue much as it is for the next twelve to twenty-four hours unless a front or low pressure region approaches the area. Ordinarily, a low pressure storm area moves at about 30 to 35 miles per hour in summer over the sea. Highs move about 10 miles an hour slower. Movement over land areas can be up to 20 miles an hour slower still, depending on the roughness of terrain. Winter adds about 5 to 10 miles an hour to the average speeds of high and low pressure areas.

In the Northern Hemisphere's Temperate Zone, the weather is controlled by low and high pressure areas—the so-called migratory pressure systems. In the United States, for example, highs and lows chase each other from west to east in an irregular, unending sequence. Systems with low pressure, the *cyclones,* are usually called *storms.* They vary in size anywhere from a devastating tornado, perhaps 100 feet in diameter, to a hurricane 100 miles across, to winter storms that measure up to 750 miles in diameter. These different cyclones have one thing in common; the winds circulate counterclockwise around their centers (clockwise in the Southern Hemisphere). Because they generally move from west to east, their front sides have warm winds bringing tropical air from lower latitudes, while to the rear their winds bring colder northern air.

Cold and warm air masses do not mix where they meet, but their interfaces, or *fronts,* produce active weather zones, with clouds and precipitation. The change from one air mass to another is usually rapid, taking place in a short distance along the ground. It is in these frontal zones that a great deal of our violent weather occurs, including many of our thunderstorms.

Between successive low pressure storms, a pattern of anticyclonic winds prevails. The weather usually quiets down, the pressure is high, and winds are gentle. In the Northern Hemisphere, the winds around a high circulate in a clockwise direction (south of the equator, counterclockwise). Bright sunshine is the rule, and skies are crisp and clear.

Using this sort of data and information, the statistical forecaster has become a master at scientifically estimating the speed and rate at which weather changes will occur. Nevertheless, a newer method of weather prediction—numerical weather forecasting—is also gaining support among meteorologists. This "quantitative" method was suggested in 1922 by meteorologist Lewis R. Richardson.

Richardson believed that he could mathematically derive the future weather based on an exact knowledge of present and past conditions. This would be more than a mere "30 percent probability of rain this evening"—it would tell *how much* rain for *how long.* His equations involved wind velocity, density, pressure, temperature, and other factors. Richardson actually did predict the weather using his methods, but he had to work for 3 months to produce a twenty-four-hour forecast. Obviously, the weather was ancient history by the time he had completed his work. Richardson estimated that it would take a team of 1,000 meteorologists, each with a desk calculator, 24 hours to forecast the weather for England 1 hour in advance. The electronic computer and other advances have helped alleviate this problem, but it is still extremely difficult to gather and convert many millions of bits of weather data into a weather report.

The first practical application of numerical weather prediction was made by the U.S. Navy. Today, information from 3,000 weather stations is fed into a computer, which prints out a twenty-four-hour forecast in 40 minutes. In the process, it performs 10 billion arithmetical operations. The work required for longer forecast periods is even greater—more than a trillion for a 100-day forecast! This is not feasible with today's equipment.

There is a great debate today between the advocates of statistical and numerical weather prediction. Numerical prediction is based on the principle of *determinism*, and its opponents believe it must fail because meteorologists cannot ever obtain enough bits of data to predict the weather with certainty. They maintain that weather really stems from many tiny factors that are lost in the mass of available weather data. Its proponents argue that such reasoning is defeatist. With enough data and sufficient understanding of atmospheric behavior, they say, a computer can be programmed to forecast the weather with great accuracy.

Just how the debate between the statisticians and determinists will be resolved remains to be seen. Perhaps, as more is learned about the weather, a synthesis of the two approaches will lead to an optimal method of weather prediction.

What are artificial wigs made of?

We live in an age of synthetics in which a stylish woman can go to the theater attired completely in man-made material, from her acrylic wig to her vinyl soles. In the not too distant future, her husband may be able to leave his all-plastic house in the morning, take a short cut across an artificial lawn of polyethylene grass to his cycolac car, and drive to work on tires of synthetic rubber.

For countless millennia, man relied on the materials he found in nature for clothing, shelter, and other necessities; now the science of chemistry provides substitutes that often surpass their natural prototypes in quality and usefulness. The enormous chemical plastics industry extrudes, molds, and draws scores of different kinds of synthetic materials to satisfy every conceivable need. Chemists can manipulate molecules to produce materials to almost any desired specification. Dynel, for example, can be produced as soft and as lustrous as human hair. Synthetic hair, of course, has the added advantage of being so moisture resistant that it can hold a hairdo even in a downpour.

Dynel, like other members of the acrylic family of synthetic fibers, is made from natural gas, salt, ammonia, and water. In addition to human hair, it can simulate textures as varied as smooth cashmere and bristly mohair.

Can monkeys talk?

Scientists who study the learning capacity of chimpanzees and monkeys are often mystified by the fact that such intelligent animals never really learn to talk. This is true even when the animals associate closely with man. In one experiment, a chimpanzee named Viki was reared like a human child in the home of a scientist couple. After six and one-half years, Viki had learned only four words: "Mama," "Papa," "up," and "cup."

Chimpanzees have no difficulty learning to communicate with gestures and noises, so some scientists have suspected that their inability to talk is caused by their brain's lack of appropriate speech centers. But recent anatomical studies have turned up another possible explanation: apes and monkeys lack a developed *pharynx,* an indispensable part of the human vocal system. Located in the human throat, the pharyngeal chamber changes shape and size continually to help produce the vowel sounds of speech. Of the

211

primates, only man has this essential accessory. Without it, monkeys may not be able to reproduce the complex sounds of human speech.

In captivity, some species of parrots and myna birds learn to mimic human speech and other sounds. One of the best mimics is the African gray parrot, *Psittacus eritheceus,* a thirteen-inch-long, pearl-gray bird with a red tail. Even though such birds acquire a fairly large vocabulary, they have no idea of the meaning of the words. For that reason, parrots and mynas do not really "talk," if the word is intended to imply communication or conversation.

Can a baby's sex be foretold before birth?

For some years, doctors have been able to predict the sex of an unborn baby by examining the chromosomes. But to do so, they had to obtain a sample of the fluid surrounding the baby, a procedure involving some risk and pain. Now a simple test has been devised to answer the tantalizing question, "Will it be a boy or girl?" The test involves taking a tiny drop of blood from the mother's finger and examining the chromosomes of the white blood cells under a microscope. The test is possible because the baby's blood mingles with that of his mother. Because it does, the blood test may provide a simple way of predicting the sex of unborn babies.

Why do stars twinkle?

You have probably heard the old rhyme:

> Twinkle, twinkle, little star,
> How I wonder what you are.

But stars themselves really do not twinkle. If you could see them from a satellite or spaceship high above the earth, you would see them shine with a clear steady light, without any indication of twinkling.

Even through the most powerful of telescopes, a star looks like a tiny point of light—as though only a single tiny ray of light betrays its presence to us. This is true despite the fact that each star is a gigantic mass of fiery matter, much like our own sun. Stars seem to twinkle because the ray of light that we see must pass through our uneven, constantly moving atmosphere.

In general, when a beam of light passes from one substance to another, it is bent off course, or *refracted*. This refraction also takes place when the light ray passes through layers of air at different temperatures. We know that our atmosphere has many layers at varying temperatures, and that the whole thing is constantly moving and changing its speed and direction. As a ray of starlight passes through these air layers it is bent this way and that in rapid succession, giving rise to the illusion we call "twinkling." This unsteadiness is similar to the quivering we see when we observe an object through hot air rising from a stove or heater.

The next time you are out on a clear night, notice how the stars near the horizon seem to twinkle more than those more nearly overhead. This is because light from the lower stars must travel a greater distance through the atmosphere than those near the zenith. This increases the probability that the light ray will be perturbed by the atmosphere.

The twinkling effect also varies from one night to the next as conditions in the atmosphere change. On some nights the twinkling is so severe that it is difficult to see the stars clearly through a telescope. The instrument magnifies the motion of twinkling, and the stars seem literally to jump about in the eyepiece.

Unlike the stars, planets do not ordinarily twinkle, but shine with a steady, unwavering light. Like the earth, they revolve around the sun and are very much closer to us than the stars. If you look at a planet through a telescope it does not look like a single point of light, but rather like a disk of light. Each point on the illuminated disk reflects light from the sun, just as a mirror might. So the light we see coming from a planet is made up of many individual light rays, not a single ray, as was the case for a star. The light from a planet is relatively steady because the wavering of one light ray is counterbalanced by the wavering of another ray in another direction. The resulting light beam, therefore, is more steady, and free of twinkling.

How old is life on earth?

Although the earth is almost 5 billion years old, rocks older than about 600 million years contain no fossils. Yet rocks only slightly younger, in the Cambrian period, 500 to 600 million years ago, swarm with fossils. At first glance, it might seem that life appeared suddenly in great variety and abundance 600 million years ago. Many scientists find this difficult to believe. The Cambrian period is just *too* rich in well-developed life forms. They feel that the complex trilobites that filled the Cambrian oceans, to take one example, must have developed during a long prior period of evolution.

Furthermore, there are telltale evidences of life in rocks that are as old as 3,000 million years. These are merely carbon deposits that *might* have been produced by algae, but they probably represent life nevertheless. So the Cambrian period is believed to mark the sudden increase in complex life forms, rather than the beginning of life. To earlier forms of life, incapable of leaving fossil records in stone, had been added a whole new range of creatures with shells and outer skeletons. These produced our earliest fossils.

No one really knows why the earlier, perhaps simpler kinds of life on earth suddenly blossomed into a torrent of diverse and complex life forms. One possible explanation tells us that a new kind of cell, or plant, might have evolved, capable of using visible sunlight to produce food in great abundance. Previously, the source of energy for life may have been the sun's ultraviolet light, which could build up complex food compounds only very slowly in the ocean.

In addition, oxygen would have been produced by the process of photosynthesis, thereby accumulating to form the earth's atmosphere. This, in turn, would have led to the development of animal life capable of using the free oxygen in the air and the oxygen dissolved in ocean water. This period, then, would have marked the explosion of life into a great variety of rich and luxuriant forms.

Another theory holds that enormous tides or glaciers in the pre-Cambrian period had ground down the mountains to virtual flatness. As far as we can tell, the earth was never before nor after as flat and low lying as in this period. It is as though a great grinding-wheel had gone over the earth, eliminating every outstanding feature. This would have erased all fossil-bearing rocks from the continents, wiping out any records of preexisting life. If this theory is true, complex forms of life may have existed before 600 million B.C., only to have all traces of this life completely eradicated before the beginning of the Cambrian period.

Scientists have given us the following chronology for life on earth. These ages are tentative at best, and will probably change as new evidence comes to light:

Object	Age
Oldest rocks	4.7 billion years
First algae	3 billion years
First animals	600 million years
Earliest vertebrates (fishes)	460 million years
First land animals	360 million years
Dinosaurs	200 million years
Mammals	160 million years
Homo sapiens	50,000 years
Egyptian civilization	6,000 years

Why do things appear backward in a mirror?

The image we see in a plane, or flat, mirror is called a *virtual image* because we cannot project it on a screen. Nevertheless, it is a simple matter to represent such an image on a scale diagram because rays of light travel in straight lines.

To reconstruct an image as seen in a plane mirror we have to consider the rays of light coming from each point on the object to the eye. To understand how this is done, imagine your eye con-

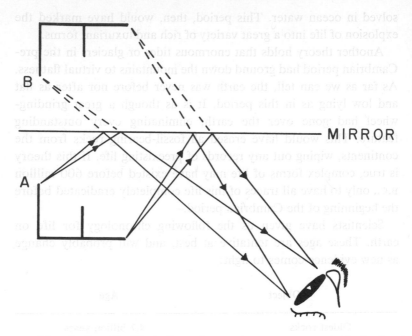

FIG. 16. A diagram illustrating why an image appears reversed when viewed in a mirror.

centrating on a tiny period on this page. Light rays coming from that dot extend outward in all directions, but very few of the rays reach your eye. The rays we are interested in form a cone, with its apex at the dot and its base equal in size to the pupil of the eye.

With that in mind, refer to point A in the accompanying diagram. The cone of light is represented by two diverging rays, which leave point A, are reflected in the mirror, and arrive at each side of the pupil. Precisely the same thing happens for every point on the letter F in the diagram.

The eye, of course, cannot take into account the fact that the light has been reflected by the mirror. So to represent any point, such as point A, we need only follow the path of the two rays that enter the eye and trace them backward to the point from which they *appear* to diverge. Thus, light coming from point A seems to come

216

from point *B,* and that is where the brain places its source. By following rays from several points on the figure, we can see that the virtual image is "backward" or reversed from left to right.

If all of this still seems quite improbable, try this simple experiment. Place a small real mirror in an upright position in the diagram, just over the line marked "mirror." You will see that the diagram is a faithful representation of how the rays behave in the real world. Furthermore, it doesn't matter where you place your eye. The letter *F* is always seen reversed. Put another way, the image of a page of print seen in a mirror resembles what we should see if we were looking at the same print through the back of a transparent page.

Can man change the climate?

Only in recent years have scientists come to believe that man may be able to change the climate over large regions of earth. Scientists have learned a great deal about the atmosphere over the past two decades. Although there are still many mysteries to be solved, the secrets of the atmosphere are surely being uncovered.

Satellites that circle the globe provide detailed pictures of cloud cover, along with measurements of radiant energy from the sun and earth. In the near future they may also provide data on temperature and humidity in the atmosphere, and perhaps even wind speed and direction.

Scientists are also discovering which factors control the general circulation of the atmosphere and what causes the circulation to change. Although many important details are still lacking, scientists have learned that the temperature difference between the equatorial and polar regions is of extreme importance. This has suggested a number of possible ways in which the circulation of the atmosphere—and, therefore, the weather and climate—can be modified.

A number of schemes have been suggested for warming the Arctic, to reduce the temperature difference between the pole and equator and change the overall circulation. The suggestion is to coat

217

the Arctic ice with a layer of black carbon dust, which would absorb more solar heat than white snow and ice. This would probably increase Arctic temperatures and cause the ice to melt. Some scientists believe that once the ice melted, it would not return. The theory is that exposed rock, soil, and water would continue to absorb relatively large amounts of solar heat, which, in turn, would prevent snow and ice from building up in large amounts. Other scientists dispute this theory, but there is little chance it will be tried out. The enormous amount of carbon black needed—about 1.5 billion tons for a layer four-thousandths of an inch thick—renders this scheme of little practical value.

Another, more feasible suggestion by Soviet engineer P. M. Barisov involves building a sixty-mile-long dam across the Bering Strait between Alaska and Siberia. He proposed pumping cold Arctic water into the Pacific Ocean. Warmer Atlantic Ocean water would then flow into the Arctic to replace it. This might lead to a small, but important, increase in Arctic temperature.

Most meteorologists agree that warming the Arctic by a small amount would change the world's overall climate and weather. Unfortunately, nobody can predict whether the change will be for the better or worse. Will deserts get more rainfall or will they become drier? Will swamps dry up or become wetter? How about the distribution of rainfall, hail, and snow in farming regions? Will a rise in sea level lead to the flooding of coastal cities? Will another Ice Age be initiated or will glaciers recede? No one knows the answers to these questions for sure.

Scientists do know that weather changes seem to have global significance. Winds in one region, for example, are accompanied by opposite winds in another. If the north winds are abnormally cold and persistent in one part of the world, then south winds are abnormally warm and persistent in another part of the world. This interdependence and unity of the atmosphere means that it may not be possible to change the climate in one part of the world without producing a series of changes in other parts of the world. Tinkering with the climate—before a more complete understanding is achieved—might well lead to catastrophe.

Before leaving the subject of changing climate, we should point out that atmospheric pollution can have an important effect on the world's climate. Perhaps the most important pollutant from this point of view is the gas carbon dioxide produced by the burning of fossil fuels. Since 1890 the amount of carbon dioxide in the air has increased about 10 percent. During that period of time the average worldwide temperatures increased almost 1°F. Although this may not seem like much when you are talking about a bowl of soup or tub of water, it represents an enormous amount of energy in the atmosphere. Calculations indicate that about half of that 1°F. temperature rise might be due to carbon dioxide. During the next few hundred years, the temperature increase could be as high as 2.5°F.

Carbon dioxide causes atmospheric heating because it can discriminate between the heat energy coming from sun to earth, and the heat energy leaving the earth. The essential point to remember is that heat rays coming from the sun are of short wavelength, while those leaving the earth are much longer. The sun's rays pass through the carbon dioxide gas with little absorption. But when the longer, infrared rays from the earth try to escape through the atmosphere, some of them are absorbed. They warm the air instead of passing through to outer space.

Of course, no one knows for sure whether the atmosphere's temperature will increase because of the increased carbon dioxide, or if it does, what effect it will have on climate. We do know, however, that the effect of increased carbon dioxide in the air needs further study.

How do camels go so long without drinking water?

Animals obtain the water they need in three ways. Two of these are the drinking of water and the use of water present in food. A third primary source is called *metabolic water,* the water produced chemically as a by-product of food digestion. This third source of water is extremely important to camels and other desert animals.

The camel has long had a legendary reputation for being able to go for long periods of time without drinking any water. Ancient writers believed that the camel had some mysterious internal water reservoir—a story that was told for so many centuries that it came to be believed. No such reservoir, however, has ever been found. Nevertheless, the camel is remarkably suited to getting along well on a minimum of water.

When green vegetation is available, camels can live for months without drinking water at all. Their food provides all the water they need. But even in the Sahara's dry summer, when little natural food is available, camels can go for a week or more without water and for ten days without food.

Camels accomplish this feat by drawing on water from their body tissues and on water produced chemically as a breakdown product of fat. The camel's hump contains up to 50 pounds of fat, which is accumulated when food and water are plentiful. As the fat is used up to supply the camel's energy needs, about 1.1 pounds of water are produced for every pound of fat used up. This is made possible because hydrogen is given off as a by-product in the breakdown of fat. Oxygen from breathing is then combined with the hydrogen to produce water. Because oxygen is much heavier than hydrogen, it does not take much hydrogen, by weight, to make a pound of water.

With the help of metabolic water, a camel can function well for a good many days, even when carrying a load. A loss of 25 percent of body weight can be tolerated under these severe conditions without serious injury. When water is again available, the camel gulps down as much as 25 gallons at one time to compensate for the water lost during the period of deprivation. It takes a period of time for the water to return to the tissues, and the fat is not immediately replaced, but the hump slowly returns to its normal size after the camel is back on a normal diet.

What is rayon?

The raw material of rayon is *cellulose,* the wonder-working giant molecule of nature. Cellulose is the material used by every plant from seaweed to redwood trees in the fibers that give plants their shape and strength. Thousands of years ago man learned to manipulate cellulose fibers to make paper and linen, but only in the past century did he discover how to break down the giant cellulose molecules and rebuild them into the first "natural" synthetics—cellophane, celluloid, rayon, and a large assortment of other products.

In 1892 scientists successfully mimicked the silkworm by chemically digesting cellulose and forming it into shiny, silklike filaments. The result was *viscose rayon,* our first man-made fabric. The new wonder cloth was as washable as cotton, yet shone with the luster and delicate texture of silk.

The first step in making viscose cellulose is to produce the so-called alkali cellulose, by reacting cellulose with lye. Combined with carbon disulfide, alkali cellulose produces a grainy orange substance that can be dissolved in caustic soda and water to produce a syrupy—or viscous—liquid, which led to the term *viscose.* Treatment with acid then changes the viscose back to cellulose again.

This regenerated cellulose of 1892 turned out to be a cellulose that is different from nature's kind. The process breaks the long cellulose molecule at several places, producing three or four synthetic molecules from a single natural one. The regenerated cellulose is still a giant molecule, or *polymer,* but smaller and somewhat weaker than the natural one. Viscose rayon, made by extruding the syrupy viscose through tiny holes into an acid bath, is still an attractive and desirable fabric for clothing.

Cellulose molecules, which comprise the cell walls of all plants, are made of long chains of glucose sugar molecules, a simple sugar that is found throughout the vegetable kingdom. Each glucose molecule consists of 6 carbon atoms, 12 hydrogen atoms, and 6 oxygen atoms arranged in a closed, six-sided structure called a ring. Such structures are common for many ordinary organic compounds. In a way not completely understood, enzymes within the cells of plants cause two glucose molecules to lose, between them, 2 hydrogen atoms and 1 oxygen atom, which are given off in the form of water. The glucose molecules then link up in the region vacated by

221

the hydrogen and oxygen atoms. This is an example of a process called *condensation polymerization*. The process is repeated over and over again by the plant, producing an extremely long cellulose molecule. The finished length varies from plant to plant, but in cotton, for example, the cellulose molecule is about 10,000 glucose units long. In wood, the molecule contains 1,800 glucose units.

Viscose rayon also led to the development of another useful product, *cellophane*. This material is the same as viscose rayon except in form. To make cellophane, the viscose is extruded into an acid bath between long, narrow slots or rollers instead of small holes. It then hardens into a thin, transparent sheet. One cellophane plant alone produces enough cellophane in one year to reach from the earth to the moon with a sheet about a yard wide.

Acetate rayon is a more lustrous form of the material than viscose rayon. It begins with the same natural cellulose used in making viscose rayon, but the molecule is chemically altered by acetic acid. The white powdery cellulose acetate is then dissolved in acetone, and the solution is extruded through fine holes directly into the air. As the acetone evaporates, filaments of acetate rayon are formed.

The main source of cellulose is wood—especially pine and spruce. It is cheap and abundant, but because it contains only 40 to 50 percent cellulose, the desired substance must be extracted by a process called *pulping*. The logs are cut into chips and simmered in chemicals that remove various resins, minerals, and tarry substances. The pulp that is left, about 93 percent cellulose, is dried into sheets to become the raw material for rayon, paper, and other cellulose products. In the United States, over 30 million tons of wood are converted into cellulose every year. Some of it goes to produce several billion pounds of rayon annually—more than 100 times the world output of silk.

Why are metals better electrical conductors than nonmetals?

There are many ways in which atoms can be bound together to form larger groupings, or *molecules*. One method involves the giving up of "excess" electrons by one substance and their acceptance by another substance that is "deficient" in electrons. Ordinary table salt, consisting of sodium and chlorine, is an example of this kind of bond. Sodium "lends" its excess electron to chlorine and each atom then forms an extremely stable structure called an *ion*. Ions have one fault, however: they are electrically unbalanced. The sodium ion, having lost an electron, is positively charged; chlorine, having gained an electron, is negatively charged. As a result, the two ions attract each other, (because opposite charges attract), and a stable, electrically neutral molecule is the result. This kind of linkage is called an *ionic bond*.

Another molecular linkage involves the allocation of "extra" electrons to more than one atom as common property. This sharing of electrons is called a *covalent bond*. A typical example of the covalent bond is the hydrogen molecule, which consists of two hydrogen atoms. Hydrogen, with one electron, requires an additional electron to reach a state of stability. When two hydrogen atoms come together, each atom shares the two available electrons with the other, thereby producing a stable hydrogen molecule.

When we examine some typical metals—iron, silver, and copper, for example—we find that their atoms combine in a different way. While the linking electrons in other materials belong only to one or two atoms, every metal atom splits off its excess outer electrons and puts them at the disposal of all. A metal, therefore, should be thought of as a structure of atomic remnants within which floats a single, plentiful pool of evenly distributed electrons.

The even distribution of fairly free-moving electrons is the direct cause of the high electrical conductivity of metals. Electrons are the smallest particles of electricity, and their motion is nothing less than an electric current. In the nonmetals, the electrons have fairly fixed positions, from which they are not easily dislodged. Metals are entirely different. The cloud of electrons is not tied to specific atoms, and can be made to move quite easily through the metal. If an electric potential, such as from a battery, is connected to the ends of a metallic wire, the electrons move easily in response to the electric force. Thus, the good conductivity of metals stems from the fact that the linking electrons are not fixed at specific places, but can flow like a fluid in a channel.

223

Before leaving the subject, it may be mentioned that electrons do not move very fast at all in a metal—their speed is usually measured in thousandths of an inch per second! It is not the electrons that move quickly, but rather the current impulse. This is analogous to what happens when a cue ball strikes a row of billiard balls. After striking one end of the row on dead center, the cue ball comes to a stop. But almost instantaneously, the ball at the other end rolls away from the pack. The two balls may not move particularly fast during this experiment, but the impulse is transmitted at a very high speed through the row of balls.

Does air pollution damage plant life?

According to a presidential report on our environment, air pollution's effects on vegetation, property, and materials cost the nation an estimated $10 billion annually. About one-half of this damage is caused by sulfur oxides, the worst culprits involved. Each year, 36.6 million tons of sulfur oxides are spewed forth by the burning and distilling of oil and coal, the smelting of various ores, and by other industrial processes. If uncontrolled, this figure will reach 126 million tons by the end of the century. Other gases particularly toxic to plants are hydrogen fluoride, ozone, chlorine, nitrogen dioxide, and hydrogen chloride.

Oddly enough, the effects of pollution on plants have been matters of concern for over a century—long before people began to worry about its effects on human health. The damage to plants ranges from relatively minor injury to complete destruction.

Plants suffer from air pollution, in a sense, because they "breathe." Poisonous gases enter their systems through openings—called *stomata*—in the leaves, as shown in the accompanying diagram. The stomata, or "breathing tubes," open in hot weather to allow water vapor to escape to the air. This is called *transpiration,* and is analogous to perspiration in a human being. These processes cool both the plant and man respectively. In cool weather, the stomata close and the plant loses water vapor more slowly.

The noxious gases enter the leaves through the stomata and

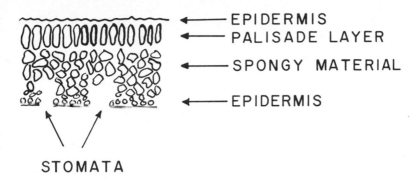

FIG. 17. Cross section of a plant leaf.

damage the internal structure of the leaves. Sulfur oxides, for example, join with water to produce sulfuric acid, one of the most corrosive substances known to man.

The destructive effects of air pollution on plants can be long lasting as well as widespread. Near Ducktown, Tennessee, sulfur dioxide downwind from industrial plants affected vegetation as far as thirty miles away. In addition, the land was so affected that now, some fifty years later, the area is still virtually bare of vegetation.

Why can't man drink seawater?

Many marine birds and reptiles are equipped with special glands that are used exclusively for salt removal. With the help of this remarkable salt gland, a gull can drink up to one-tenth of its body weight of seawater and get rid of the excess salt in about three hours. If a man were to drink an equivalent amount of seawater—two gallons—his body would dehydrate itself trying to flush out the excess salt.

No animal can tolerate a body-salt concentration of more than 0.9 percent. Any salt in excess of this amount is eliminated in the urine. Human kidneys are not able to concentrate more than 2.2 percent salt in urine, and so cannot cope with seawater with its 3.5 percent salt content. The horse can concentrate only 1.5 percent salt in its urine, so, with its inefficient kidneys, it cannot drink

225

water from certain brackish supplies that are quite fit for human consumption.

The camel can cope with heavy doses of salt, almost twice the concentration of seawater. The whale, a mammal that lives in the ocean, also has kidneys efficient enough to allow it to drink seawater without harm.

How far can telescopes see into space?

The most powerful optical telescope in the world is the Hale telescope located on Mount Palomar near Los Angeles, California. This reflecting telescope is 200 inches in diameter and was dedicated on June 3, 1948. It is operated jointly by the California Institute of Technology and the Carnegie Institution of Washington, D.C. The telescope was financed by the Rockefeller Foundation, and cost $6.5 million to construct.

The Hale telescope, and other giants of its kind, are not conventional telescopes in the sense that an astronomer normally looks through them to bring the stars closer. They are really powerful and elaborate astronomical cameras. The truly amazing feature of the 530-ton Hale telescope is that it can be aimed at a chosen star and controlled so accurately that it follows the star unerringly across the nighttime sky. To do this, it moves automatically throughout the night, compensating for the rotation of the earth, the orbital movement of the earth around the sun, and the travel of the sun in its own spinning galaxy, the Milky Way.

Like an ordinary camera, the Hale telescope is really a "light accumulator." It remains focused on a given part of the sky for several hours at a time, thereby accumulating light on a highly sensitive photographic film. This provides bright images of stars and other celestial objects, which would be much too faint to be seen by the human eye. The eye, of course, cannot "accumulate" light over a long period of time. As soon as light reaches the retina, it is changed into an electrical signal and sent off to the brain. A photographic emulsion, on the other hand, operates on a different principle. The effect of the light falling on the film accumulates

226

over a period of several hours, building a stronger and stronger image the longer the film is exposed to light. By this means, a reflecting telescope, such as the one on Mount Palomar, can "see" stars and galaxies at a distance of several billion light-years from the earth.

A *light-year* is the distance that light can travel in a year at a speed of 186,000 miles per second—approximately 6 million million miles. Used in this way, the Hale telescope is at least a million times as powerful in detecting stars as the human eye alone.

In observing a galaxy at a distance of 2 billion light-years, the telescope records an image of light that left its source 2 billion years ago. This enormous period of elapsed time is almost half as great as the age of the earth. Another way of emphasizing the amount of time involved is to note that the light began its voyage across space eons before prehistoric animals left their earliest fossil remains on earth. Because it took so long for light to travel from these distant galaxies to earth, the very objects that are recorded on the photographic films may not even be in existence today! We can only be certain that the image we project on a photographic plate tonight is a true representation of the way the celestial object looked 2 billion years ago.

What are fossils?

One kind of fossil merely consists of the remains of a plant or animal. The remains may include bones, teeth, or perhaps the entire animal preserved in ice or by some other means. Fossils also exist in the form of prints, such as leafprints and footprints, inscribed in rocks. Cavities with the shape of human bodies were discovered in hardened volcanic ash at Pompeii, Italy.

A petrified fossil is formed when the remains of a plant or animal turn to stone. Water dissolves away the original plant fiber or body structure. Minerals then replace the bone or fiber, creating a likeness in stone of the original plant or body. Petrified wood is a common example of this kind of fossil.

Fossils are useful to scientists in determining the age of rock

227

formations in which they are found. Paleontologists have pretty well worked out the chronology of the different life forms that once inhabited the earth. They know, for example, that flying reptiles evolved into birds during the Jurassic period some 170 million years ago. The fossils of extinct species of plants and animals, therefore, are samples from a known progression of life on earth. Each type of fossil represents a definite time in the evolution of life, because that life form lived only during a certain span of the earth's history. So the discovery of a particular fossil in a rock stratum implies that the rock was deposited or formed during the corresponding time period.

Why does the Gulf Stream have such a warming effect on climate?

Man has long known that "rivers" flow in the oceans. Some are cold currents of water from Arctic regions and others are warm currents of water from the tropics. These streams vary in width, depth, and speed. They generally flow in stable, well-defined "channels," and they exert continual, long-term influences on the environments of the land masses they skirt.

Scientists have calculated that, if the temperature difference between a warm current and the adjacent ocean is 20°F., every cubic mile of the warm current gives up an amount of heat that corresponds to the burning of 7 million tons of coal. One such enormous heat exchanger is the Atlantic's warm Gulf Stream, which gives the British Isles and parts of Norway a temperate climate while Labrador, at the same latitude on the other side of the Atlantic, is a frozen land.

Warm ocean currents are not the only means by which water transports heat from the tropics to higher latitudes. To illustrate, consider what happens when water evaporates from the surface of the ocean in the tropics. This change in state from liquid to vapor requires a great amount of energy, which is absorbed by the vapor. The vapor then plays the role of a heat-carrying vehicle, which follows the circulating air currents flowing away from the equator. Some of it moves northeasterly until it reaches a latitude of about

30 degrees. There, cooling, it may sink and meet a cold air current from the Arctic. The mixing of the disparate air masses results in a storm, and the vapor condenses into water. This transformation releases all of the heat energy absorbed in the tropics, thereby warming the air and the land on which it falls.

What is the Mohorovičić discontinuity?

Scientists believe that the inner core of the earth consists of a solid sphere of iron and nickel about 1,600 miles in diameter, surrounded by a liquid layer of the same materials about 1,350 miles thick. Surrounding this metal core is a layer of solid rocky material about 1,780 miles thick called the *mantle*. The upper 420 miles of the mantle is brittle enough to fracture from time to time and cause earthquakes. The inner part of the mantle is so plastic that it bends instead of breaking.

Above the mantle, at a depth that varies between 3 and 31 miles beneath the surface, is an abrupt change called the *Mohorovičić discontinuity,* after its discoverer. It probably represents a change in the composition or character of the rock, for at that depth the velocity of sound waves generated by earthquakes suddenly increases from 4 to 5 miles per second.

The Mohorovičić discontinuity is the lower surface of the earth's crust. The crust is thin under the oceans, it increases to about 22 miles in thickness under the continents, and it is thickest under mountain systems.

Are animals color blind?

Vision is one of the five basic senses of the animal kingdom, but not all animals see the same things. A major variability in their responsiveness to light is the range of the spectrum they see. For example, bees and many other insects are sensitive to a wide range of ultraviolet light, but most light we see as red is quite invisible to them. But what about all the red flowers that are clearly so attractive to insects? Actually, few of the flowers that attract insects

229

are really red—those we see as red or purple also reflect a great amount of blue, and it is the blue that the insects see.

Scientists use simple experiments to learn about vision in insects. One involves the European poppy, a popular wild flower that looks simply bright scarlet to us, but bees and other insects are obviously attracted to it. The experiment is performed by picking two poppies, and in the field of poppies, flattening them out on a board. One is covered with a filter that transmits only ultraviolet light. The other flower is covered with a filter that transmits neither ultraviolet nor visible light. Both flowers now look black—that is, invisible to our eyes. But the insects alight only on the first flower, because they can see the ultraviolet light reflected from its petals.

As far as vision goes, the world's appearance varies greatly from one kind of animal to another, because their eyes rarely have exactly the same range. Because the bee sees ultraviolet light, a flower displays a completely different pattern to him than to man. On the other hand, some flowers that seem red to us are black to the bee because its eyes do not respond to the longer light waves at that end of the visible spectrum. If the waves are longer still, where red turns into infrared, man too goes "blind," yet the diamondback rattlesnake and other pit vipers have no trouble perceiving it.

Actually, no animal has yet been found whose eyes can really see infrared light, but certain snakes have two pits below the eyes that contain a thin membrane rich in nerve endings. There are 3,500 such nerve endings in each pit, or 100,000 times as many as man has on an equal area of skin. Using these extremely heat-sensitive organs, a pit viper can detect, from eighteen inches away, a tumbler of water only a few degrees warmer than the surrounding air. Rattlesnakes will actually strike at such objects, probably mistaking them for prey.

Why are the continents higher than the ocean floor?

Have you ever wondered why the surface of the earth is so irregular, with the continents projecting upward the way they do? On the average, around the world today, the continents project almost three miles above the ocean floors. And evidence suggests that a comparable difference in elevation has persisted ever since the continents were formed. What, then, keeps these massive continental blocks from sinking until they are level with the rest of the earth's surface? The answer seems to be the same as to why a cork floats: in each case, the objects are buoyant because they are less dense than the material in which they are immersed.

Archimedes' Principle tells us that a body having a given volume will float in water if it weighs less than an equal volume of water. If it weighs more than an equal volume of water, it will sink. Thus, a cork floats because a given volume of cork weighs less than the same volume of water.

In the case of the floating continents, it is the earth's mantle of rock that plays the part of water to the colossal continental corks. Taken overall, the earth's crust consists of a spherical shell of a rock called *basalt,* into which vast blocks of granite rock, which make up the continents, are embedded. The oceans are located in the low areas between the continents. Granite, the principal material of the continents, is about 20 percent lighter than the mantle material under the basalt. Basalt, on the other hand, is only 10 percent lighter. The continents thus must ride higher above the mantle than does the crust's basaltic, basement layer.

The idea that a continent—or any major land mass, such as an island—floats on the mantle rock is known as the theory of *isostasy.* The theory has received direct verification in an unexpected event: the entire Scandinavian peninsula is slowly rising out of the sea! Pressed down for so long by enormous glaciers during the Ice Age, Scandinavia has been rising ever since the glaciers departed some 9,000 or 10,000 years ago. Scandinavia is thought to stand today nearly a thousand feet higher than it did under the heavy burden of the ice cap. Measurements indicate that parts of the peninsula are currently going up at the rate of 3 feet per century. It may yet have as much as 650 feet to go before reaching equilibrium.

What is polywater?

Chemists have discovered—much to their astonishment—that ordinary water has an exotic relative that is almost half again as heavy as water, and has the consistency of Vaseline. This new form of water, called *polywater,* is thick and indestructible, and at least one scientist fears that it might run wild outside the laboratory—converting the world's supply of water into a gooey substance that would not support life.

Polywater is made in a vacuum when ordinary water vapor condenses inside hair-thin tubes. The viscous liquid boils at 920°F. and freezes at −40°F. Even at that cold temperature it congeals into a glasslike solid with no similarity to ice. Once it is made, polywater is not affected by air. It dissolves in water, but can be recaptured by boiling away the ordinary water.

Scientific studies show that this bizarre material is an entirely new kind of substance—a polymer of water—hence the name *polywater,* for short. Polywater is composed of the same atomic ingredients as the ordinary kind—2 hydrogen atoms linked to 1 oxygen atom. But many individual units of H_2O are linked together in polywater by new bonds to form the giant supermolecules that chemists call *polymers.* All of our synthetic plastics and fibers are made in the same manner, by the linking together of many small molecular units into large polymers.

The news of polywater's properties led one scientist to warn that it may be extremely hazardous. If it ever escapes from the laboratory, he warns, it may be able to grow until it replaces all of our natural water. Other less fearful scientists urge studies to find practical uses for it. Chemists are now trying to find out if polywater exists in nature, perhaps in cells of the human body.

How much energy do we receive from the sun?

With the exception of nuclear reactors, practically everything that does any work on earth depends on energy derived from the sun. The amount of solar radiation that falls on one square inch just above the earth's atmosphere amounts to about one watt, enough to operate a few pocket radios, but hardly enough to operate a small flashlight bulb. If we scale that figure up for the entire earth, it amounts to 170 billion megawatts. (A *megawatt* is 1

232

million watts.) Only about 45 percent of that amount, or 75 billion megawatts, reaches the earth, the remainder being reflected or absorbed by the clouds and atmosphere. About one-quarter of that 75 billion megawatts is used each day to evaporate 260 cubic miles or 1 billion billion tons of water, mostly from the surface of the ocean. About 7 billion megawatts are absorbed by plants, but only 0.3 billion megawatts are used in photosynthesis to manufacture plant food. About 2 billion megawatts are used to produce the winds and ocean currents, and the rest of the incoming energy is reradiated back into space.

Does climate have any effect on the size of men and animals?

Song sparrows are common all over North America, but those found in Alaska are considerably larger than their cousins that live in the hot areas of the Southwest. This disparity is a result of a tendency in evolution known as *natural selection,* which tends to perpetuate slight differences among individuals in a population if the differences are advantageous. For example, smaller birds or animals have a harder time than larger ones in keeping warm in cold climates. This is because small animals have more skin area (by which heat is lost) per ounce of weight than their larger relatives. In a hot region, on the other hand, small size is an advantage, helping to keep birds cool.

The same process of natural selection operates on the slopes of tall mountains, where climatic extremes exist within a mile or two of each other. This results in horizontal bands of animal and plant life, each adapted to its own particular altitude.

Even man has been influenced by natural selection. Mongolians are unlike Caucasians in that they tend to have shorter legs and arms and thicker bodies. Anthropologists speculate that these differences came about over many thousands of years, during which a large group of human beings was trapped north of the Himalayas by the Ice Ages. Another human example is found in the Andean Indians of South America, who, through natural selection, have become uniquely adapted to the harsh conditions of high altitude life. At the 13,000-foot tableland where they live, the air pressure is only 8 pounds per square inch, compared with 15 pounds per square inch at sea level. To compound the difficulties of these people, the temperature drops below freezing almost every day of the year. To overcome the problem of low air pressure, the Indian has developed a pair of oversize lungs in an extra-large chest. To meet the problem of cold, his body has changed, over countless generations of mutations, to give him short arms and legs so that his blood has a shorter distance to travel. In addition, his extremities have so many blood vessels that he can walk barefoot in the snow without discomfort.

If man, throughout his existence on earth, had not been so skilled in adjusting to various harsh environments by the use of fire, shelter and clothing, racial differences probably would be greater than they are. Groups of people would have had to adapt to their harsh environments if they had not learned to counteract them. Furthermore, man would then not have been able to travel throughout the world and interbreed as he has done.

Today, man lives everywhere except where perpetual ice and snow keep him away, even on Tibetan heights, where sea-level dwellers labor to catch their breath. Mountain people have larger hearts than valley people, and blood that is richer in red cells. Clearly, climate does have a significant effect on man, and on the animals that help him populate the earth.

How are diamonds formed?

Few materials look less similar than coal and diamond, yet both are made of the same chemical element, carbon. No one knows for sure what goes on deep in the earth where the seemingly magical transformation from soft carbon to hard diamond takes place. But experiments show that, to make diamonds, carbon must be subjected to temperatures of 5,000°F. or more, and to pressures of over a million pounds per square inch. These conditions prevail about 240 miles down inside the earth.

Once formed, diamonds are brought to the surface by molten

234

magma during volcanic eruptions. When the magma cools, a plug of the material—called a *diamond pipe*—is left in the earth's crust. The pipe contains a mass of bluish rock, called *kimberlite,* which is seeded with diamonds.

Long before the discovery of diamond pipes near Kimberly, South Africa, in the 1870s, miners in Brazil and India had found diamonds scattered in dried-up river bottoms. Such deposits were formed by swiftly running water, which picked up the diamonds from volcanic pipes and dropped them miles away. Africa is rich both in diamond pipe mines and in alluvial beds, and produces several tons of the precious stones per year—practically all of the world's annual output. About 80 percent are used industrially, because diamond is the world's hardest material, as well as a valued ornament to beauty.

Can food be made from coal and gas?

Scientists at West Virginia University believe that tiny microbes that eat gas, petroleum, and coal may someday help to answer mankind's shortage of proteins. Although soybeans are the cheapest form of protein available today, they may be supplemented in the future by a process in which bacteria convert *hydrocarbons* into proteins. (Hydrocarbons are compounds of hydrogen and carbon.)

Proteins are basically a combination of carbon, oxygen, hydrogen, and nitrogen. They are built up or synthesized by plants, animals, and such microorganisms as bacteria. The real trick to the synthesis of proteins is finding the necessary carbon. Plants, with the help of sunlight, extract carbon from the carbon dioxide in the air. Animals, in turn, obtain carbon from plants. But certain bacteria can obtain carbon directly from the hydrocarbons contained in fuel.

The most plentiful sources of hydrocarbons are gas, coal, and oil. The problem with coal is the presence of cancer-inducing impurities, which would have to be removed at considerable expense. Crude oil has already been used to synthesize edible proteins, but the oily residue must be separated from the proteins before they can be used. This, too, is expensive. Gas, on the other hand, has neither of these drawbacks. It contains no harmful impurities, and any unused gas merely bubbles away, avoiding the separation problems associated with crude oil.

In a practical process, natural gas and air are passed through a culture of bacteria, water, and certain minerals. The gas is almost 100 percent methane (1 atom of carbon joined with 4 atoms of hydrogen). Methane provides the bacteria with the required carbon and hydrogen, and air provides oxygen and nitrogen. As the bacteria grow, they produce vitamins, amino acids, and other useful by-products. The bacteria themselves are removed from the culture and processed directly into edible proteins.

The proteins are in the form of a crystalline powder with no taste or smell. It can be added to flour to make bread or to other foods as a protein supplement.

In a related field, researchers have also developed a process in which waste vegetable matter, such as alfalfa leaves, can be converted to a protein-rich food by bacteria. This product is now being used as a protein supplement in livestock feed.

There are literally thousands of species of bacteria that can convert hydrocarbons into proteins and vitamins. They are most easily found in the soil near gas and oil wells, or around harbors and beaches where oil spillage has occurred. The selection of the proper strain of bacteria has thus far been done by trial and error, a time-consuming and expensive proposition. When this problem is overcome, scientists hope that the price of such proteins will become competitive with soybeans.

What causes the earth's magnetic field?

The study of seismology has found the inside of the earth to contain an outer core, probably of molten iron and nickel, surrounding a solid center. The earth's magnetic field is thought to be produced by the flow of electric currents in the liquid core.

The principles behind this theory of the earth's magnetism are no different from those which explain the operation of an ordinary

236

electric generator or dynamo. The first principle involves the close relationship between electric current and magnetic field: electric currents are always surrounded by magnetic fields, and magnetic fields are generated by electric currents. The second principle is called *electromagnetic induction:* when an electrical conductor, such as a wire or molten interior of the earth, is moved through a magnetic field, a current of electricity is induced to flow in it.

The power required to generate the earth's magnetic field is not large—on the geophysical scale—and probably comes from motions within the molten outer core. These motions are the result of convection, perhaps caused by heat generated by relatively small amounts of radioactive elements deep in the interior of the earth. The fluid motions are thought to generate electric currents by electromagnetic induction, as in a dynamo.

In a dynamo, coils of wire mounted on a shaft are moved through a magnetic field by turning the shaft. Ideally, if the wires offered no resistance to the current, and if the moving parts were frictionless, the dynamo could be coupled to an electric motor so that the two would run forever. The motor would turn the dynamo shaft, and the dynamo would generate the electric current to run the motor. In the real world, however, friction and resistance are inevitable and energy must be provided from outside to keep the system running.

The dynamo theory of the earth's magnetic field tells us that a motor-generator combination—comparable, but widely different in actual detail—exists in the molten interior of the earth. Because this imagined dynamo, like all real ones, is less than wholly efficient, energy must be provided to keep it going. This energy comes from convective or circulating movements that may arise in the outer liquid core from the intense heat of the smaller, inner core. Because of the earth's rotation, the motions in the liquid core are complex swirling ones. The symmetry caused by the planet's rotation accounts for the fact that the earth's magnetic axis is approximately lined up with its geographic axis. Such a dynamo in a liquid sphere has yet to be demonstrated in the laboratory, however.

Through its magnetic field, the earth's core extends its influence all the way to the surface and beyond. Modern measurements in space prove that the earth's magnetic forces reach out into space for thousands of miles before fading away into insignificance. This region of influence, called the *magnetosphere,* plays an important role in deflecting the many bursts of charged particles continually emitted by the sun.

How high is the highest spot on earth?

The top of Mount Everest in Tibet was first measured accurately by a British survey team in 1852. At 29,002 feet, it became the highest place in the world. After corrections were later made for gravitational anomalies, the corrected height was taken to be 29,141 feet. Later, when measured by a party of Indians in 1954, its height was 26 feet higher still.

Had Mount Everest risen 26 feet in a century? That is hard to say. Even with the most advanced instruments, mountain measuring is a tricky business. Measurements are made optically using a surveying transit, which can only be accurate if its base is absolutely level. The leveling is done by means of a plumb bob or spirit level, both of which depend on gravity. But the great mass of the mountain has its own gravitational field, which pulls the plumb bob off the vertical direction by a tiny amount. This could cause a significant error in the calculations. The shape of the earth is another problem. The earth is not exactly spherical, being about 27 miles thicker at the equator than through the poles. This must also be taken into account. Finally, the atmosphere itself turns light rays off course, playing tricks with the angles that surveyors measure. At times such atmospheric effects can cause errors of a few hundred feet.

For these reasons, the recorded measurements of high mountains can be off the true figure by anything from a few feet to a few hundred feet. This uncertainty is illustrated by the method used to arrive at the first accepted height of Mount Everest. Six measurements were made of the peak, each from a different place. All were different, the highest being some 36 feet greater than the lowest. When all six were averaged, the figure turned out to be 29,000 feet—exactly. The surveyors were unwilling to publish this "round figure," fearing that posterity would take it to be an estimate rather than an "exact" measurement, so they arbitrarily added 2 feet to lend credence to their results!

How high is the highest spot on earth? No one knows exactly, at this moment, to the last foot, but 29,000 feet is probably close enough for most purposes.

Index

243

246

72 73 74 75 10 9 8 7 6 5 4 3 2 1